Exploring
Gender
in
Hate
Crime
Law

Gendered Hate

Jessica P. Hodge

Northeastern University Press | BOSTON

Northeastern University Press

An imprint of University Press of New England

www.upne.com

© 2011 Northeastern University

All rights reserved

Manufactured in the United States of America

Designed by Katherine B. Kimball

Typeset in Minion by Integrated Publishing Solutions

For permission to reproduce any of the material in this book, contact Permissions, University Press of New England, One Court Street, Suite 250, Lebanon NH 03766; or visit www.upne.com

Library of Congress Cataloging-in-Publication Data appear on the last printed page of this book.

5 4 3 2 1

*To my nephews, Javan and Brogan:
My hope is that you will know a world
with less violence and hate.*

Contents

Preface and Acknowledgments ix

1 Why Does Gender Matter? 1

2 Hate Crime Legislation: The Past and Present 20

3 Developing the Gender Category: "It Just Made Sense" 43

4 Enforcing the Gender Category: "Is Gender Even on Their Radar?" 64

5 Where Do We Go from Here? Policy Implications and Directions for Future Research 94

APPENDIXES
  Appendix A: Methodology 113
  Appendix B: New Jersey Bias Crime Statutes 123
  Appendix C: New Jersey Senate Bills 1146 and 402 127
  Appendix D: New Jersey Bias Crime Legislation Effective as of March 13, 2008 136
  Appendix E: Interview Guides 146
Notes 151
Bibliography 161
Index 175

Preface and Acknowledgments

Approximately seven years ago I first discovered my interest in hate crimes, particularly gender-motivated hate crimes. The topic intrigued me because violence against women continues to be a significant social problem, yet there is no consensus on the appropriate response to this problem within the academic literature or within federal and state policies. Over the past several years I have spent considerable time researching and writing about gender-motivated hate crimes, and I admit that there were occasions when I wondered if it was time for me to move on to a different topic. Perhaps because of the lack of attention to gender-motivated hate crimes within the academic literature, or because of the public's lack of knowledge and interest, I began to seriously doubt the relevancy of my work. However, the horrific events of Tuesday, August 4, 2009, not only reminded me of why I first became interested in the topic of gender-motivated violence, but they also served as one of my key motivations to finally complete this project.

It was on that date when George Sodini walked into a fitness center in Pittsburgh, Pennsylvania, with the sole purpose of murdering women. The tragedy was an obvious gender-motivated hate crime: Sodini wrote on the Internet about his feelings of hate for women, and he selected a fitness class in which he could purposely target women for murder. In the end, three women were killed and several others injured, simply because they were women. Despite the tragic events of that day, there was little to no discussion within the media or among the general public about how the violence directed at these women had been a result of their gender. None of the women had a prior relationship with Sodini; indeed, none of the women even knew him. He had simply selected his victims because they were women. Even so, very few people addressed the fact that these women were victims of a gender-motivated hate crime, and it was this lack of discussion that reminded me of the two main reasons for this research.

First, gender-motivated violence needs to be talked about. Violence against women, like the Sodini murder spree, is rarely discussed within the media or by the general public, which demonstrates just how little consideration is given to such violence either nationally or globally. Second, gender-motivated violence needs to be studied. Although women are victims of violence on a daily basis, scant research explores how the gender category of bias crime legislation could serve as a tool to combat such violence. It is my hope that this book will prompt conversations and assist people interested in eliminating such violence.

I relied on the support of many people during the research and writing of this book. The project started when I was a graduate student at the University of Delaware, and as the chair of my dissertation committee, Susan L. Miller provided generous support and feedback through many drafts. I am very thankful for Susan's patience as my mentor and my friend. I would like to thank my editors, Claire M. Renzetti and Phyllis Deutsch, of the University Press of New England. I am grateful for their guidance as I worked to turn my dissertation into a relevant and readable manuscript. I would also like to thank Beverly A. McPhail, of the University of Houston, for her feedback; her comments helped improve the quality of the final product.

In addition, I would like to thank the investigators, prosecutors, legislators, and members of special interest groups who served as respondents for this work. Without them, this research would not have been possible, and I appreciate their willingness to share their time and experiences with me. I would also like to thank my colleagues in the Department of Criminal Justice and Criminology at the University of Missouri, Kansas City; they were all very supportive while I finished the manuscript, and I feel very blessed to be a part of the university. I also must thank Sam Scaggs, a graduate student there; his keen eye and attention to detail was an incredible help during the editing stage.

I would also like to thank my dear friends and family who have helped me throughout the past several years. Without the encouragement of my "sister in crime," Maggie Leigey, I am not sure I would have gotten through this process. She is an amazing scholar and friend. I owe special thanks to my University of Delaware friends, especially Nicole Bracy, Lauren Barsky, Bonnie Wu, Rita Poteyeva, and Cami Turner. They provided support during many stages of this project. I am also grateful for my new Kansas City friends. They not only provided encouragement during the final stages of the project, they also provided relief when fun and relaxation were needed. And last but definitely not least, I want to thank my wonderful family. It is because of their unwavering faith and support that I am even writing these acknowledgments. Although my family did not always understand what I was researching or writing, they continued to ask questions about my progress and they never doubted my ability to achieve my goals.

It is because of you all that I finished this book, and I thank you all from the bottom of my heart.

Gendered Hate

1 | Why Does Gender Matter?

> Cary Stayner plotted for a year to rape and murder and targeted two other groups of women before he spontaneously dragged three Yosemite National Park tourists into his fatal game of horrors . . . Days before he killed the three women, he said he had assembled a murder kit in a backpack consisting of a rope, a roll of black duct tape, a gun and a long, serrated knife. He had just been waiting for the right moment to use it.
> —S. Finz and K. Fagan, *"Stunning Details in Stayner's Confession"*

> In 1994, a young woman at the Virginia Polytechnic Institute was raped in her dorm room by two varsity football players, Antonio Morrison and James Crawford. During the attack, Morrison said to the woman, "You better not have any fucking diseases." Afterwards, in the cafeteria, Morrison was heard bragging how he "liked to get girls drunk and fuck the shit out of them."
> —D. Hasenstab, *"Is Hate a Form of Commerce?"*

> In 1989, at the University of Montreal in Canada, Marc Lepine murdered 14 women in an engineering class before killing himself. During the shooting rampage in which he deliberately separated the women from the men, he shouted, "You're all fucking feminists!"
> —B. A. McPhail, *"Gender-bias Hate Crimes"*

Some men deliberately target women with violence. While the above examples are a few of the more well-known cases in which women were attacked because of their gender, as a group, women experience violence in staggering amounts on a daily basis. For example, two to four million women in the United States are victims of domestic violence each year (Valente, Hart, Zeya, and Malefyt 2001, 285). Violence committed by intimate partners or former partners is the leading cause of injury to American women (Atkins, Jurden, Miller, and Patten 1999). Studies also show that rape and other forms of sexual assault happen frequently and are a devastating experience for many women (O'Toole, Schiffman, and Edwards 2007, 195; Pendo 1994). As the National Violence Against Women Survey revealed, one in every six women have been victims of rape (Tjaden and Thoennes 2006). More specifically, approximately twenty-one million men and women reported being forcibly raped at some point in their lives, 86 percent of whom were women. In addition, men were more likely than women to be perpetrators of forcible rape (Tjaden and Thoennes 2006).

Although these numbers demonstrate the extent to which women are victims of violent crime, it is a fact that men are more likely than women to be victims of violent crime overall. According to national crime data, males are victims of violent crime at a much higher rate than females (Federal Bureau of Investigation 2009a). For example, of the 14,137 murder victims in 2008 for whom the gender was known, 78.2 percent (11,059) were male (ibid.). What these numbers fail to illustrate, however, is the fact that although women are less likely than men to be victims of violent crime in general, women are significantly more likely to be victims of a particular subset of violent crime. Indeed, what these numbers fail to show is the extent to which violence directed at women is gendered.

Recent national statistics on crimes such as rape and sexual assaults reveal that 84 percent of the victims are women and 16 percent are men (Truman and Rand 2010). The gendered nature of intimate partner violence is also apparent when looking at national victimization rates. According to a Bureau of Justice Statistics report (Catalano 2007), 22 percent of nonfatal violent crimes against females aged twelve and older were committed by intimates, compared to only 4 percent of nonfatal violent crimes against males of the same age. Other estimates are that approximately 50 percent of all murders of women in the United States are committed by intimate partners (Campbell et al. 2003), and that men are the perpetrators of 95 percent of violent acts between intimates (Taylor 1996). Even taking into account the limitations of victimization data and, more specifically, the underreporting of male victims of sexual assaults and domestic violence, the gendered nature of violence against women is clear: violence against women is primarily committed by men. Put simply, when women are victims of violent crime, the majority of offenders are male; conversely, when men are victims of violent crime, the offenders are rarely female. In fact, the degree to which women are victims of gender-based violence is so overwhelming that being female is considered "the risk factor" (Heise 1989, 6; cited in B. Perry 2001, 26).

The consequences of gendered violence are extensive and damaging, not only to the millions of women experiencing such violence, but also to the millions of women who fear victimization. These numbers are particularly alarming when one acknowledges that half of the population is targeted for a specific subset of crimes, crimes that have historically been used by offenders to exert power and authority over their victims. On one hand, it can be argued that offenders of interpersonal violence must exert some level of power over any victim (say, a robbery victim) in order to "succeed" in the act. On the other hand, unlike in the case of a robbery that may be motivated by financial gain, sexual assaults and domestic violence are often motivated by the sole desire of the offender to maintain control over the particular victim. In other words, there is no other motivation for the violence except to reinforce the victim's subordinate status within the relationship or within society in general. In fact, these crimes are often called "misogynistic acts of violence" because of their gendered pattern (Miller 1994, 231).

Although violence against women is not a new phenomenon, its pervasiveness has only recently become recognized as a national problem deserving further attention on the federal and state levels. The word "recently" is telling, as it was only in 1994 that Congress enacted the Violence Against Women Act (VAWA), the most comprehensive legislation in U.S. history to address this issue.[1] Despite the passage of VAWA, however, neither scholars nor federal and state policymakers agree on the best response to gender-motivated violence. The inclusion of bias crime legislation within this discussion is still relatively new, and the way gender fits in the hate crime discourse continues to be debated.

What Is a Hate Crime?

The term "hate crime" is a relatively novel classification within criminal statutes. Throughout history, people and property have been purposely selected as targets simply because perpetrators fear or hate a perceived or actual group characteristic, yet it was not until the late 1970s that the first hate crime law emerged. The first state-level law was enacted in California in 1978 (Jenness and Broad 2005, 39). A few states soon followed California's example, yet such legislation became common only in the late 1980s. As Best explains: "In the late 1980s, opposition to violent attacks on minorities coalesced in campaigns to criminalize 'hate crimes'" (1999, 57). Looking for a meaningful way to describe such violence, journalists and policy advocates developed the term "hate crime" (Green, McFalls, and Smith 2001). The new criminal classification of "hate crime" quickly evolved, and now nearly every state includes some form of bias crime provision in its statutes.

Since the enactment of the first bias crime statute, these laws have taken many forms, with immense variation among the states (Jenness and Broad 2005, 39; B. Perry 2003, 386; Weisburd and Levin 1993–94). An offense is generally considered a hate or bias crime if a person or property is purposely selected due to an actual or perceived group characteristic.[2] This characteristic motivates the offender or offenders to select a certain target because of the bias or hatred felt toward the target's particular attribute. State and federal bias crime laws vary, but commonly they enhance penalties for a crime—such as assault—if the offender is also convicted of a hate crime.[3] With a penalty-enhancement statute, offenders may receive a sentence two or three times longer than what they might have received if the offense had not involved the bias element. For instance, in Minnesota, a misdemeanor assault motivated by bias elevates the crime to a fourth-degree felony, thereby increasing the punishment (Minnesota Statute 609.2231, Subd. 4). In Missouri, a charge of first-degree property damage found to be motivated by bias raises the crime from a class D felony to a class C felony, again enhancing the penalty (Missouri Revised Statute 557.035).

As with the definition of a bias crime, states vary in which status groups are listed as possible victims of bias. For instance, disability is protected under California's hate crime statute, yet it is not included in the model definition provided by the Anti-Defamation League (2001). The most common protected categories are race, color, national origin, and religion (Jenness and Broad 2005, 42). Other status categories—such as sexual orientation, gender, gender identity, age, disability, and political affiliation—appear less frequently in state statutes and are often more controversial. In fact, both policy-makers and scholars disagree as to which groups to include in federal policies and state-level bias crime statutes. For example, sexual orientation is often not included within state statutes because some legislators are reluctant to legitimize or protect what they consider a "lifestyle" (Green, McFalls, and Smith 2001).[4]

Categories such as gender and disability do not receive the same level of support as the more traditional categories like race, ethnicity, and religion. Even individuals who consider themselves supportive of hate crime laws sometimes question the validity of including certain protected groups. Because gender is not universally considered a core group, it has taken longer for this category to be incorporated into state statutes. For instance, although California included gender as a status category in 1978 (McPhail 2003, 263), and both Alaska and New York included gender as a protected group in 1982 (Jenness and Broad 2005, 72), gender was generally not included in state statutes until the mid-1990s. In fact, the Anti-Defamation League did not include gender in its model statute until 1996 (2001). When asked why the organization initially excluded gender, Steven M. Freeman, director of the league's Legal Affairs Department, explained:

> It would not be accurate to say that gender was first excluded, and then we had a change of heart. It would be more accurate to say that after we had some experience with the statute, the question was raised internally as to whether it should be broader than originally drafted. When we brought to our lay leadership the question of whether to include gender, the vote was affirmative. (quoted in McPhail 2002b, 130)

Although gender has not traditionally been considered one of the classic categories of bias crime legislation on either the federal or state level, advocates for including gender recently won a victory on the federal level. With the passage of the Matthew Shepard and James Byrd, Jr. Hate Crimes Prevention Act (HCPA) on October 28, 2009, gender and sexual orientation, gender identity, and disability are now included as categories on the federal level ("Hate Crimes Expansion Covers Gender, Orientation, Disability" 2010). The law addresses both the effects of hate crimes on interstate commerce and the lack of state resources, or the unwillingness of state officials, to thoroughly investigate and prosecute such crimes. More specifically, the HCPA now permits federal law enforcement officials to become involved in investigations and prosecutions when local agencies seek assistance or when state hate crime laws do not include the categories of gender, gender identity, sexual orientation, or disability. This provision is especially important for the gender category because of the reluctance to include it on the part of some state and federal policymakers, as well as legal scholars and other academics.

The inclusion of gender in bias crime statutes has encountered much skepticism among both supporters and opponents of hate crime laws. However, as demonstrated by the examples and the statistics provided at the beginning of this chapter, women are victims of gender-bias offenses simply because they are women. Of course, not all crimes against women are motivated by gender, just as not all crimes against different racial or religious groups are motivated because of the victim's particular identity. Furthermore, not all men engage in violent behavior—more specifically, not all men engage in violence against women. However, that fact does not lessen the need to recognize the similarities between bias offenses motivated by gender and other types of bias offenses (B. Perry 2001, 83).

Gender-bias crimes affect women collectively, similar to the way that burning a cross or vandalizing a synagogue affects an entire racial or religious community.

The act does not just affect one individual; rather, it affects an entire group, making the targeted community feel fear and, sometimes, a sense of inferiority. Women are constantly aware of their vulnerability and status as potential victims. For instance, even women who have not been victims of rape are affected by the fear of being raped in the future (Gordon and Riger 1989; Senn and Dzinas 1996). The fear of rape is so strong among women that it surpasses the fear of other types of crimes (Softas-Nall, Bardos, and Fakinos 1995) and significantly restricts the activities of women (such as, going out at night) much more than the activities of men: "Indeed, it is difficult to imagine many other social problems that affect so many people in such a direct way" (Warr 1985, 249).

When hearing of another woman's being raped or assaulted, women often experience feelings that go beyond sympathy or concern for the victim. Understanding that the victim's gender was a motivating factor for the offense, women recognize just how easily they could be the victim of a similar crime.[5] These feelings are similar to how a gay man might feel on hearing that someone was attacked because of that person's actual or perceived sexual orientation, or how a Muslim might feel when hearing that someone was attacked due to the person's religion. When such violence occurs, the act not only harms the specific victim of the crime; the harms of the offense extend outward into the targeted community and general society.

Although the victim of a crime motivated by money (such as a robbery) often elicits compassion and concern from others, individuals who hear about the offense often have no residual feelings of fear or anger. Put differently, although people may have sympathy for or empathize with the victim, it is easier for people to distance themselves from the offense as they did not experience the direct pain or loss. However, because bias crimes are directed at a particular social identity and motivated because of an offender's dislike of the particular characteristic, when learning of a bias offense, people within the targeted group naturally fear similar victimization. Members of the targeted group often sense an increased threat to their personal safety. Indeed, one of the key justifications for hate crime laws is the heightened psychological trauma and sense of vulnerability among the victims and members of the targeted community, such as depression, anxiety, and feelings of helplessness and isolation (Lawrence 1999, 63). As Lawrence explains:

> The victim of a bias crime is not attacked for a random reason—as is the person injured during a shooting spree in a public place—nor is he attacked for an impersonal reason, as is the victim of a mugging for money ... A bias crime thus

attacks the victim not only physically but at the very core of his identity. It is an attack from which there is no escape . . . This heightened sense of vulnerability caused by bias crimes is beyond that normally found in crime victims. (40)

The similarities between gender-motivated crimes and the more classic hate crimes, such as crimes directed at someone's race or religion, become apparent when one recognizes that violence directed at women affects women as a group—the harm of the criminal act extends to other members of the female gender. For example, after several women were murdered and mutilated at the University of Florida in Gainesville in 1990, women throughout the university community were afraid to stay in their own neighborhoods (Center for Women Policy Studies 1991, 10; cited in Miller 1994, 231). Another example is when a series of rapes occurred near the University of Missouri in Kansas City, in late 2009 and early 2010. Although the sexual assaults did not occur on the campus, "many women on campus [were] on edge over the attacks" (Pepitone 2010). This is also true for domestic violence. As a telephone survey of 1,000 women ages 18–70 revealed, more than half of the women surveyed (54 percent) worried that they or someone they know would be a victim of domestic violence (Harutyunyan 2008). Lorraine Cole, the chief executive officer of YWCA USA, commented: "These are truly frightening survey findings . . . that so many women live in such fear of domestic violence is shocking" (ibid.).

Since violence against women remains a critical issue within our society, it is imperative that we continue to develop tools that could address this problem. The inclusion of gender within bias crime statutes is one of these tools. This book underlines the importance of including gender within federal and state hate crime statutes, and provides academics and policymakers with the knowledge they need to bring gender to the forefront of hate crime discussions.

Gender as a Protected Group: The Contentious Debate

In response to growing concern about hate crimes, Congress passed the first federal law specifically related to bias crimes, the Hate Crime Statistics Act (HCSA) of 1990 (Federal Bureau of Investigation 1999). The act required the Department of Justice to annually collect and publish data reported from local law enforcement agencies (Gerstenfeld 2004, 28; Jenness and Broad 2005, 37). Until the recent passage of the HCPA, the HCSA required the Department of Justice to collect data on only those hate crimes motivated by race, ethnicity, religion, disability, and sexual orientation (Federal Bureau of Investigation 2007). With the passage of the HCPA, the attorney general is now required to collect data on the new categories of gender and gender identity (Anti-Defamation League 2010). However, despite the fact that forty-nine states (every one except Wyoming) have some form of a hate crime law, only twenty-six states and Washington, D.C., include gender as a protected group in their hate crime statutes (Anti-Defamation League 2008).[6] Consequently, much of the debate within the discourse of bias crime legislation is whether gender should be included as a protected group. McPhail observes: "Although gender is frequently becoming a part of the hate crime policy template, its fit within the hate crime paradigm remains controversial" (2002b, 130).

The controversy surrounding gender and hate crime legislation is multifaceted, perhaps more so than past debates regarding status groups that are now included. Arguments against the addition of gender as a protected group maintain that, because of the extent of violence against women in this country, these crimes would overwhelm already congested courts and would make the gathering of statistics too cumbersome. Furthermore, opponents argue, gender-motivated crimes do not fit the "typical" hate crime criteria; in other words, factors used to assess whether bias was involved in an offense are largely irrelevant to crimes such as domestic violence or rape. However, many scholars argue that it is imperative to include gender within the paradigm of hate crimes. Goldscheid explains:

> Although our country historically has treated these crimes as personal, family law matters, they inflict harm much like other bias crimes. They affect women as a group, not just as individuals, collectively influencing and limiting women's choices about everything from where to work or study, to how and when to travel. The chill on women's life choices is palpable: violence fundamentally restricts women's sense of citizenship and freedom. (1999, 125)

One of the arguments against the inclusion of gender-motivated violence in hate crime legislation is that those who commit crimes against women do not really "hate" women, "at least in the same sense that white supremacists hate blacks and Jews" (Gerstenfeld 2004, 49). It is because of this logic that many critics do not believe that gender-motivated crimes fit within the "typical" bias crime rationale. If a hate crime is due to an offender's prejudicial attitudes about or animus toward another individual or group, critics question how one can argue that a man hates all women, or that crimes of rape and domestic violence are always motivated by hatred of women. Indeed, this perspective is apparent in the following words of Senator Orin Hatch, a Utah Republican, during the congressional hearings on VAWA:

> Say you have a man who believes a woman is attractive. He feels encouraged by her and he's so motivated by that encouragement that he rips her clothes off and has sex with her against her will. Now let's say you have another man who grabs a woman off some lonely road and in the process of raping her says words like, "You're wearing a skirt! You're a woman! I hate women! I'm going to show you, you woman!" Now, the first one's terrible. But the other's much worse. If a man rapes a woman while telling her he loves her, that's a far cry from saying he hates her. A lust factor does not spring from animus. (quoted in Gaffney 1997, 259)

Critics claim that these crimes should not be considered within bias crime statutes because of the difficulty in deciphering which rapes are motivated by an animus toward a particular gender. McPhail explains: "Clearly rape myth acceptance and ignorance by policy makers play a role in not understanding gender-based violence. The socialization of sex roles, gender stereotypes and expectations, the historic legacy of minimizing violence against women, and the male justification of rape all play a part in not recognizing violence against women as a hate crime" (2002b, 132). Many scholars point out the difficulty of finding a sexual assault or domestic violence case that is not motivated in part by an inherent gender bias, and they argue that such crimes are used as a way of intimidating women and reinforcing a sexually stratified social hierarchy (Weisburd and Levin 1993–94, 38). Indeed, sexual assaults and domestic violence are often considered as analogous to such crimes as cross burnings and lynchings, crimes historically used to enforce a racially stratified social hierarchy (Angelari 1994; MacKinnon 1991).

Research has demonstrated that sexual assault, particularly rape, can often be interpreted as a hate crime. Like other "traditional" bias crimes against racial, ethnic, or religious minorities—in which violence is used to gain revenge over an entire group of individuals—gender-motivated violence is often a way for men to punish all women. For instance, in their interviews with convicted rapists, Scully and Marolla (1985) found that men used rape to punish and revenge themselves on women as a collective class. In other words, the victims represented all women; no victim was viewed as just an individual female. The rapists believed that they had the right to discipline and punish women, and they chose to use rape as a method of displaying their dominance. One rapist said:

> I wanted to take my anger and frustration out on a stranger, to be in control ... I hated the victims because they probably messed men over. I hated women because they were deceitful and I was getting revenge for what happened to me. (quoted in Scully and Marolla 1985, 257)

Research also demonstrates that men use violence within intimate relationships as a way to control and dominate their partners, and that this violence is most often perpetrated by males against females (Belknap and Potter 2006, 173). As a result, scholars argue that domestic violence should also be considered a gender-motivated hate crime (Goldscheid 1999; Goldscheid and Kaufman 2001; Issacs 2001; McPhail 2002b; Miller 1994, 231; Weisburd and Levin 1993–94). Like sexual assaults, domestic violence cases exhibit several factors that fit within the bias crime criterion. For example, as Isaacs explains, "much domestic violence also has its source in negative attitudes, in this case attitudes about the subordinate place of women relative to men in society and the appropriateness of using violence to keep them there" (2001, 31). Also, like those who commit sexual assaults, perpetrators of domestic violence are seldom punished, which, conveys the message that their behavior is acceptable.

State courts have recognized the parallels between domestic violence and other bias crimes and have used the gender category within state hate crime statutes to enhance penalties for offenders. For instance, one judge in New Hampshire used that state's bias crime law to increase the sentence for a man with a history of violence toward women (Weisburd and Levin 1993–94). Because of his established pattern of abuse of women, Richard Towne received a sentence for assault that was more than double what he would have received otherwise. A Massachusetts court has also used a pattern of abuse as evidence of gender bias. In this case, affidavits submitted by the defendant's wife and other former partners demonstrated a history of both physical and emotional abuse, which led the court to issue an injunction under the state's bias crime law (Goldscheid 1999).

Despite the limited success in using the gender category in domestic violence cases, critics continue to claim that because most of the crimes against women are not "random" violent acts and are committed by acquaintances or intimate partners, they do not fit into the hate crime paradigm. Opponents argue that gender should be excluded as a protected group because the victim is not interchangeable—meaning that the offender is not looking for just any random woman (Carney 2001; Weisburd and Levin 1993–94). Gelber comments: "Perhaps because crimes against women are often perpetrated by someone whom they know, it is difficult to conceive of those crimes as motivated by hatred towards women" (2000, 283). In fact, when discussing whether rape should be included as a gender-motivated offense, some scholars have argued that only certain types of rape (such as cases of rape by a stranger) be considered as bias crimes. Because the victim is unknown to the offender in stranger rape cases, these cases more readily fit the hate crime rationale due to the interchangeability of the victim. McDevitt argues:

> With respect to race, *any* black family that moves into certain neighborhoods will likely be attacked. With respect to sexual orientation, *any* man thought to be gay who happens to walk down a particular street will in all likelihood be assaulted. Similarly, gender-motivated hate crimes should include those attacks in which the offender is looking for *any* woman. By this criterion, acquaintance rape and acts of domestic violence, no matter how despicable, would be excluded from consideration as hate offenses. Only random attacks against women would be included. (quoted in Levin and McDevitt 2002, 21)

However, most supporters of including gender argue that the lack of a prior relationship is not necessary for the existence of a bias-motivated offense and that, in fact, many "traditional" hate crimes are also perpetrated against acquaintances. Victims of bias crimes are often not chosen at random; rather, the crimes are directed at a specific individual (Goldfarb 2003). McPhail explains: "Unfortunately many hate crimes are perpetrated on neighbors and coworkers. Making a prior relationship a disqualification of hate crime status would exempt these crimes as well" (2002b, 132). A Bureau of Justice Statistics report (Harlow 2005) says that just over half (52 percent) of all victims of a violent hate crime were victimized by strangers or persons they recognized only by sight. Therefore, if a prior relationship were to disqualify bias crimes not committed by strangers—almost half (48 percent) of violent bias crimes—it would ignore the reality that the experiences of these victims were no less significant than the experiences of those who did not know the offender. In fact, the prior relationship makes these crimes more heinous, due to the victim's shattered sense of community and social familiarity (Pendo 1994, 168).

Furthermore, as Carney explains, "to argue that females are not interchangeable in the commission of a rape is to ignore how many women try to alter their lifestyles to avoid becoming a victim of a rape precisely because they are aware of their vulnerability" (2001, 342). In other words, because women are conscious of their vulnerability, they are always mindful of their actions so as to reduce their chance of being a victim. Miller notes: "Safety is only partially assured within prescribed bounds—restricted by daylight, type of neighborhood, choice of clothing, and the like. Women learn these boundaries early and they learn to fear" (1994, 232). Therefore, through the use of fear and violence, crimes such as rape reinforce women's position within the social structure as they are forced to take specific steps in order to avoid victimization. This fear is similar to that often felt by gays and lesbians when disclosing their sexual orientation to others. Because of the heterosexist social structure in which we live, gays and lesbians often must hide their orientation for fear of victimization.

Opponents of the inclusion of gender, however, argue that such laws are not necessary to protect women from violence. Critics point out that many laws currently address domestic violence and sexual assault, making additional legislation redundant (Gerstenfeld 2004, 49; McPhail 2002b). However, proponents assert that the current laws addressing domestic violence and sexual assaults do not cover all possible forms of gender-bias crimes. For instance, the Stayner and Lepine examples provided at the beginning of this chapter were neither crimes of sexual assault or domestic violence, yet they clearly were motivated by gender bias: Lepine murdered fourteen women at the University of Montreal because he blamed his academic and personal failures on women. Horrific cases such as this could not be officially designated as hate crimes if gender were not covered by bias crime laws.

Another act of violence directed at women that would not be covered under current domestic violence or sexual assault laws was the tragic event that occurred on October 2, 2006, at an Amish school in Pennsylvania. Before he went to the school, Charles Carl Roberts IV, a thirty-two-year-old milk-truck driver, admitted to his wife that he had molested two young girls twenty years earlier, and that he was thinking of molesting someone again (Gandy 2006). At the school, Roberts separated the girls and the boys and let the boys go free before he began shooting. After killing five young girls and seriously wounding five others, Roberts fatally shot himself. According to Jeffrey Miller, the state police commissioner, Roberts attacked the girls as a way to seek revenge for something that had occurred in his past ("Fifth Girl Dies after Amish School Shooting" 2006).

A third example of how current domestic violence and sexual assault laws fail to cover all forms of gender bias crimes occurred on August 4, 2009, at a Pittsburgh health club. George Sodini, a forty-eight-year-old white man, entered an aerobics dance class (which he purposely selected because all the members of the class were women) and opened fire, randomly killing three women and injuring eleven more, before turning the gun on himself ("Three Pennsylvania Women Killed in Hate Crime" 2009). It was discovered soon after the murder spree that Sodini had maintained an Internet blog detailing his hatred for women and his plans for seeking revenge on them. He blogged about how he had been driven into a depression because of his lack of success with women, how he could not understand why women ignored him, and the fact that he had not had a girlfriend for more than twenty years.

Even though this was an obvious gender-bias offense, there was little to no acknowledgement in the media of the fact that his actions constituted a hate crime directed at women. When discussing this lack of concern for gender-motivated violence, one *New York Times* columnist wrote: "We have become so accustomed to living in a society saturated with misogyny that the barbaric treatment of women and girls has come to be more or less expected" (Herbert 2009). Even if there had been a consensus that Sodini had committed a gender-motivated hate crime, the incident could not have been officially labeled as such because Pennsylvania did not then (nor does it now) include gender as a category covered by the state's bias crime statute.

Despite the controversy surrounding the inclusion of gender in hate crime legislation, little empirical research has been conducted on this topic. Indeed, a study of prosecutors in Texas soon after gender was added as a category to that state's hate crime law (McPhail and DiNitto 2005) may be the only study to focus specifically on the inclusion of gender. As gender continues to be a controversial issue within the hate crime discourse, empirical work needs to explore the complexities surrounding the creation and implementation of gender categories within hate crime laws. By exploring these issues in New Jersey, this book provides information that will be useful to scholars interested in the hate crime debate and policy-makers interested in combating violence against women.

Who Are the Victims of Gender-Motivated Violence?

It is necessary to note that domestic violence and sexual assault cases do not involve only female victims and male perpetrators. Research has demonstrated that men are also victims of domestic violence (Hamel 2007) and that same-sex assaults also occur (Renzetti 1992). This book, however, takes a macro-oriented, feminist approach to examining gender-based violence. The argument throughout this book is that some men in our patriarchal society use gender-motivated violence to dominate and control women; therefore, the book focuses on treating male violence against women as a bias crime.[7] This perspective does not deny that same-sex violence occurs, or that women are sometimes the offenders;

however, it is widely acknowledged by both scholars (Dobash et al. 1992; Miller 2005; Stanko 1993) and practitioners such as shelter workers (Belknap and Melton 2005) that women are more likely to be the victims of male perpetrators.[8] Reed and her colleagues explain:

> A multitude of quantitative and qualitative research studies as well as volumes of health and criminal justice data from across the globe clearly demonstrate that male intimate partner violence (IPV) against women and girls is an issue of tremendous public health and human rights significance worldwide. (2010, 348)

The feminist approach has been criticized for failing to explain same-sex interpersonal violence, particularly within lesbian relationships, since this form of violence undermines the notion that men alone are responsible for dominating women and that the problem lies in the patriarchy of society. The feminist approach has also been criticized for ignoring the fact that women may also be violent within intimate relationships. Nevertheless, research has shown that, in heterosexual relationships, gender is "overwhelmingly the defining factor" for the source of power and control (Perilla et al. 2003, 20; cited in Miller 2005, 26). Some men use violence against their female partners when the women fail to meet their physical, sexual, or emotional needs, and the men's masculine identities are reinforced by their ability to control partners as a result of the violent acts (Anderson and Umberson 2001). Conversely, research has demonstrated that in same-sex relationships, power is a function of many variables—such as education, class, and ethnicity (Perilla et al. 2003, 20; cited in Miller 2005, 26; see also Renzetti 1992).

While not ignoring the facts that same-sex violence occurs in both domestic assaults and sexual assaults, and that women can also be violent, the gender disparities involved in such violence are clearly evident: men are overwhelmingly the perpetrators of violence against women. Moreover, research demonstrates that when women are violent within intimate relationships, they use violence to defend themselves or their children, or as a means of expressing anger or frustration based on past abuse (Miller 2005),[9] whereas men use violence to assert dominance and to control or punish their partner (Barnett, Lee, and Thelan 1997; Hamberger et al. 1997). Because violence directed at women by men continues to be a serious issue, affecting millions of women in this country, it is critical that we continue to find ways in which to eradicate such violence. One means of eliminating it is to recognize the bias element within gender-based offenses and to treat such crimes as gendered hate crimes, prosecuting and punishing offenders accordingly.

The Current Scholarly Focus

Although there are no official national statistics regarding the number of gender-motivated bias crimes reported throughout the country, states that include gender in their hate crime statutes occasionally provide their own statistics. For example, according to the 2007 Minnesota crime report, provided by the Minnesota Department of Public Safety (2009), only one gender-bias crime occurred in 2007, compared to 27 religious-bias crimes during the same period.[10] In California, there were 25 gender-bias crimes reported in 2007, compared to 263 bias crimes motivated by sexual orientation (California Department of Justice 2008).[11] Finally, in New Jersey, one gender-bias crime was reported in 2007, compared to 392 racially motivated crimes during that same year (New Jersey State Police 2008).[12] The variance between these numbers is significant and worthy of further exploration. Why are more bias crimes relating to race and religion reported than gender-bias crimes? Are few gender-bias crimes reported simply because not many offenses have been committed that fit in the gender category?

Although critics of the gender category may argue that this is the case, others would disagree, pointing to recent crimes. For example, like the Sodini murder spree in the Pittsburgh health club, many individuals believed the shooting rampage in the Amish school was a gender-motivated hate crime. Although the violence committed by Roberts was directed specifically at young girls—as noted above, he killed five and seriously wounded five others—the incident was not reported as a gender-bias offense by law enforcement officials or by media covering the tragedy. In fact, as the columnist mentioned before observed: "There would have been thunderous outrage if someone had separated potential victims by race or religion and then shot, say, only the blacks, or only the whites, or only the Jews. But if you shoot only the girls or only the women—not so much of an uproar" (Herbert 2009). Perhaps, then, there are other reasons for the small number of reported gender-bias crimes, such as the public's being unaware of the existence of a gender category in the bias crime statutes. Another question worth exploring is how crimes such as domestic violence and sexual assaults fit in the gender category: are these offenses considered gender-bias crimes by police and prosecutors?

Other factors may also be responsible for the small number of gender-bias crimes reported by law enforcement. Investigators may be unsure of what a gender-bias case looks like, or what evidence is needed to designate an offense as motivated by gender bias. Or prosecutors may be reluctant to pursue cases as gender-motivated offenses because these cases do not match their criteria of a "typical" bias crime, even if the evidence points in the direction of bias. This certainly seems to have happened with Texas prosecutors (McPhail and DiNitto 2005; McPhail and Jenness 2005–6). But has it happened elsewhere? McPhail and Jenness note that "very little" is known about what influences prosecutorial action (or inaction) related to hate crime (2005–6, 92). In order for the gender category to be a viable part of hate crime legislation, and an effective tool for combating gender-motivated violence, we need further research on this topic.

The Research Setting

This book is intended to fill a gap currently existing in the literature on the development and enforcement of the gender category in hate crime legislation. New Jersey was chosen to be the case study for a number of reasons.

First, New Jersey is one of twenty-six states to include gender as a protected group in its bias crime statute (Anti-Defamation League 2008). California included gender within its bias crime statute in 1978 (McPhail 2002b); Alaska and New York did so in 1982 (Jenness and Broad 2005, 72). New Jersey took the same action on August 15, 1995, when Governor Christine Todd Whitman signed legislation that expanded the state's definition of bias-motivated offenses to include gender and disability as enumerated categories (Hester 1995).

Second, although gender was not included until 1995, New Jersey enacted a hate crime law in 1981, one of the first states to do so (Vitale 2002), and New Jersey's attorney general's office has required law enforcement agencies to collect data on bias crimes since 1988. According to this mandate, all law enforcement agencies are required to report bias-motivated offenses to the Division of State Police's Uniform Crime Reporting Unit on a monthly basis (New Jersey State Police 2000). These numbers are compiled into an annual report that is sent to the Federal Bureau of Investigation (FBI) and made available to the public through the office of the state's attorney general.[13]

Third, New Jersey is one of the more progressive states in the country when it comes to the implementation and enforcement of bias crime laws. For example, New Jersey reported one of the highest numbers of bias incidents for 2006 and 2007 (Federal Bureau of Investigation 2007, 2008).[14] Although it is possible that these statistics mean a larger number of bias crimes occurred within the state as compared to other states with lower numbers, many scholars have argued that the opposite is true. Bell made a relevant discovery in her research:

In addition to being blamed for driving the overall crime rate up, hate crime units or other police officers responsible for enforcing hate crime law are not likely to be lauded for their enforcement efforts when they identify a large number of "hate crimes"; a high hate crime rate makes a city look more bigoted rather than more tolerant and progressive. (2002, 98)

Therefore, rather than reflecting a more bigoted state, high bias crime statistics may reflect greater diligence among law enforcement officers when investigating and reporting such crimes. Although New Jersey reports one of the highest numbers of bias incidents in the country, it may be due to the dedication of the state's law enforcement officials that these crimes are recognized and reported.

Finally, New Jersey implemented the first program in the country in which juvenile bias offenders had to complete a rehabilitation program, and it was one of the first states to implement formal police policies specifically related to bias crimes (Levin 1992–93). In addition, the New Jersey legislature created a state office focused solely on bias crimes. The Office of Bias Crime and Community Relations (OBCCR) was responsible for developing bias crime training programs for law enforcement officers, designing educational programs for schools and communities, and overseeing bias crime investigations throughout the state. Although the OBCCR was recently closed, information regarding educational programs and training is still provided on its website.[15] For all these reasons, New Jersey was an excellent case study for a further exploration of the use of gender in bias crime legislation.

To examine the inclusion and application of the gender category, the book relies on qualitative methods such as a content analysis of media accounts and legislative histories, and interviews with key criminal justice personnel, political figures, and advocacy group members. The following discussion highlights these methods; in addition, Appendix A gives a complete description of the methodological approach utilized in this study.

Content Analysis

To explore the creation of hate crime legislation in New Jersey, specifically in regard to the inclusion of gender as a status group, I analyzed the content of various public records pertaining to the development of this legislation. I obtained legislative histories using the New Jersey State Legislature website and the Lexis-Nexis Academic database; materials were also obtained from the New

Jersey State Library. The content analysis also involved newspaper articles pertaining to bias crimes, including those related to gender. I obtained these articles from the Lexis-Nexis Academic database and from the archives of two leading New Jersey newspapers. As this study also examined how the gender category has been portrayed by the media since its inclusion in the state's bias crime statute, I analyzed the content of newspaper articles written after the law's passage. These newspaper articles were also obtained using the Lexis-Nexis Academic database. Overall, the sample consisted of seventy-two newspaper articles.

Interviews

Based on previous research on bias crimes, I hypothesized that there would be a variety of definitions and opinions throughout the state regarding such offenses, and the specific practices of each jurisdiction would vary depending upon the organizational and community contexts. Therefore, I conducted interviews with a variety of subjects, from different counties and municipal agencies. Of the nineteen individuals interviewed for this study, six were county prosecutors, six bias crime investigators, six representatives of special interest groups, and one key legislator actor. I supplemented the data obtained from the interviews with three completed surveys from country prosecutors,[16] e-mail correspondence with a member of the state's General Assembly, and telephone communications with a former member of the staff of Senator Jack Sinagra, one of the original sponsors of the bill to include gender and disability in the bias crime statute. Thirteen of the twenty-four subjects were male, and eleven were female.

Organization of the Book

To understand why gender is included as a protected group in some states but not others, one must first examine the process by which hate crime legislation is initially created within a jurisdiction and how it garners support and opposition from multiple constituencies. Chapter 2 examines this process, providing a review of the literature on the development of hate crime law. The chapter examines bias crime legislation as a social movement, focusing on how claims-makers—such as media, advocacy groups, and politicians—frame such legislation. The chapter also reviews the literature on the enforcement of hate crime laws, utilizing prior research to highlight the importance of organizational and community contexts for successfully investigating and prosecuting bias crimes.

By revealing the intricacies involved in the passage of this type of legislation, the discussion provides the basis for exploring the complexities specific to the gender category.

The research conducted in New Jersey is discussed in chapters 3 and 4. Chapter 3 analyzes the legislative history and newspaper accounts to explain how the gender category came to be included in New Jersey law. Interviews with key players provide context for this process. Chapter 4 discusses how the gender category has been enforced in New Jersey since the enactment of the law, again examining newspaper accounts and describing interviews with members of special interest groups, bias crime investigators, and county prosecutors. Finally, chapter 5 synthesizes the findings from the previous two chapters and suggests policy implications and directions for future research.

2 | Hate Crime Legislation
The Past and Present

> A person who has been singled out for victimization based on some group characteristic ... has, by that very act, been deprived of the right to participate in the life of the community on an equal footing for reasons that have nothing to do with what the victim did but everything to do with who the victim is. In short, a bias attack is as much an attack on the victim's persona as on the victim's person ... By their very nature, moreover, these harms are not confined to the actual victim. Because bias crimes are triggered by the victim's membership in a larger group, the feelings of vulnerability and injustice created by bias crimes are frequently and understandably shared by other members of the group.
> —*American Civil Liberties Union amicus curiae brief in support of the petitioner in Wisconsin v. Mitchell, 508 U.S. 476 (1993)*

Hate crime policy is a complex topic. Not only do scholars and policymakers debate the effectiveness of hate crime legislation, they also debate which groups should be protected by the laws. As demonstrated in the previous chapter, one of the most controversial issues is whether gender should be included as a protected group. To understand how gender fits within the hate crime domain, it is helpful to understand the development and enforcement of hate crime legislation in general.

The Hate Crime Statistics Act

The HCSA, the first federal law specifically related to bias crimes, was passed by Congress in 1990 (Federal Bureau of Investigation 1999). Although the HCSA did not make hate crimes federal offenses, it did require the Department of Justice to annually collect and publish data reported from local law enforcement agencies (Gerstenfeld 2004, 28; Jenness and Broad 2005, 37; Weisburd and Levin 1993–94).

In the FBI's most recent report, there were 9,168 bias-motivated offenses reported by participating agencies (Federal Bureau of Investigation 2009b). The majority of offenses involved intimidation, assaults, and forms of destruction, damage, or vandalism; law enforcement agencies also reported seven murders and eleven rapes. More than half of the reported hate crimes involved racial bias (51.3 percent, or 4,704), followed by bias against sexual orientation (17.6 percent, or 1,617) and religion (17.5 percent, or 1,606). These proportions are similar to those in previous years' reports. However, local law enforcement participation in the process is voluntary; therefore, the true count of hate crimes throughout the country is unknown.

The HCSA also directed the attorney general to establish guidelines for data collection and to establish what evidence was necessary to demonstrate a bias-motivated offense (Jacobs and Potter 1998, 39; Pendo 1994).[1] The original act required the Department of Justice to collect and report data on crimes motivated by race, ethnicity, religion, and sexual orientation, but in 1994 the act was amended to include disability (Center for Women Policy Studies 2001). The category of gender was not added until the recent passage of the Matthew Shepard and James Byrd, Jr. Hate Crimes Prevention Act (HCPA) in October 2009 (Anti-Defamation League 2010).

The initial exclusion of gender from the HCSA was not due to a lack of effort by advocacy groups dedicated to women's issues (McPhail 2002b). Before the passage of the act, a group called the Coalition on Hate Crimes Prevention was formed in order to establish the prevalence of hate crimes, and then to sponsor the act (McPhail 2002b). The coalition consisted of civil rights, religious, and gay and lesbian groups and law enforcement organizations (Angelari 1994); yet, as McPhail observes, "women's groups were notably absent" (2002b, 128). Interestingly, both the National Organization for Women and the National Coalition against Domestic Violence attempted to participate in the coalition in order to modify the bill to include gender; however, the coalition members voted to exclude the gender category and canceled all subsequent meetings with the women's rights groups (Angelari 1994; McPhail 2002b). The coalition argued that gender should be excluded because lobbying for its inclusion would have delayed passage of the bill, would not have improved the collection of data on domestic violence or rape, and might even have made collecting data too difficult, due to the prevalence of gender-bias crimes (Angelari 1994, 83).

Hence, during the first set of congressional hearings in 1985, testimony revolved around the three core categories of race, ethnicity, and religion. In 1986, during the second set of hearings, Congress heard testimony about violence against gays and lesbians. However, gender was not included in the act despite the written testimony of Molly Yard, then president of the National Organization for Women, explaining that the majority of violence committed against women occurs at the hands of men, that rape and domestic violence are tools of oppression to keep women subordinate, and that other social movement groups often compare the harms resulting from these crimes to the harms resulting from other forms of hate crimes (McPhail 2002b).

The exclusion of gender outraged many advocates and scholars. As Angelari points out, it was ironic for the coalition to argue that it was imperative to include sexual orientation in the act so that crimes against gays and lesbians would not be seen as less significant or less reprehensible than crimes against other groups, and at the same time to fail to recognize that by excluding gender, they were in essence relegating crimes against women to the same secondary position (1994, 85). Furthermore, Sheffield notes:

> This law [the Hate Crime Statistics Act], noteworthy in that it represents a far-ranging consensus about the need to address hate-violence in America, and historic in that it recognizes that violence against gay and lesbian people is a crime of hatred and bigotry, is seriously flawed by its omission of sexual violence. Counting hate crimes against women would reveal that 52 percent of the population is in serious jeopardy. The exclusion of sex-hate as a form of hate-violence is not only a profound denial of the most pervasive form of violence in the United States but an attempt to deny the reality of patriarchal/sexist oppression and its interaction with other structures of power and privilege such as race, class, and sexuality. It is an attempt to have it both ways: that is, to rage against such hate-violence when the victims are male (and occasionally female) and yet to protect male superiority over women. The denial of sexual violence as a hate crime is purposeful for the status quo, for it would be detrimental to the social order to define men's violence against women as a serious, hate crime. (1992, 395–96; cited in Jenness and Broad 2005, 143)

Although gender is no longer excluded from the HCSA, it now becomes a question of when states will join the FBI in collecting data on gender-motivated hate crimes. As previously mentioned, a few states already provide such statistics, but a broader effort must take place in order for the category to receive the recognition it needs to become a viable tool for law enforcement officials.

The Hate Crimes Sentencing Enhancement Act

Because the Hate Crime Statistics Act was solely a law about collecting data, Congress passed the Hate Crimes Sentencing Enhancement Act in 1994. Similar to the state penalty enhancement statutes, the new act increased penalties for bias-motivated federal offenses, requiring sentences to be enhanced by at least three offense levels (Angelari 1994; McPhail 2002b). Unlike the HCSA, however, the Hate Crimes Sentencing Enhancement Act did include gender as a protected category, along with the other previously listed groups. Under this law, the federal government can investigate and prosecute bias-motivated crimes that occur in national parks or on other federal property—in other words, crimes that are under federal jurisdiction. However, because of the act's limited scope, federal criminal prosecutions for gender-bias crimes are rare (Gerstenfeld 2004, 29).

The Violence Against Women Act

Also in 1994, Congress sought to address violence against women specifically. After four years of hearings and the accumulation of data regarding the extent to which women are affected by violent acts, Congress enacted the Violence Against Women Act of 1994 (Valente et al. 2001). Congress recognized the need for federal legislation to address the inadequacies and inherent biases in states' legal systems having to do with violent acts against women (Goldfarb 2000; Hagan 2001; MacKinnon 2000; Pendo 1994).

During the four years before the passage of VAWA, Congress heard testimony from over a hundred witnesses and collected statistics from a variety of sources (Goldscheid 2000; see also Goldfarb 2000, 2003; Hagan 2001; Hasenstab 2001; Valente et al. 2001, 285). Those who testified included law professors, attorneys, representatives of national organizations and corporations, and survivors of rape and domestic violence. Corporation executives testified about how domestic violence significantly affected their employees (leading to absenteeism, poor job performance, increased medical claims, and so forth) and said it was necessary to develop programs to deal with the effects of domestic violence. Rape victims testified about how their lives had been drastically affected by their traumatic experiences (including dropping out of school, lost interest in and focus on their education, and the fear of retaliation from their attackers after reporting the rape). Domestic violence experts testified about the detrimental effects of domestic violence and rape, stating that women are disproportionately the victims of these crimes. Congress also heard testimony from representatives of medical and health associations demonstrating that the pervasiveness of violence against women contributes to enormous healthcare costs throughout the country due to the number of physical, mental, and emotional injuries sustained by victims.

In addition, Congress received numerous reports on how women are often treated unfairly within state legal systems by law enforcement officials, prosecutors, and judges (Hagan 2001). And Congress heard testimony on how women are frequently blamed for the battering they experience or the rapes they suffer. The testimony revealed how domestic violence continues to be considered a private matter by many criminal justice officials, regardless of educational efforts and changes in policies. For example, one former prosecutor told the story of a woman seeking to press charges against her husband. Although she still had a black and swollen eye from his abuse, she was told by the judge:

> Ma'am, I credit your testimony, and I am convinced that your husband assaulted you in violation of the law. As a result, I am authorized to award you a civil protection order, which could order him to stay away from you and stop hurting you. But I am not going to do that today. Because you have children together, you're going to have to find some way to cooperate with each other to raise them. So, I want you to go home and try to work things out in private. And I suggest that you go see a movie I saw recently, "Mrs. Doubtfire," where Robin Williams and his wife decide to separate, but still manage to find a creative way to work together when it came to their children. (quoted in Epstein 1999, 6–7)

Through the passage of VAWA, Congress addressed the flaws and deficiencies in state laws in several ways, and provided assistance for victims of gender-motivated violence. The act included several provisions that revised and expanded federal laws, provided grant money for state programs, and added new federal programs to deal with victims of violence motivated by gender (Angelari 1994; Hagan 2001; Stolz 1999). Yet the most significant provision of VAWA— a section to be struck down as unconstitutional by the Supreme Court—was the civil rights remedy enacted by Congress under the Commerce Clause and Section Five of the Fourteenth Amendment.[2]

Congress passed the remedy (section 13981 of VAWA) in order to give victims of gender-motivated violence an opportunity to seek redress within the federal courts.[3] The provision enabled victims of gender-motivated violence to bring a civil suit against the perpetrators in order to recover compensatory and punitive damages, injunctive and declaratory relief, attorney's fees, and other assistance deemed appropriate by a court (Goldfarb 2003), even if the defendant had not been criminally charged, prosecuted, or convicted (Goldfarb 2000). As Congress discovered in its numerous hearings, "this financial compensation is necessary to cover the costs borne by victims of violence against women, including medical and mental health treatment, job retraining, loss of property and assets, and a host of other financial and physical injuries" (Valente et al. 2001, 298).

Although proponents of the civil rights remedy hailed it as a huge success because it acknowledged gender-motivated violence as a denial of women's right to equality (Goldfarb 2000), it was the most controversial provision of VAWA (Hasenstab 2001). Some considered the remedy to be inherently class-biased, since only women who could afford to bring a civil suit against their offender could receive financial remuneration, and often batterers have few or no assets to turn over to their victims (Goldscheid 2003; Regan 1999). Even more controversial was Congress's constitutional authority to enact such a provision. This was the question the Supreme Court sought to answer when it granted certiorari in the case of *U.S. v. Morrison* (529 U.S. 598, 2000).

The Court received this case in 1999, four years after Christy Brzonkala, a female student at Virginia Polytechnic Institute (Virginia Tech), had filed a complaint with the school's judicial committee that she had been assaulted and repeatedly raped by two football players, Antonio Morrison and James Crawford, in her dormitory room during the fall of 1994. During the school-conducted hearings, Morrison admitted having sexual conduct with Brzonkala despite the fact that she had told him "no" twice. Morrison was found guilty of sexual assault by the judicial committee and received a two-semester suspension, but the committee determined that there was insufficient evidence to punish Crawford. Morrison appealed his suspension through the university's administration, claiming that his due process rights had been violated at the hearing. During a second hearing, the judicial committee once again found Morrison guilty but reduced his offense from "sexual assault" to "using abusive language." In the hearings, Brzonkala testified that the assailants had threatened her during the offense and stalked her afterward. Moreover, Morrison was overheard by other students stating in the dormitory dining hall that he "liked to get girls drunk and fuck the shit out of them" (Hasenstab 2001, 993). Morrison appealed his second conviction, and in August 1995, Virginia Tech's senior vice president and provost dismissed Morrison's punishment and allowed him to return to the university (ibid.). After Brzonkala learned from a newspaper that Morrison would once again be attending classes with her, she dropped out of school.

In December 1995, Brzonkala filed suit against Morrison, Crawford, and Virginia Tech in the U.S. District Court for the Western District of Virginia, claiming that the manner in which her case had been handled by the university violated Title IX of the Education Amendment Act[4] and that the attack by Morrison and Crawford violated section 13981 of VAWA. The district court dismissed her claims, ruling that the section was unconstitutional because Congress did not have authority to enact this section under either the Commerce Clause or Section Five of the Fourteenth Amendment (Hasenstab 2001). However, in 1998, the Fourth Circuit Court of Appeals reversed this decision and reinstated Brzonkala's claims; that court concluded that section 13981 was constitutional and that her claims sufficiently indicated a motivation of gender animus. Yet, after rehearing the case, the court vacated its original decision and upheld the district court's ruling. Consequently, the Supreme Court granted certiorari to rule definitively on whether section 13981 of VAWA was indeed constitutional.

On May 15, 2000, the Supreme Court ruled that Congress did not have the authority under either the Commerce Clause or Section Five of the Fourteenth Amendment to enact the civil rights remedy (Hagan 2001). In the majority opinion written by Chief Justice William Rehnquist, the Court decided that violence against women was not economic in nature (MacKinnon 2000), nor was it an activity that substantially affected interstate commerce (Wethington 2001), thus it was inappropriate to regulate the violence under the Commerce Clause. Moreover, because section 13981 was intended for use against private individuals—rathter than designed to prevent transgressions by the states—the Court concluded that it violated Section Five of the Fourteenth Amendment (Bono 2001). Although the majority recognized that the act was supported by numerous congressional findings, it did not consider the voluminous record to be sufficient for upholding section 13981. As a result, one of the most significant pieces of legislation to address violence against women was rendered powerless.

The Matthew Shepard and James Byrd, Jr. Hate Crimes Prevention Act

More recently, perhaps due to the limitations of the Hate Crime Sentencing Enhancement Act and the repeal of the civil rights remedy in VAWA, a more inclusive bill was passed to address the inadequacies of existing federal law in dealing with hate crimes nationally. The bill, originally proposed in 1998, went through several revisions (Gerstenfeld 2004, 28). It was titled the Local Law Enforcement Hate Crimes Prevention Act during the 2007 congressional session (Human Rights Campaign 2009) and was later titled the Matthew Shepard and James Byrd, Jr. Hate Crimes Prevention Act (HCPA).

As discussed in the previous chapter, the act requires the Justice Department to collect data on crimes motivated because of the victim's actual or perceived gender, sexual orientation, gender identity, or disability. Perhaps more important, the law permits the federal government to assist state and local police departments with investigations of hate crimes on a broader scale. Whereas in the past the federal government was limited to the investigation and prosecution of bias crimes based on a victim's race, ethnicity, or religion, or to hate crimes committed on federal property (such as a national park), the newly enacted HCPA allows state and federal agencies to coordinate their efforts on a larger number of cases, particularly when state agencies cannot, or refuse to, investigate alleged bias crimes. The original bill was passed by the Senate in 2000 and went through several congressional sessions before being passed by the House (Center for Women Policy Studies 2001). Finally, after more than a decade of lobbying by various advocacy groups, the bill became law with President Obama's signature on October 28, 2009.

The Creation of Hate Crime Laws

The National Landscape

In *Making Hate a Crime*, Jenness and Grattet claim: "To understand the initial issue creation phase of the formation of the hate crime policy domain . . . it is important to examine how the anti-hate-crime movement successfully engaged in an organizational and ideological struggle to place discriminatory violence on the public agenda" (2001, 18). As the authors explain, the anti-hate-crime movement can be linked to the social changes created by two larger movements: the civil rights movement and the victim's rights movement (20). Because of the civil rights movement of the 1960s and 1970s, a discourse developed involving the rights of racial and ethnic minorities, women, and gays and lesbians. These movements shared a commitment to reducing discrimination against minorities and successfully framed violence directed at minorities as a form of discrimination (26). As a result, the civil rights movement, the women's movement, and the gay and lesbian movement created awareness throughout the country, generated significant media and legislative attention, and overall, framed bias-motivated offenses as a contemporary social problem.

The victim's rights movement also facilitated the creation of the anti-hate-crime movement. The crime victim's movement emerged on the national landscape due to a concern about rising crime rates and decreased confidence in the legal system. The public perception was that victims of violent crime were not receiving the justice, nor were criminals receiving the punishment, they deserved. By 2000, almost every state and the federal government had enacted laws that in many cases were called the "victim's bill of rights" (28). These laws essentially prescribed the response of government agencies to victims of crime: victims are to be treated with dignity, respect, and fairness; victims are guaranteed the right to be heard at the various stages of the criminal justice process; victims are to be protected from intimidation, harassment, or abuse from the defendants; and so forth. However, as Jenness and Grattet explain, the connection of the crime victim's movement with the anti-hate-crime movement was surprising, as the former is typically considered a conservative social movement, very different from the liberal civil rights, women's, and gay and lesbian movements. The authors note that "although it makes for strange bedfellows, this allegiance has proved crucial to the formation of an anti-hate-crime movement" (2001, 27).

Jenness and Grattet also explain the implications that hate crime legislation has for theories of policymaking, which often emphasize three factors: demand factors, interest groups, and political context (168). According to the demand factors theory, legislation is created as a response to a pressing social problem. In the case of hate crime policies, this theory would suggest that legislators and other policymakers create laws in reaction to increases of bias-motivated behavior (ibid.). For example, a jurisdiction may enact a hate crime statute in the aftermath of a horrendous crime motivated by bias. This is often called a "triggering event," as it triggers the public to demand attention to the issue, garners significant media attention, and often results in some form of action taken by the government. However, this theory is problematic due to the inconsistency with which jurisdictions enact such legislation. For example, the state of Wyoming does not have a hate crime statute, even though it experienced a widely publicized murder of a gay college student, Matthew Shepard, in 1998.

The interest group theory, however, "envisions the policy process as a competition between differentially empowered groups of actors who define a problem, dramatize its importance, and promote solutions to remedy it" (Jenness and Grattet 2001, 170). Interest groups have varying political and organizational power, thus the group that manages to keep the attention of the public and the media is more likely to see its efforts result in new legislation. This theory is useful in explaining why certain groups have received protected status within hate crime legislation. Because the general public accepts the intentions of some interest groups (such as religious organizations) more willingly than the intentions of others (for instance, advocacy groups for gays and lesbians), the former groups are more likely to receive acknowledgement in the policy-making arena. This holds true with hate crime legislation: bias against religion is included in most states' statutes, whereas bias against sexual orientation is often not.

Finally, Jenness and Grattet argue that political context, or the political environment, is the most important means by which social issues are recognized as potential policy items.[5] As the authors explain, the legal culture and policy-making traditions of a jurisdiction provide resources for interest groups and policymakers to use in framing issues so that their proposals are accepted (174). Furthermore, the adoption of a policy in other jurisdictions makes adopting it also an act of conformity by a legislature once an issue becomes institutionalized as a social problem (177). According to this perspective, state legislatures may enact hate crime statutes due to the pressure of conforming to federal legislation or other states' actions.

Symbolic Purpose

Many scholars also argue that hate crime laws are created as a symbolic tool used to educate the public on the moral and social norms of a community (Gerstenfeld 2004, 21–23). Gerstenfeld writes: "Of all the arguments made in support of hate crimes legislation, the symbolic argument is perhaps the most frequently given" (22). Some scholars argue that hate crime laws are a form of "symbolic politics" (Jacobs and Potter 1998, 66). They assert that politicians use bias crime legislation as a way to send messages to important groups of constituents. For example, politicians pass hate crime legislation in order to send a message to the lobbyists that they empathize with the lobbyists' issue and will support bias crime laws to combat the violence directed at their group.

Politicians also use hate crime legislation to send a message to the public that they are against prejudice and bigotry, and to demonstrate their moral character to their constituents. Finally, politicians utilize hate crime legislation to send a message to actual and potential bias crime offenders. By passing such laws, politicians tell offenders that their actions are not tolerable and that if they do offend, they will be severely punished (Jacobs and Potter 1998, 67–68). Indeed, Jacobs and Henry argue:

> Politicians have enthusiastically climbed aboard the hate crime epidemic bandwagon. Denouncing hate crime and passing sentencing enhancement laws provides elected officials with an opportunity to decry bigotry. Politicians can propose anti-hate legislation as a cheap, quick-fix solution that sends powerful symbolic messages to important groups of constituents. (1996, 376)

In her case study of the Violence Against Women Act of 1994, Stolz (1999) argues that symbolism is a main component of legislation. For example, she concludes that VAWA was enacted to educate the public about domestic violence—specifically, that it is a crime. Another symbolic function was to communicate a message of reassurance to victims of domestic violence and a threat to offenders. Stolz also argues that the legislation served as a moral educator—sending a message that gender-motivated violence was a violation of civil rights, just like racism was. And finally, VAWA served as a model for how to combat domestic violence on the state level. More broadly, Stolz conjectures that federal legislation is often implemented due to the public's concern about a crime problem, and not necessarily in response to interest group lobbying, narrow constituency politics, or changes in the composition of Congress.

Internal Determinants versus Regional Diffusion

Jenness and Grattet (1996) reinforced the importance of examining the symbolic nature of hate crime legislation by examining the utility of the internal determinants model and the diffusion model in explaining the adoption of hate crime laws. The internal determinants model claims that internal factors—such as the political, economic, and social characteristics of a state—explain why a specific state adopts a new policy; on the other hand, the diffusion model posits that external factors—such as the influence of neighboring states—play a role in why new policies are adopted (134). Utilizing logistic regression analyses, the authors examined how various structural and political variables predict the probability that a state will pass bias crime legislation.

Interestingly, they found that neither structural nor political variables sufficiently explain whether a state will enact such a law. For instance, in their analysis of structural variables, the authors discovered that measures of urbanization, immigration, and violent crime are not good predictors of enacting hate crime legislation (1996, 144). Furthermore, the authors found no evidence that passing a hate crime law is a response to economic decline (145). They also discovered little support for the effect of state politics on the adoption process:

"The probability of adopting a bias-motivated violence and intimidation law does not seem to depend upon the degree to which states are committed to establishing and protecting group rights, the presence of minorities in politically influential positions, or the capacity of the state to engage in institution-building" (ibid.).

Since the data did not support the argument that structural and political factors alone influence whether a state enacts hate crime legislation, Jenness and Grattet argued that future work must address the symbolic realm of the state (1996, 147).[6] More specifically, the authors argued that symbolic factors such as media attention, triggering events, and the role of social movement organizations must be investigated in order to fully understand the development process of hate crime legislation.

Building upon the work of Grattet, Jenness, and Curry (1998), Soule and Earl (2001) examined the influence of intrastate characteristics (that is, the internal determinants model) and interstate characteristics (the regional diffusion model) on the development of hate crime legislation. However, Soule and Earl diverged from past studies both theoretically and methodologically: the authors did not assume that states are equally influenced by other states' adoptions, or that all previous adopters had an equal effect on the remaining potential adopters. Rather, Soule and Earl argued that "some states are more important referents to the diffusion process; thus their actions might be more infectious than others. Other states might have characteristics that make them more susceptible to the enactment of a hate crime law once it has begun to diffuse" (282).

Employing regression analyses, Soule and Earl found that wealthier states were more likely to pass hate crime laws: "Apparently, during economic upswings, states are more expansive toward subordinate groups and are more likely to pass laws to protect them from hate or bias-related crime" (293–94). The authors also discovered that the more Democratic a state legislature is, the sooner it will enact bias crime legislation, and that states with a great deal of media attention to hate crimes were also quicker to enact such laws; yet neither the percentage of liberal voters nor the percentage of nonwhite citizens increased the speed of passage of hate crime laws. Interestingly, Soule and Earl also found that states that had previously enacted a civil hate crime law or data collection law were slower to enact a criminal hate crime law. This contradicted the authors' hypothesis: "This unexpected finding may result from the fact that some states have adopted civil or data collection laws in an attempt to quell concern over hate crimes without taking the powerful and important step of criminalizing hate crimes ... [and] that the data collection laws and civil redress laws might provide a 'shield' or a 'buffer' for states reluctant to criminalize hate crimes" (294).

Soule and Earl also obtained interesting findings in regard to the susceptibility and infectiousness of states in passing hate crime laws. For instance, contrary to what Grattet, Jenness, and Curry (1998) found, Soule and Earl observed that "the adoption of a criminal hate crime law in a region actually decreased the rate of subsequent adoptions within that region" (2001, 296). The authors reasoned that "this could be because the states are more aware of their region-mates' actions and if the process of getting one of these laws passed was controversial, it may have, in essence, scared off other states who were paying attention to the process" (ibid.). Also, Soule and Earl found that some states—such as those that had repealed sodomy laws—were more likely to pass criminal bias crime legislation. Moreover, the authors discovered that some states were more infectious than others in passing hate crime law, particularly because of the media attention garnered during the decision-making process. In sum, the authors claim that in regard to the enactment of hate crime laws, some states are leaders and some are followers (297–98). Soule and Earl explain:

> Like Grattet and colleagues (1998), we emphasize the importance of understanding that states are not independent from one another; the actions of one state can (and do) affect subsequent actions by other states. State lawmakers do not exist in a vacuum; rather they pay attention to what others are doing, especially with regard to controversial laws such as criminal hate crime laws. (2001, 298)

A Case Study Approach

Utilizing a different approach from the aforementioned quantitative studies, Becker (1999) examined the symbolic nature of hate crime legislation through a historical analysis of Ohio's ethnic intimidation law. In particular, he explored the role of triggering events, interest group activity, and the media in the development of the Ohio legislation. Through interviews with key players in the law's enactment and an analysis of media accounts and archived documents such as legislative records and press releases, Becker discovered that interest group activity, media campaigns, and a specific triggering event all significantly influenced the enactment of the ethnic intimidation law.

First, Becker explained the role of a specific triggering event: in an interview with the senator who originally sponsored the bill, Becker discovered that the senator had been motivated to author the legislation after a cross burning incident in his district (1999, 252). Becker also found that various interest groups played a role in the development of the legislation, by offering support in the form of written testimony to legislative committees and newspaper editorials. Notably, Becker did not find any groups that had opposed the bill. Indeed, the only individual opponent was a Republican representative from Cincinnati, and he was not against the statute but disagreed with the punitive damages that it allowed victims to recover (255).

Becker also discovered that the media affected the law's formation in two ways: news coverage of events, which may have sensitized the public to the issue, and the media campaigns of various advocacy groups, such as the Anti-Defamation League. Specifically, he found that media coverage of bias-related incidents increased during the period he examined, on both the state and the national levels. Becker explained: "The intensive coverage of specific incidents may have influenced Ohioians' [sic] perceptions of hate crimes and hate group activity, which may have led to a perception that a problem existed and the conclusion that legislative intervention was required" (256). Furthermore, Becker learned through his interviews that the media had been used to garner support for the law. The senator sponsoring the bill said it was "standard practice for him to educate the media, solicit editorial support, and utilize the media when attempting to pass new legislation" (257). Thus, Becker concluded that his research demonstrated the importance of triggering events, interest group activity, and the role of the media in the creation of hate crime legislation.

The Enforcement of Hate Crime Law

> It is clear that differences in the number of hate crimes reported in various regions do not simply reflect differences in the number of criminal acts motivated by bias. They may instead reflect different incentives to call acts of bias to the attention of local authorities, as well as different incentives that influence law enforcement agents to respond to, and to report, hate crimes.
> —R. McVeigh, M. R. Welch, and T. Bjarnason, "Hate Crime Reporting as a Successful Social Movement Outcome"

How do law enforcement officials' perceptions of certain cases influence whether they are investigated or prosecuted? For years researchers have sought answers to this question. A great deal of research has explored the variables that influence the decisions of police officers (for example, see Chappell, MacDonald, and Manz 2006; Mastrofski, Ritti, and Hoffmaster 1987; Novak et al. 2002; Sherman 1980). Another considerable body of research has examined the factors that influence the decisions of prosecutors (for example, see Albonetti 1987; Hirschel and Hutchinson 2001; Spears and Spohn 1997; Spohn, Beichner, and Davis-Frenzel 2001). However, in many ways hate crime laws create a unique dilemma for law enforcement officials, and researchers have only begun to study this phenomenon.

As explained in the quote above, the official count of hate crimes in a jurisdiction does not accurately reflect the actual number of incidences. There are many reasons for this discrepancy. For instance, victims of bias crimes face various challenges when deciding whether to go to the police (Finn 1988); victims may be fearful of retaliation if they report the crime, or they may wonder if the authorities will respond appropriately to the crime, as law enforcement officers may be prejudiced themselves. Another reason for this discrepancy, as explained in the quote, is that officials also encounter many different incentives for responding to hate crimes, as well as for reporting such incidents.

Police Response to Hate Crime Laws

As hate crime laws were implemented throughout the country, questions arose about their effectiveness. For instance, critics of bias crime legislation questioned whether these crimes could be accurately identified as such, much less thoroughly investigated by police (Jacobs and Potter 1998). Various studies have since examined how police departments enforce hate crime statutes (Bell 2002; Boyd, Hammer, and Berk 1996; Culotta 2002; Franklin 2002; Grattet and Jenness 2005; Haider-Markel 2004; Jenness and Grattet 2005; Martin 1996; McVeigh, Welch, and Bjarnason 2003; Nolan and Akiyama 2004), and this research has revealed a number of important findings.

In one of the first studies to examine police response to hate crimes, Martin (1996) compared the law enforcement approach to bias crimes and its approach to other crimes. She gathered case reports from two jurisdictions, New York and Baltimore. Her findings showed that "the responses of the two law enforcement agencies to bias crimes reflect the differences in their communities, organizational approaches, and state laws" (471). For instance, in New York, an investigator assigned to a specialized bias crime unit responded to all suspected bias incidents, subsequently becoming responsible for the cases. The investigator worked closely with precinct detectives and victims and, if an arrest was made, followed the case through the criminal justice system (461). In contrast, the Baltimore Police Department did not have a specialized unit; instead, individual beat officers were responsible for investigating alleged bias offenses. Cases deemed to be possible bias crimes were then reviewed at a monthly meeting attended by various official representatives.

Martin found that the Baltimore police placed "less emphasis on solving crimes and apprehending offenders than on gathering information to enable the police to identify trouble spots, act to reduce intergroup tensions, and provide assistance to victims and to the community" (471). Hence, as Martin explained, it was not surprising that the proportion of arrests for bias crimes was only "slightly higher" than for nonbias crimes. However, in New York, the priority for the investigator was to solve bias crimes, and more resources were invested to make that possible; consequently, the arrest rate was "markedly higher" for bias crimes compared to nonbias crimes (471). Martin concluded:

> The success of a bias-crime program ultimately rests both on victims' willingness to report offenses and on patrol officers' ability and willingness to respond to and report bias motivation when they encounter it. This ability and willingness, in turn, requires effective training and clear policies that reward officers for identifying bias cases rather than penalizing them with burdensome paperwork. (477)

Building upon Martin's work, Boyd, Hammer, and Berk (1996) also examined law enforcement response to hate crime laws. Through interviews and observations, the authors explored the decision-making practices of detectives in two large urban police departments. Boyd, Hammer and Berk discovered that many officers were not in favor of the new hate crime policy, for several reasons. For instance, the policy increased the bureaucratic requirements—such as additional paperwork—imposed upon them. The authors explained: "Many interviewed officers, detectives, and commanding officers expressed resentment over the demands placed on them by the new policy, seeing it as another bureaucratic imposition that takes officers away from their 'real' crime-solving duties" (827). Others expressed concern about determining motive in hate crime cases, and a few officers even "expressed the belief that hate crimes should not be considered crimes at all. They are just 'human nature' or the normal expression of hostility among people living in crowded conditions" (827).

When comparing the two police departments, Boyd, Hammer, and Berk found that the procedures for dealing with hate crime incidents varied considerably. Like Martin, the authors found that different departments had different procedures for both reporting and investigating bias crimes. In one of the departments that Boyd, Hammer, and Berk studied, both the commanding officer and the senior detective considered hate crimes to be conceptually different from all other crimes; thus special precautions were taken to accurately identify possible bias crimes, and clear procedures were implemented to process such cases. However, in the second department, patrol officers received no additional training or instruction on bias crimes, as they were not considered any different from other crimes. In fact, "true" hate crimes (for instance, cross burnings) were considered to be so infrequent that preoccupation with such crimes would take away from "real" police work. Hence, Boyd, Hammer, and Berk concluded that "the constitution of an incident as a hate crime is deeply intertwined with the social context in which its detection, investigation, and classification occurs" (848).

Nolan and Akiyama also explored how organizational and community contexts affected law enforcement activity, in a study utilizing focus groups and surveys. The authors discovered five common factors at both the department and officer levels that influenced how police officers enforced and reported hate crimes. For example, among the department-level factors, the authors found that hate crime laws were more likely to be enforced if the majority of the officers in the department shared attitudes and beliefs about hate crime reporting. More important, hate crime laws were more likely to be enforced if the police officers perceived that citizens wanted them to report hate crimes, and if they believed that the community would appreciate the efforts that the department made to deal with these crimes. The authors also discovered that few resources—for instance, training and support staff—were allocated to enforce hate crime legislation if the police officers did not perceive that these crimes were a priority for the department (2004, 98–100).

Among the individual-level factors, Nolan and Akiyama discovered that the degree to which a police department's policies and procedures supported hate crime reporting was a significant factor in the enforcement of these laws. In other words, the authors found that if a department did not have a hate crime reporting policy, or had a policy that was not enforced, officers were not likely to report these crimes. Moreover, the authors found that the officers' own beliefs about their departments' commitment to hate crime reporting were significant factors in the enforcement of such laws, and "one measure of this commitment is the amount of training resources directed to hate crime investigating and reporting" (2004, 100).

More recently, Bell (2002) affirmed that organizational and community contexts significantly influence the enforcement of hate crime laws. In her qualitative study of one large metropolitan city, Bell found that law enforcement officers often felt conflicting pressures from their community and department in regard to the enforcement of hate crime laws. For example, officers were often pressured by their department to enforce hate crime laws; yet they simultaneously felt pressured to keep hate crime statistics low. Moreover, as Bell explained, "organizational pressures may provide incentives for police to fail to comply or to comply only minimally with the law. Police may not enforce the law because efficiency demands that limited resources be allocated to activities they believe more deserving of official action" (2002, 14).

Bell also discovered that police officers were often pressured by members of the community to not enforce hate crime legislation against certain subgroups within the city. For example, she reported that certain segments of the community continually fought against desegregation and as a result, made it very difficult for police officers to enforce hate crime laws in these areas of the city. Bell found that many officers felt that the hate crime laws were created to enforce the ideals of the society, but were not necessarily to be enforced on the street.

Finally, Bell observed that detectives were very careful about which cases to bring under the hate crime law, as they did not want to weaken or "wear the law out." One detective clarified this reasoning to Bell: "The civil rights law has teeth. It's there to bite you on the butt. If you bring cases with lousy evidence and language, the law loses its teeth" (quoted in 2002, 153). Thus, detectives invoked the law when they had a "good case." These cases often involved language indicative of a bias motivation, and a credible victim who was injured or frightened (154).

Jenness and Grattet (2005) took an innovative approach to this area of research by studying what they call the "law-in-between," or the time between the enactment of hate crime legislation and the active investigation of such crimes by law enforcement officials. Specifically, the authors asked: "What types of law enforcement agencies and community environments yield formal policies designed to articulate an agency's definition of hate crime, as well as the specific protocols the agency advocates for handling hate crime cases?" (2005, 339). To answer this question, Jenness and Grattet examined both community and organizational factors that might influence whether an agency developed a hate crime policy. The authors solicited policy information from 397 police and sheriff agencies throughout the state of California, with a response rate of 91 percent. Interestingly, of the responding agencies, almost half (44.7 percent) claimed that they did not have a written hate crime policy. Reasons given for not having an explicit policy included: the lack of need for a hate crime policy, because there were very few, if any, such crimes in the jurisdiction; an administrative delay in developing a policy, despite the fact that California had had a hate crime statute for almost two decades; and an ability to enforce hate crime law with existing policies, because hate crime policing procedures were not considered any different from regular policing procedures (2005, 350).

Through logistic regression analyses, the authors found that community factors, such as the crime rate and community demands (for example, human relations commissions), were not sufficient predictors of the adoption of hate crime policies (2005, 354–55). However, the authors also found that organizational factors were instrumental for developing polices—specifically, organizational perviousness was crucial to this process.[7] In other words, external factors, in combination with the degree to which the organization was amenable to innovation, influenced the likelihood of having a hate crime policy. As a result, the authors argued that future research needs to explore how hate crime policies influence the likelihood that police officers accurately identify and respond to hate crimes (356). This is particularly important because, as noted, almost half of the responding agencies did not have a hate crime policy—in fact, many of the agencies that chose not to respond to the authors' survey may have done so because they did not have a written policy either.[8] In other words, if the policies do assist police officers in responding to hate crime incidents, agencies should develop explicit policies.

Prosecutors' Response to Hate Crime Laws

Compared to the research conducted on police response to hate crime laws, little empirical research has examined prosecutors' responses to such laws. The lack of empirical studies is partly due to the difficulty of obtaining such data on a statewide or national level (Phillips 2006) and is "in large part a function of the newness of the criminal category and of the lag time between changes in the legal world and scholarship devoted to understanding such changes" (Jenness and Grattet 2001, 147). This is unfortunate, as prosecutors are the legal actors who determine whether or not to add the additional charge of a bias crime.

Researchers have attempted to find out why so few cases are prosecuted as bias crimes. For instance, through interviews with forty individuals—including law enforcement officials, representatives of constituency organizations, and researchers who had conducted studies related to hate violence—Finn elucidated four specific challenges that prosecutors face when enforcing hate crime statutes. First, prosecutors must prove the crime was motivated by bias. As departments often lack the necessary resources to sufficiently investigate bias crimes, it is difficult to obtain the needed evidence. Therefore, prosecutors rely on the following guidelines for determining whether a crime was motivated by bias: (1) common sense (for instance, a cross burning on the lawn of a minority family obviously suggests racial bias); (2) the language used by the suspect; (3) the severity of the attack; (4) a lack of provocation; (5) a previous history of similar incidents in the area; and (6) the absence of any other motive (1988, 14).

Another challenge that prosecutors face is uncooperative witnesses or victims. Many victims do not want to proceed with an investigation; they would rather just move away from the area. The third challenge confronted by prosecutors is the use of special defenses during trials. For example, defendants have been acquitted in the past by using a "homosexual panic" defense, or for claiming self-defense or temporary insanity in response to an alleged sexual advance. Finally, Finn explained that prosecutors often face judges who do not want to give out the severe sanctions associated with the bias crime charge, particularly if the offender is a juvenile. Hence, Finn concluded:

> Prosecutors are in a pivotal position to both promote targeting of bias crime among police and judges and to sustain whatever efforts law enforcement and the judiciary are already devoting to hate violence offenses. While ultimately it requires the concern of all three criminal justice system actors to significantly alter how bias crime offenders are handled, district attorneys can play a major role in initiating and promoting change in this area. (1988, 15)

More recently, Bell offered similar reasons for why prosecutors find it difficult to prosecute such crimes. First, prosecutors explained that these crimes are often more challenging than regular cases because of the added burden of proving motive (2002, 161). Not only is it necessary to determine a suspect and find evidence of guilt, but prosecutors also need to prove why the crime was committed. Prosecutors also found these cases difficult because witnesses often did not want to come forward, especially in communities where the prosecution of hate crimes was unpopular (162). And in cases where there were corroborating witnesses, judges were sometimes unwilling to convict on the bias charge (ibid.).

Because of these challenges, Bell found that prosecutors, like detectives, often look for what is considered a "good case." One assistant district attorney explained: "[A good case] has a repeat offender. It occurs in an area where this type of thing has happened before, the victim and the perpetrator are of different races and there is no other reason for this to have occurred" (2002, 165). Bell suggested that the focus on the strongest cases might result from district attorneys' offices emphasizing positive win-loss records for promotions and subsequent elections.

In one of the few published studies that focused specifically on the prosecution of hate crimes, McPhail and Jenness (2005–6) examined how prosecutors decided to implement the hate crime law in Texas. Through sixteen interviews with prosecutors, the authors found that a range of factors influenced the decision-making process. The authors separated the factors into two groups: factors that prosecutors readily identified as influential in the decision-making process, and factors that prosecutors denied were influential (96). Factors readily identified by prosecutors included reasons such as the facts of the case and the strength of the evidence; whether the burden of proving the bias element was worthwhile in securing a higher punishment; whether hate was the sole reason for the crime, or whether there might have been multiple motives; whether the case fit the prosecutors' idea of a "typical" hate crime (like the dragging death of James Byrd Jr.); whether the potential benefits of adding the hate crime enhancement, such as a longer sentence, outweighed the potential costs for the prosecutor, including additional work; and whether prosecutors wanted to send a message to both the targeted community and potential hate crime offenders.

Although these reasons were openly acknowledged by prosecutors, McPhail and Jenness (2005–6) discussed other factors that might influence the decision-making process but that were either denied or minimized by the prosecutors in their study. For instance, prosecutors denied that conviction rates or electoral politics played a role in the decision-making process. And prosecutors minimized the extent to which pressures from the community or media influenced their decisions. The authors also discovered that the prosecutors' own identities and experiences had limited influence on the decision-making process. Specifically, the majority of the prosecutors denied that either their racial identity or their gender played a role in their charging decisions.

In the past, empirical studies have essentially disregarded how law enforcement officials respond to the gender category. Previous studies acknowledge that police and prosecutors often look for the "perfect" case when enforcing bias crime laws (Bell 2002; Boyd, Hammer, and Berk 1996), yet researchers have not fully explored how these officials respond to cases that do not fit the "typical" hate crime mold. Thus, we have little information about how criminal justice professionals handle the complexities of investigating and prosecuting gender-motivated bias crimes. McPhail and DiNitto (2005) made what was probably the first attempt to fill this gap in the literature.

Through in-depth interviews with prosecutors throughout the state of Texas, the authors examined prosecutors' knowledge of the state's new gender-bias status category and their willingness to charge offenses against women under the new law. McPhail and DiNitto discovered that prosecutors were uninformed about gender-motivated bias crimes; many expressed surprise that gender was even included within the hate crime law. For example, when first asked about the gender category, several prosecutors associated "gender" with "sexual orientation." McPhail and DiNitto also found that prosecutors were reluctant to ascribe violence against women to hate. Rather, prosecutors considered the violence to be motivated by a desire for power and control; consequently, they had difficulty prosecuting such crimes under the category of a gender-bias hate crime. One prosecutor mentioned that most men killed women while expressing love—not hate—for them, concluding that these crimes were not consistent with the hate crime criterion (2005, 1173). Another prosecutor explained that a married rapist could not be a bias crime offender because "in her judgment, having a successful relationship with one woman in his life seemed to dispel the notion that he hated women in general" (1173–74).

In addition, McPhail and DiNitto discovered that most prosecutors did not believe that women were a stigmatized group, like other targets of hate crimes. In fact, many prosecutors expressed concern for men as a group. The authors observed:

> It is interesting to note that this concern with the "opposite" group did not arise in discussions of other categories. That is, when speaking of race, no prosecutor referenced White people, or when speaking of sexual identity, no one mentioned protecting heterosexuals. (2005, 1171)

Moreover, prosecutors argued that bias against women would be hard to prove, and that legislators had included gender as a political act to appease certain constituents (2005, 1174). In sum, "the majority of prosecutors could not envision using gender as a status category in a hate crime enhancement" (1176).

As demonstrated throughout this chapter, many factors come into play for both the development and the enforcement of hate crime laws. Furthermore, as illustrated by the one study to explore prosecutors' perspectives of the gender category (McPhail and DiNitto 2005), this category presents many unique challenges for law enforcement officials. Because of these challenges, it is imperative for researchers to further examine the complexities of the gender category. Past research has explored the development of the gender category on the national level (for example, see Jenness and Broad 2005); however, research has not yet examined the process by which the gender category is included within state statutes. And although McPhail and DiNitto (2005) provided an analysis of prosecutors' perspectives of the gender category, their research was conducted soon after the category was added to the state's law and did not include other perspectives, such as those of investigators and members of special interest groups.

Given the paucity of knowledge about the enforcement of the gender category in hate crime law, this book thus fills a gap in the literature regarding the gender category. The first two chapters have laid the foundation for understanding the development and enforcement of hate crime legislation; the next three chapters focus specifically on the case study of New Jersey.

3 | Developing the Gender Category
"It Just Made Sense"

> Crimes motivated by hate and bias tend to erode the basic fabric of society. Bias incidents having a racial, religious, ethnic, sexual, or gender component as well as crimes against individuals with a handicap, manifest themselves in a wide spectrum of criminal activities. These bias incidents jeopardize the active and open pursuit of freedom and opportunity. They attack our citizens based on their race, religion, ethnic heritage, sexual orientation, handicap, or gender.—*New Jersey Police Department, "Bias Incident Summary," 2006*

In 1981, New Jersey became one of the first states to enact a hate crime law (Vitale 2002). Like many early state statutes on hate crimes, this law was added to the general harassment and simple assault statutes, in the part of the criminal sentencing code concerning the criteria for an extended term of imprisonment.[1] In 1990, the legislature passed the Ethnic Intimidation Act to increase sentences "in cases where the offender acts 'at least in part, with ill will, hatred or bias' toward his victim because of the victim's race, color, religion or sexual orientation" (Bean 1993, 4). The purpose of the act was essentially to upgrade harassment and simple assault charges from misdemeanors to fourth-degree indictable crimes, when bias was involved (ibid.).

Then, in 1995, through Senate Bill 402, the language of the Ethnic Intimidation Act was changed from "at least in part, with ill will, hatred or bias" to "with a purpose to intimidate" as a result of the 1992 U.S. Supreme Court decision in *R.A.V. v. City of St. Paul*, 505 U.S. 377 (Hester 1995; Phillips 2006).[2] With this change of words, the statute no longer criminalized personal viewpoints (that is, expressions of contempt and hatred) protected under the First Amendment; rather, the revised statute punished actions with the intent to intimidate based on one of the protected group characteristics. With these revisions, New Jersey's statute complied with the U.S. Supreme Court ruling in *R.A.V.*

However, in a 2000 landmark case, *Apprendi v. New Jersey*, 530 U.S. 466, the U.S. Supreme Court deemed New Jersey's law to be unconstitutional (Vitale 2002).[3] The Court decided that the defendant's due process rights had been violated since the decision to increase the sentence had not been determined by a jury. As a result of this decision, the New Jersey state legislature repealed the then-existing hate crime statute and adopted a new bill that created a separate crime of bias intimidation. This bill was signed into law by Governor John O. Bennett on January 11, 2002 (Vitale 2002). The new crime of bias intimidation (see N.J.S. section 2C:16-1 in Appendix B) must be charged and prosecuted as a separate offense, and a conviction of bias intimidation typically elevates the underlying crime one degree higher than the original status: "As a separate offense, a charge of bias intimidation is now treated as any other crime and the defendant is afforded all of the protections of the Sixth and Fourteenth Amendments, including the right to be tried by a jury on that specific crime and a right to a finding of guilt 'beyond a reasonable doubt'" (Vitale 2002, 368). The bias intimidation statute is New Jersey's current hate crime law.

The Inclusion of Gender

On October 21, 1992, Jack Sinagra and Joseph Kyrillos in the New Jersey Senate and Harriet Derman and Jeff Warsh in the Assembly introduced the bias intimidation bill to add gender and disability as protected statuses to the then-existing hate crime law, and to eliminate the value-laden words found to be unconstitutional in *R.A.V. v. St. Paul* (Haydon 1992). In 1993, a civil remedy measure was attached to the bill,[4] and on May 13 the Assembly passed the bill unanimously, without floor debate (Marsico 1993d).

On May 24 a senate panel released legislation to expand the hate crime statute to include gender and disability. Senator Sinagra called the failure to include gender or handicap within the bias crime definition a "technicality" and a "flaw" in the law (quoted in "Panel Votes to Include Gender"1993). The legislation was pending on June 12, when the civil remedy measure was signed into law (Marsico 1993b). Approximately eight months later, the Senate Judiciary Committee unanimously endorsed the measure and sent the bill to the full senate for final consideration (Marsico 1994). On June 13, 1994, the legislation passed the Senate with a vote of thirty-seven to two ("Anti-bias Bill Forwarded," 1994).

Governor Christine Todd Whitman did not sign the bill into law until August 15, 1995. Although the bill had been introduced almost three years earlier, the inclusion of gender was unremarkable according to two key female legislative actors, neither of whom remembered any controversy surrounding its addition to the hate crime statute. Indeed, when asked why gender was added, one of them stated: "It just made sense."

However, the process of including gender was noteworthy. Although there was little disagreement about whether gender was an appropriate addition to the bias crime statute, there was debate about what types of gender-bias crimes should be covered. Specifically, lawmakers debated whether sexual offenses should be included as gender-motivated bias crimes (this debate is examined in the following section). In the end, the gender category was included with a distinct exemption. Subsection d of the current statute states:

> *Gender exemption in sexual offense prosecutions.* It shall not be a violation of subsection a. if the underlying criminal offense is a violation of chapter 14 of Title 2C of the New Jersey Statutes and the circumstance specified in paragraph (1), (2), or (3) of subsection a. of this section is based solely upon the gender of the victim.

According to this exemption, a bias intimidation charge cannot be attached to a charge of sexual assault if the motivating factor was solely the victim's gender. In other words, "to find a defendant guilty of bias intimidation in a sexual assault case, the bias must be based on the victim's race, color, religion, handicap, [or] sexual orientation" (Vitale 2002, 370).[5] The reasons for this exemption, as well as the reasons for the inclusion of gender, are revealed through the analysis of legislative histories and newspaper accounts, as well as through interviews with legislative actors, prosecutors, investigators, and interest group members.

The Impetus behind the Gender Category

The political context, the media, triggering events, and interest group activities all played a role in the inclusion of gender in New Jersey's bias crime statute.

Political Context

Innovative Political Environment

As one of the first states to enact a hate crime law, New Jersey had proved itself receptive to legal innovation. When gender began to be considered as a possible category, in the early 1990s, the legislature had already demonstrated its interest in bias crime laws with the passage not just of the hate crime law in 1981 but also of the Ethnic Intimidation Act in 1990. Two interviewees explained that the New Jersey legal climate has always been pioneering in regard to bias crimes:

> I think you have a liberal-minded type of legislature who would be more attuned to bias crimes. In a whole lot of other states, I would guess—maybe I'm wrong—discounting states like California, I would imagine that we probably have stronger bias crime laws in New Jersey than most states. (male interest group member)

> New Jersey in particular is one of the most diverse states in the nation, [and has] generally been in the forefront of the laws against discrimination, relatively progressive. And that's why you often find New Jersey does a relatively good job around bias crimes. (male county prosecutor)

This innovative political environment was evident two years prior to the inclusion of gender in the criminal statute, when the legislature enacted the civil remedy measure described above, which permits the victims of bias crimes to seek legal redress in civil court. Since gender was included in this civil statute, lawmakers had already addressed the importance of recognizing gender in hate crime legislation. Moreover, the passage of the civil remedy law in 1993 occurred in the same period in which federal hearings were held on the Violence Against Women Act (discussed in chapter 2). During the early 1990s, New Jersey lawmakers were certainly aware of this potential federal legislation, and although gender had been excluded from previous federal hate crime legislation (such as the Hate Crime Statistics Act of 1990), it was increasingly becoming a part of the federal discourse on hate crimes. The timing of these discussions undoubtedly influenced the New Jersey legislature's decision to include gender as a protected category in the civil remedy law and, subsequently, in the criminal statute.

The establishment of the Office of Bias Crimes and Community Relations (OBCCR) within the Division of Criminal Justice provided additional evidence of New Jersey's innovative political environment during this time. Under the directive of Governor Jim Florio, the state's attorney general created this office in 1992 (New Jersey, Office of the Governor, 1993). The first statewide office in the country to focus on bias crimes, the OBCCR was responsible for investigating and prosecuting hate crimes throughout the state, for implementing training programs for law enforcement officers, and for educating the public and schoolchildren about hate crimes. A priority of the governor's office, the OBCCR benefited from the substantial political support it received during this time. For example, on the same day that the civil remedy measure was signed into law, Governor Florio and Attorney General Robert Del Tufo announced an expansion of the OBCCR, stating that the office was to acquire two new investigators and would train additional county and local investigators (Marsico 1993b). Because of this political support, the office played an influential role in how bias crimes were handled throughout the state. Therefore, the creation of the office, in addition to the passage of the civil remedy law, illustrated that the issue of hate crimes was a priority for high-ranking political officials, further demonstrating the receptive political environment in New Jersey at this time.

The passage of the civil remedy law also provided politicians with an opportunity to inform the public about the importance of hate crime legislation. Governor Florio expressed the significance of such legislation through emotional statements such as: "We cannot legislate decency, but we will not tolerate hatred. Whether they involve a gun, a fist or just a can of spray paint, hate crimes are the most corrosive crimes because they tear at our communities and families in divisive ways" (New Jersey, Office of the Governor, 1993). Attorney General Del Tufo also expressed the importance of hate crime laws: "We're still at a point in our society where we need to have more of a commitment to caring and healing" (quoted in Marsico 1993b).

By using powerful statements against hate crimes, political actors framed bias crime legislation as a necessary tool to combat bigotry and violence within society. Because the civil statute was enacted before the criminal statute, political actors used the passage of the former to reinforce the importance of hate crime legislation. By emphasizing the deleterious effect of hate crimes on communities, these political actors ensured that any opposition to the proposed crime bill faced both political and public scrutiny. Furthermore, as gender was included in the civil law, it established a discourse within the political and public arenas regarding the inclusion of gender in hate crime legislation.

Symbolic Purpose

As discussed in chapter 2, hate crime legislation was initially a liberal-oriented issue, as it stemmed from social movements such as the civil rights movement, the women's movement, and the gay and lesbian movement. However, one reason for the success of the hate crime movement was its unexpected alliance with the more conservative crime victim's movement (Jenness and Broad 2005). The convergence of these movements facilitated support across the political spectrum. In fact, all four of the original sponsors of the New Jersey bill to include gender were Republicans. The bill to revise the existing hate crime law was part of the anticrime package of the Republican majority in the legislature (Marsico

1993d), yet it enjoyed bipartisan support within the Senate and the Assembly. This is a testament to how politicians, both liberal and conservative, used hate crime legislation as a way to appease constituents concerned with combating crimes motivated by bias.

Passing the legislation gave both Republicans and Democrats an opportunity to condemn violence motivated by hate and to send a message to voters about their commitment to civil rights. In doing so, Republicans and Democrats not only showed a commitment to civil rights, which is considered a relatively liberal cause; they simultaneously garnered support for the crime victim's agenda, which is a more conservative cause. Therefore, by supporting the hate crime law, lawmakers appeased constituents on both ends of the political spectrum. Notably, this was all accomplished without having to expend political capital, as the political environment in New Jersey was predominantly in favor of the hate crime bill.

Politicians were also aware of the symbolic power of hate crime legislation and used it to reinforce their support of the crime-fighting agenda. For instance, after the Assembly unanimously passed the bill, Assemblywoman Derman, one of the original sponsors, said: "It probably is (largely) symbolic. But when it comes to the implementation, if there is a harsher penalty, then so be it . . . hate is insidious" (quoted in Marsico 1993d). Furthermore, Assemblyman Warsh said: "It's beyond symbolism . . . it sends a message that these types of crimes won't be tolerated" (quoted in Marsico 1993b). As the proposed bill was included in the majority's anticrime package, it gave lawmakers a symbolic piece of legislation to use in addressing constituents' concerns about the reported increase of hate crimes throughout the state. Therefore, by supporting the hate crime bill, politicians appeared tough on crime and simultaneously committed to civil rights.

Securing Political Support
Interviews with key actors confirmed the importance of the political context for the development of New Jersey's hate crime law. One male interest group member succinctly stated: "Politics definitely play a role. Legislation is political, so politics are important." When asked about the purpose of including the gender category, three interviewees mentioned that this type of legislation gave politicians the opportunity to secure support from important interest groups, particularly groups interested in combating gender-motivated violence, such as the National Organization for Women, the Coalition against Sexual As-

sault, and the Coalition for Battered Women. One male interest group member explained:

> The reality is that people will say that you have these crimes, because politically it is a point-scoring piece of legislation. I'm not demeaning any legislatures, but you have a state like New Jersey and you're looking for the support of the National Organization [for] Women or organization of rape crisis centers, and you strongly support or introduce bias crime legislation against women, I think you've picked up a strong supporter in those groups.

The importance of securing the public's support was also mentioned as a reason for the inclusion of gender. One male bias crime investigator observed:

> If they know they are going to be running for position and they have a lot of female voters in their area, they might want to sweeten the pot by putting something that would—you know, where they could tell their constituents, "Well, hey, I tried to get an addition to whatever so we could give women free access to marriage counselors and stuff like that, but the rest of the committee did not want to go along with me." But it's still in their political arena. Nobody votes for anything against women and children, because you know, it looks bad on your résumé.

This view was supported by evidence from newspaper articles and legislative histories. An analysis of this material turned up no overt opposition specifically to including the category of gender. This was surprising since the category had generated much debate on the federal level during the enactment of the Hate Crime Statistics Act a few years earlier. Furthermore, as the gender category is not without its critics, one would have expected more discussion on the state level of the appropriateness of including gender in the state hate crime law. However, the only opposition to its inclusion came from people concerned about hate crime laws in general. The concerns revolved around the constitutionality of such legislation, particularly whether it violated the First Amendment. For example, one defense attorney, representing a man convicted of a race-motivated bias crime, argued that the law was unconstitutional because it violated free speech and was too selective, even with the proposed changes in the bill. The defense attorney, Louis Kady, said: "It's still selective. It's political. What about bald men? What about fat people?" (quoted in Marsico 1993c)

Interestingly, one month before the legislature introduced the bill to include gender, Kenneth Goodman, an assistant deputy public defender who opposed all hate crime laws, used the absence of the gender category to support his argument that such legislation was unconstitutional. Goodman had represented a teenager who pled guilty under the harassment statute for spray painting ethnic slurs on several cars and a garage. The *Star-Ledger* reported that Goodman "argued that the law improperly protects only certain classes of people, noting, for example, that a person who launches anti-Semitic slurs to intimidate a Jewish family could be charged with bias-related harassment, while no such charge could be filed against a person who spewed anti-female slurs, since gender is not among categories safeguarded by the statute" (O'Neill 1992).

Although this statement was made prior to the introduction of the bill to include gender, it demonstrates that the gender category was already a part of the hate crime discourse in New Jersey. The statement also illustrates that legal actors were mindful of the gender category, despite its absence from New Jersey's hate crime law at the time. Given that awareness on the part of political and legal actors and the lack of direct opposition in the political arena to the inclusion of gender, it appears that the New Jersey political context was indeed a receptive environment for the expansion of the state's bias crime statute. Put simply, it appears that the inclusion of gender was the result of good timing and an innovative political climate.

Role of the Media

In addition to a political environment that was receptive to the proposed bill to include gender and disability, the media was also a significant force in the development of the legislation, influencing public opinion about hate crimes and providing a forum for politicians and activists to discuss their respective agendas. One male prosecutor explained the importance of the media in the development of New Jersey's hate crime law:

> Well, I think that the legislature, although they would deny it, is always worried about what public reaction is going to be. And certainly, public reaction is mediated through what the reporting is. So, the media certainly has a large role in helping to shape public opinion. So, I think it is quite important because the media is one of those groups . . . the legislature has to answer to.

Therefore, even though the political environment was receptive to the expansion of the hate crime law, it was imperative that such legislation was portrayed favorably in the media, in order to secure political and public support.

Favorable Reporting on Hate Crime Legislation

The content analysis of media accounts prior to the passage of the law demonstrated the role that the media played in the development of the legislation. Between 1990 and 1995, twenty original articles or editorials about gender and bias crimes appeared in the archives of the Newark *Star-Ledger* and the Trenton *Times*. Seven of these twenty pieces provided specific support for the proposed bill that expanded the hate crime law to include gender. These articles quoted political actors' explanations of the importance of expanding the hate crime legislation. For instance, on June 12, 1993, the *Star-Ledger* published an editorial titled "The Price of Hatred," calling the inclusion of gender and disability "a welcome step that is needed." Furthermore, on December 23, 1993, the New Jersey State Commission on Racism, Racial Violence and Religious Violence issued a report arguing for the inclusion of gender and disability in the state hate crime law (Reilly 1993).

Only two articles reported opposition to the new law, and notably, in neither case was the opposition specifically directed at the gender category. In one of the articles, Senator John Scott, a Republican from Bergen County, expressed concern about the meaning of bias terms: "They mean different things for different people. I think we're going down a dangerous path" (quoted in "Panel Votes to Include Gender" 1993). In the second article, a defense attorney criticized the legislation for being political and too selective (Marsico 1993c). Although these two articles reported opposition to the hate crime law, the comments were imbedded within articles overwhelmingly in favor of the proposed bill. Indeed, the opposing viewpoints appeared to be added in order to provide balance to the debate, yet the articles clearly offered more arguments in favor of the legislation.

Past research has shown how crime-related issues are politically constructed in the media (for example, see Beckett 1999), and the fact that more articles were written in favor of the legislation demonstrates the positive narrative perpetuated by the media in regard to the proposed bill. The positive slant is important, as members of the public often form their opinions on social issues based on what is reported in the media. If the newspapers had offered a negative account of bias crime legislation, the public would have been less likely to support such laws, in turn making it less likely that politicians would vote for them. However, since hate crime laws were discussed favorably in the newspaper articles, often with statements by politicians on the importance of bias crime legislation, it is apparent that the media spun a positive narrative around the proposed crime bill.

The Construction of a Social Problem

The media also played a role in constructing hate crimes as a pressing social issue in New Jersey. In the few years before the passage of the law, the media frequently reported an increase in hate crimes throughout the state. The content analysis of twenty articles published during this time showed that six explicitly mentioned an increase in bias incidents. For example, one article explained that "campus bias crime has become a hot issue at colleges throughout New Jersey and the rest of the country" (Peet 1990). The article reported that New Jersey ranked second in the country in the number of reported anti-Semitic incidents during the previous year. Another article noted that the number of bias incidents recorded in the New Jersey State Police Uniform Crime Report "rose significantly" between 1988 and 1991, from 593 to 976 (Marsico 1993c). By repeatedly reporting an increase in bias incidents, newspapers presented hate crimes as a growing problem throughout the state, a problem that demanded action by politicians and criminal justice officials.

However, despite the media's constructing hate crimes as an increasing social problem, only one of the twenty articles specifically mentioned violence directed at women and showed how gender-motivated violence fit in the context of hate crimes. The article described how the director of the OBCCR had spoken to "more than 200 women at a forum of the National Council of Jewish Women" and had "recounted several incidents of prejudice to women" (Freeman 1994). Except for this article, the newspapers did not present violence directed against women as an increasing social problem, in the way they had with both racial and religious bias crimes.

While the media provided a favorable view of hate crime legislation, constructing the crimes as an important social issue, the fact that gender-motivated violence was only mentioned once in this context is a telling example of how little attention was given to this category. Moreover, it demonstrates that the category was included in the law with minimal fanfare, further evidence that the inclusion of gender was primarily due to opportune circumstances, such as the timing of R.A.V. and the desire of state politicians to amend the state's bias crime statute, in addition to the numerous congressional hearings on the extent of violence against women that facilitated the passage of the Violence Against Women Act. It is also interesting to note that the limited coverage of gender-motivated violence foreshadows how little consideration the gender category received, by both the media and law enforcement officials, after its inclusion in the bias crime statute. As the next chapter will show, this lack of media attention ultimately affected how law enforcement officials perceived gender-motivated violence fitting in the hate crime framework and how they did (or did not) use the gender category.

In sum, the inclusion of gender was not due to concern over an increasing number of gender-motivated hate crimes; rather, it was primarily due to favorable conditions within the political and legal contexts. Although gender-motivated violence was not discussed at great length, the media's construction of other forms of hate crimes as a growing social problem played a role. Put simply, the media facilitated the passage of the hate crime law by providing a forum for political actors to promote their agenda, by increasing awareness of the number of bias incidents throughout the state, and by portraying the increase of hate crimes as a growing problem in need of attention.

Triggering Events

Triggering events, such as a highly publicized crime, often play a significant role in the development of hate crime law.[6] Interestingly, no specific crime occurred in New Jersey to facilitate the inclusion of the gender category. When asked whether there was an incident that triggered the addition of gender, none of the prosecutors, investigators, or interest group members interviewed could recall any such event. There was also no mention of a gender-bias incident in the newspaper accounts prior to the passage of the law. Although there may not have been a particular crime in the state that triggered the inclusion of gender, two significant court cases and the massacre of fourteen women at the University of Montreal seemed to influence the addition of gender to New Jersey's hate crime statute.

Influential Court Cases

As previously discussed, the bill to include gender was introduced in the New Jersey Assembly following the U.S. Supreme Court decision in *R.A.V. v. St. Paul* in 1992. The New Jersey statute's language requiring prosecutors to prove intent of "ill will" and "hatred" was considered a violation of the First Amendment because it prohibited an expression of thought, not just the criminal act resulting from a thought. Hence, the bill was introduced to make New Jersey's statute comply with the standards set forth in *R.A.V.*

The Supreme Court decision in *R.A.V.* provided the state legislature with an opportunity to revise the existing statute without having to expend political capital. As previously demonstrated, the prevailing political mood in the state was in favor of such revisions, so lawmakers could endorse the bill without encountering any controversy. Indeed, they appeared to avoid criticism within the political arena by showing support for the bill. Had it not been for *R.A.V.* and the widespread political agreement regarding hate crime legislation, the bill might not have even been proposed, and the opportunity to include gender might not have presented itself. *R.A.V.* acted as a triggering event because the decision required revisions in New Jersey's hate crime law, which presented an opportunity to include additional categories.

Although the decision in *R.A.V.* motivated the legislature to revise the language in the hate crime law, the proposal to expand the law to include gender and disability appeared to be the result of a case decided by the state's Superior Court. Senator Sinagra, one of the bill's sponsors, told a *Star-Ledger* reporter that the legislation was proposed in response to the Superior Court judge's ruling (Haydon 1992). In this case, Judge Joseph Sadofski had struck down New Jersey's statute as unconstitutional because of its similarity with the St. Paul ordinance deemed unconstitutional in *R.A.V.* In his ruling, the judge said that New Jersey's law might have passed constitutional muster if it had punished criminal conduct without specifying any categories of victims (O'Neill 1992).

Therefore, by expanding the legislation to include gender and disability, the proposed bill protected two additional categories of people often targeted due to a specified group characteristic. While not necessarily acceptable to Judge Sadofski, the proposed law satisfied the standards set forth in *R.A.V.* by removing the value-laden language that the Supreme Court had deemed unconstitutional. Because claims-makers such as politicians and interest groups were most concerned that the new law would pass constitutional muster, and not necessarily concerned with the inclusion of additional categories, the legislature was able to expand the law by presenting these revisions within the discourse of rectifying the statute to comply with constitutional standards.

A Case of Gender-Motivated Violence

These two court cases were triggering events within the legal context, and a specific incident also acted as a triggering event, according to one of the key legislative actors involved in the development of the bill. Specifically, a 1989 case at the University of Montreal demonstrated the necessity of including gender as a category in the bias crime statute. This legislative actor explained:

> I think it was not too long after there was a student in Canada who shot up a classroom, an engineering classroom, while shouting that women shouldn't be engineers. And we were using that as an example of something that would be a bias

crime against women. If he had been shouting racial epithets, he would've been charged with a bias crime. But because he shouted, you know, epithets against women, if this all had happened in New Jersey, it wouldn't have been a bias crime. And we just thought that was an injustice to women to not acknowledge that there is societal discrimination against them and that it leads to criminal acts.

Although this incident had not occurred within the state, this legislative actor still used it as an example of why it was important to include gender in the hate crime law. Interestingly, no other interviewees mentioned the case; and in a search of New Jersey newspaper archives between 1989 and 1995, only three articles in the Newark *Star-Ledger* and the Trenton *Times* mentioned the massacre at the University of Montreal.[7] Of the three articles, only two were written before the passage of the hate crime law; one article discussed a vigil at Rutgers University marking the one-year anniversary of the murders (Casey 1990), and the other discussed how the incident had facilitated efforts to reduce violence on television within Canada (Associated Press 1993). Despite the limited coverage of the case by New Jersey's newspapers, the incident generated a considerable amount of national media attention during this period. The incident may have influenced other political actors, thus arguably serving as a triggering event in New Jersey.

Interest Group Activities

Interest group activities also played a role in adding gender to New Jersey's bias crime statute. Previous research has shown that interest group activities were pivotal in the developmental process of new legislation (for example, see Becker 1999), but interest groups were not as significant in the inclusion of gender in New Jersey's hate crime law. The role of interest groups was limited because their influence was unnecessary: as already discussed, the political and legal climate, in addition to the media, were already in favor of the proposed bill.

The only interest groups mentioned in the newspaper accounts prior to the passage of the law were supportive of the bill. These groups included the New Jersey branches of the Anti-Defamation League, the American Civil Liberties Union, the American Jewish Committee, and the American Jewish Congress. Notably, these groups did not explicitly support the inclusion of gender; rather, they supported the bill because it reworded the existing statute to comply with the U.S. Supreme Court decision in *R.A.V.* Although these interest groups did not directly show support for including the gender category, their approval of the proposed bill indirectly supported the addition.

It is interesting to note that during this time the Anti-Defamation League did not include gender in its hate crime model, yet the New Jersey branch of the league indirectly supported the inclusion. The fact that the league did not challenge the addition of gender, despite the fact that its own model did not include the category, further demonstrates that gender was added as part of a larger issue. Since the interest groups were more concerned with revising the law to pass constitutional muster, the inclusion of the gender category generated little fanfare. However, as these groups have considerable influence in New Jersey, if they had opposed the law or the inclusion of gender, it is likely that some form of debate would have occurred. More specifically, if these groups had opposed the law, the political actors in New Jersey would have had to expend greater effort to garner support for the proposed bill.

While the aforementioned groups indirectly supported the inclusion of gender, one other interest group, the Commission on Sex Discrimination in the Statutes, unequivocally argued for its inclusion—in particular, the inclusion of sex offenses motivated by gender bias. According to a former member of the group, the commission had been established after the legislature failed to pass the state-level Equal Rights Amendment. The commission was established by the governor to examine state statutes and recommend changes to the legislature to remove any overt sex discrimination. The group reviewed various laws, including family law, employment law, and criminal law, and found the exclusion of gender in the bias crime statute to be discriminatory. This female commission member explained:

> So one of the things the commission found when it was studying the criminal law was that there was not an enhancement for gender bias. And that was kind of [in] vogue at that point. So the commission recommended that there be an enhancement for bias crimes. And that would include gender bias. We thought, if you're going to enhance crimes that are being motivated by bias, then you had to acknowledge that racial bias wasn't the only kind of bias there was. And we thought it should track our antidiscrimination law in the state, which is very broad, and include what the federal law and most state laws [had], in terms of categories of bias. And so we thought it was a little strange to just decide that you can enhance a penalty for someone who committed a racially motivated crime but not one that was motivated by gender.

The fact that the commission was the only interest group to directly argue for the inclusion of gender demonstrates the minimal role that interest groups played in this process. Besides the commission's efforts, the interest groups that were involved played a relatively passive role. The groups expressed support for the proposed bill; however, as explained above, their support was primarily focused on the rewording of the statute to comply with the *R.A.V.* decision, and their support for including gender was only indirect. The interest groups did not need to expend financial and political capital to ensure passage of the law since the political environment was already receptive to the proposed bill. Had that not been the case, it is likely that the interest groups would have played a more prominent role.

Notably, the Commission on Sex Discrimination in the Statutes was not only concerned about adding gender to the hate crime law, it was also concerned with the conditions in which the category was included. While the bill was going through the Senate, the executive director of the commission, Melanie Griffin, testified before the Senate Judiciary Committee. She urged the committee to apply the law to sexual offenses (Marsico 1994). However, as the *Star-Ledger* reported, "Jane Grall, the attorney general's legislative counsel, pointed out that such considerations already are 'part and parcel of sex offenses' and that adopting Griffin's amendment means 'perhaps some overlapping'" (ibid.). In the end, despite the commission's urging, sexual offenses were exempted from the bias crime statute if committed solely because of the victim's gender.

This fact demonstrates the limited influence that the commission had on the development of New Jersey's hate crime law. As the female commission member explained, "it's an uphill battle whenever you want to mess with something that the attorney general isn't promoting." The outcome might have been different had other groups focused on gender-motivated violence—like the Coalition against Sexual Assault, the Coalition for Battered Women, and the National Organization for Women—worked together to attract media attention. However, the passage of the law occurred before the Coalition against Sexual Assault was organized as a formal group, and the Coalition for Battered Women appeared to not view this issue as relevant to its agenda.[8] If other interest groups had expressed concern about the exclusion of gender-motivated sex offenses, these crimes might have been included in the hate crime law. However, the view of the Attorney General's Office that the inclusion of gender-motivated sex offenses would be "overlapping" with existing criminal statutes would probably have prevailed, due to the office's political influence on the state legislature.

The Gender Exemption in Sexual Assault Cases

Gender-motivated sexual assaults are exempted from the bias crime statute. However, if a sexual assault is committed against someone based on one of the other enumerated categories, then a bias crime charge can be attached to the offense. Several interviewees, including investigators, prosecutors, and interest group members, provided insights into why gender-motivated sexual assaults were specifically exempted from the bias crime statute—in addition to the opposition of the Attorney General's Office.

Inconsistency with the "Typical" Hate Crime Model

Three prosecutors and one interest group member believed the exemption resulted from the original intent of the bias crime statute. As the original intent of New Jersey's hate crime law was to criminalize acts of vandalism and harassment directed at someone's race, ethnicity, religion, or sexual orientation, these individuals argued that the legislature did not believe that sexual assaults conformed to the traditional definition of a bias crime. Two of the male county prosecutors explained:

> [The legislature] probably thought of bias crime as something a bit more traditional—that is, coming in the legacy of civil rights legislation. And although they wanted to protect women, they did not see sexual assaults in the same way as they saw a hate crime.

> I also think that the way we traditionally conceptualize biased crimes is based on race and ethnicity, and to a lesser extent, sexual orientation. It does not encompass what we usually think of as gender, as male-female gender . . . We don't usually think of bias, in the bias crime context, as encompassing the things that motivate sexual assault. You know what I mean? It's a separate category of assault and behavior. The bias crime statute grew up out of this category of cases that was largely racially motivated. And then secondarily motivated by sexual orientation, crimes against homosexuals and things like that.

These individuals surmised that gender-motivated sexual assaults were exempted because the crimes did not fit the traditional conceptualization of a hate crime. In talking about the original intent of the law, all four used examples such as burning crosses and painting swastikas on synagogues to explain what crimes the law was originally intended to include. As the majority of these crimes fall in the categories of race, ethnicity, and religion, they easily fit in the conventional notion of a hate crime. However, since sex offenses are not considered to be crimes directed specifically at an individual because of his or her race, ethnicity, or religion (the "typical" categories), such offenses did not conform to the traditional conception of a bias crime.

Another reason for the exemption of gender-motivated sexual assaults was because sexual assaults and bias crimes were considered to have separate motivations. Two male investigators and one female interest group member explained that rape was not considered a hate crime because it is an offense in which a perpetrator wants to exert power and control over a victim. The motivation of power and control was viewed separately from the motivation of hate; thus, rape was believed to stem from a completely different mind-set. In fact, the motivations of power and control were not believed to be applicable to other types of bias crimes. One of the two investigators noted that a race-based assault he was investigating had not been motivated by the perpetrator's intent to assert power over the victim; rather, the crime had been motivated by a dislike of the victim's race. Even in response to further questions, the investigator did not perceive the motivations of power and hate as interchangeable.

It is noteworthy that the motivation of power and control was viewed as distinct from the motivation of hate, particularly since the statute defines a hate crime as an act committed with the purpose of intimidating an individual because of his or her membership in one of the enumerated categories. By purposely intimidating someone, the offender is ultimately exerting power in a show of domination; also, arguably, an individual would not be able to intimidate another person without having the power to do so. However, the motivation of sexual assaults was considered by legal actors to be separate from the motivation of hate since they did not move beyond the cursory definition of a hate crime. In the example of the race-based assault mentioned above, the investigator considered hate to be dislike of a particular group characteristic; he did not perceive the perpetrator as having acted out of a desire to intimidate or dominate the victim. By adhering to this superficial definition of a hate crime, legal actors fail to recognize that bias crimes go beyond an intense dislike for someone, and that such crimes are committed in order to enforce a social hierarchy that is biased toward a particular group. Consequently, sexual assaults are not perceived as hate crimes because legal actors often do not acknowledge that some men use rape as a means of reinforcing a male-dominated gender hierarchy. Two interviewees, one male investigator and one male interest group member, argued that sexual offenses were not about power and control at all, but rather about sexual gratification. The male interest group member stated:

> For argument's sake, some would argue that men—for example, serial rapists—hate all women because it's not a sexual act, but more a power issue. Well, that's a whole other issue and I don't necessarily agree with that. I've heard it for so long and for

so often. You have to understand the physiology of males, that aggression, that sexual force within, are so intertwined that you really can't separate that physical urge that overtakes someone in these cases that we have, if they commit a murder and a rape. I think there is a sexual release to it, not normal as we know it, but that's why they've chosen a woman. Not because they just totally want to dominate or control, but I think there's a physiological, sexual urge that is somewhat propelling. A lot of people may disagree with me, but so be it.

It is somewhat encouraging that three of the interviewees believed rape had been exempted from the statute because it was considered to be motivated by power and control. Feminists have fought hard to change the antiquated perception that rape is merely an act of sexual release, and to change the way sex offenses are handled within the criminal justice system. Since these individuals used words such as "power" and "control" to describe the motivation of rape, it demonstrates that the women's movement has been partially successful in changing law enforcement officials' perspective.

At the same time, however, it is very discouraging that two of the male interviewees continued to use the archaic argument that rape is an act of sexual gratification in order to explain why such offenses are not considered hate crimes. This argument is especially disheartening since the one male interest group member blatantly disregarded the issue of power as a motivation for rape. This perspective is fueled by a sexist understanding of why men rape women, a view that has been reinforced through decades of rape myths and victim blaming.[9] Unfortunately, it is clear that some law enforcement officials still have this perspective.

According to these interviewees, gender-motivated sexual assaults were exempted from the bias crime statute because the motivations for these crimes were viewed as separate from the motivations of other forms of bias offenses. More specifically, these interviewees surmised that the legislature excluded gender-motivated sex offenses because such crimes did not fit within the original intent of the law, and because such crimes are motivated by power and control, or even sexual gratification. If these assumptions are correct, it would appear that the legislature did not view gender-motivated sexual assaults as being on the same level as sexual assaults motivated by one of the other enumerated categories. By failing to recognize that women are targets of such crimes because of their gender, the legislature ignored the way crimes such as rape affect women as a group, just as more "traditional" bias crimes affect entire communities and not just the individual victim. Moreover, by excluding such offenses from the bias crime statute, the legislature disregarded the gender animus present in sexual offenses, thus perpetuating the false—and often sexist—perceptions of why some men choose to rape women.

Pragmatic Reasons

The majority of the interviewees—including investigators, prosecutors, and interest group members—also postulated that gender-motivated sexual assaults were exempted from the bias crime statute due to pragmatic reasons. For instance, one female interest group member surmised: "Maybe [the legislators are] saying, it looks like it would be a gender crime most of the time, so we're going to eliminate that." A male member of a different interest group agreed with this conclusion:

> Maybe because they look upon it as a run-away train—that is, every time someone would be convicted of sexual assault against a female, that in essence, they would have to argue that it's a gender-bias crime.

According to this perspective, the legislature exempted gender-motivated sexual assaults because of the potential burden on the criminal justice system. As the next chapter will discuss, prosecutors, investigators, and interest group members expressed concerns about pursuing sexual assaults as gender-bias crimes primarily due to the difficulty of proving gender bias in such cases. Therefore, it may be that gender-motivated sexual assaults were exempted from the statute so that the category did not present difficulties for law enforcement officials.

This is seemingly a legitimate argument, but history demonstrates that politicians are rarely influenced by the realities of the criminal justice system when passing new legislation. When passing harsh sentencing laws (such as "three strikes" legislation), politicians do not seem to consider the spatial and financial consequences that such laws have on the correctional system (like the prison overcrowding that became a significant issue after the passage of "three strikes" laws). As the inclusion of gender-motivated sexual assaults was the only apparent controversy related to the addition of the gender category, it appears that the legislature simply removed a divisive issue, thereby ensuring the bill's smooth passage. Political actors were more concerned about revising the law in order to pass constitutional muster; consequently, there was little concern about gender-motivated violence.

Half of the interviewees also argued that gender-motivated sexual assaults were exempted because there were already laws to address those crimes, and the penalties associated with the offenses were already severe. In fact, four of the nine prosecutors and three of the six investigators speculated that the legislature exempted the crimes because they were already covered under a separate statute and because sex offenses were already felonies. One male prosecutor explained:

> I think there were technical issues there, and they did not want to go delving into the sexual assault statute. They may have done it as a way of just simplifying the process so as to not create an issue with sexual assault. They just carved it out in one way or another. In other words, there might not have been any theory behind it all. It may have been purely practical.

It is interesting to note that men were the majority of those who suggested that gender-bias sex offenses were exempted from the statute because other laws already addressed such crimes. Perhaps even more interesting, however, was that five of the ten interviewees who offered this conclusion, including prosecutors and investigators, did not agree with the exemption. Rather, these five, including both men and women, believed that gender-bias sexual assaults should be considered as hate crimes. One of the male investigators explained:

> I thought it should have been a part of it. I thought it should have been intact . . . They figure this is strong if we just leave it as aggravated sexual assault. We'll charge him with rape and that will give him as much time as if we had another statute in regards to bigotry and hate. It's almost like taking a double bite from the apple. No, it's not. You need to attach that extra punishment.

Of the four interviewees who explicitly agreed with the exemption, three of them were male—one investigator and two prosecutors. The one exception was a female prosecutor. The facts that male interviewees were more likely both to suggest that gender-bias sex offenses were exempted for pragmatic reasons and to agree with the exemption highlight how sexual assaults continue to be viewed through a gendered lens.

As the legal profession continues to be dominated by men, violence against women remains a second-tier crime, not worthy of the same legal consequences as crimes committed primarily against men. Although the majority of rapes are committed against women, and these crimes affect women collectively, such crimes do not receive the same symbolic classification as other forms of bias crimes. Because the label "hate crime" generates significant media and public attention, failing to label sexual offenses as such perpetuates the lack of consideration these offenses receive within the national discourse. After a bias incident, there is often discussion about the crime that serves to educate the public. If sexual assaults were appropriately labeled as hate crimes, a similar discussion could occur in regard to rape and other forms of gender-motivated violence that would educate the public about the actual nature of rape and discredit common rape myths.

Moreover, by exempting gender-bias sexual assaults from the hate crime law, the New Jersey legislature not only dismissed the idea that men rape women in order to prove their masculinity and to reinforce a social hierarchy, but they also ignored research showing that many rapists express hatred toward women as a group, not just hatred toward a specific victim (for example, see Scully and Marolla 1985). By failing to recognize the value of treating gender-bias sexual assaults in the same manner as other forms of bias crimes, the patriarchal view of such crimes continues to prevail, and female victims of bias crimes are not afforded the same legal legitimacy as other victims of bias crimes. In the end, this treatment not only obscures the gender animus within sexual assaults, it also reinforces the notion that antifemale violence is common and just part of the natural order of society.

As discussed throughout this chapter, the inclusion of gender in New Jersey's hate crime law was ultimately a product of opportune circumstances. In the succinct explanation of one key legislative actor, quoted above: "It just made sense." Although it may have "made sense" for the legislature to include gender in the statute, pragmatically, the category of gender conflicts with how law enforcement officials conceptualize bias crimes. The next chapter elucidates how the gender category has been enforced in New Jersey since its addition to the bias crime statute.

4 | Enforcing the Gender Category
Is Gender Even on Their Radar?

"It's not hate that kills people—it's indifference."—*Author unknown*

New Jersey's bias crime statute was expanded to include gender on August 15, 1995. However, according to the state's annual crime reports, only four gender-bias incidents were recorded between 1999 and 2008—and, interestingly, these incidents were recorded in the state's most recent reports, published after the current study was conducted.[1] In comparison, during the same period 3,521 race-bias incidents, 2,589 religious-bias incidents, and 579 offenses motivated by sexual orientation bias have been reported.[2] Furthermore, as the disability category was added to the bias crime statute at the same time as the gender category, it is interesting to note that twenty-five disability-bias incidents have been reported between 1999 and 2008.

Why were no gender-bias incidents in New Jersey's annual crime reports prior to this study? Are law enforcement officials not investigating offenses as possible gender-bias crimes, or have there just have not been any incidents that fit into this category? Furthermore, if domestic violence cases are not exempted from the hate crime statute, like gender-motivated sexual assaults (as discussed in the preceding chapter), why are these offenses not considered gender-bias crimes? Finally, what is the purpose of having the gender category if it is not utilized by law enforcement officials? This chapter explores the answers to these questions.

Gender and Hate Crime Law: The Proving Grounds

The fact that there had not been any gender-bias cases in the state's annual crime reports raises the question: are law enforcement officials in New Jersey aware of the gender category? Or, as one male interest group member asked: "Is gender even on their radar?" None of the fifteen prosecutors and investigators interviewed for this study had experience investigating or prosecuting a gender-bias offense, and the majority of them were uncertain of the definition of a gender-bias crime. For instance, one male prosecutor admitted: "I can't think of what would be included as gender-biased, honestly." One female prosecutor said that when her supervisor had asked her to participate in a study about the gender category, she did not even know what a gender-bias crime was:

> I said to him, I'm not actually sure what this means. So, I'm not sure what a gender-biased thing would be. Like, oh, "you're ugly"? I'm not sure what—if you could tell me what you mean by gender bias, I'll tell you whether or not we've had anything like that.

This uncertainty about the gender category was particularly evident in the subjects' discussions of the types of bias crimes with which they did have experience. It became apparent throughout the interviews that gender was an uneasy fit with hate crime for most of the subjects, as the category and the corresponding offenses—particularly domestic violence and sexual assaults—were inconsistent with what they recognized as "typical" hate crimes.

Inconsistent with Prior Knowledge

When asked what types of bias crimes were the most common in New Jersey, the majority of interviewees mentioned race-bias crimes, specifically crimes against African Americans. The next most common types of bias crimes related to religion or sexual orientation. These responses are not surprising: they are similar to the numbers consistently found in the state's annual crime reports, and these types of hate crimes are the most commonly reported on the national level as well.

The fact that these are the most commonly reported hate crimes perpetuates the idea that bias offenses must fit in one of these categories in order to be easily identified as a hate crime. For instance, when asked about their professional experience with bias crimes, all of the interviewees could readily cite a hate crime case involving race, religion, or sexual orientation. As these three categories have all been part of New Jersey's hate crime law from the beginning, it is not surprising that investigators and prosecutors find it easy to classify bias incidents according to such categories.

However, the gender category has been included in the hate crime law for over a decade, and one would assume that these legal actors would have had the opportunity to use the category at some point. Yet, because gender-bias offenses are not considered "typical" hate crimes, investigators and prosecutors continue to be uncertain about the gender category and how these crimes fit in the hate crime framework. One male prosecutor said:

> As you probably know, most bias crimes are committed by—well, the largest percentage are committed by juveniles, they tend to be prank type crimes, misdemeanor type crimes, have a big impact on the community. But, in other words, the lion's share of those crimes that law enforcement thinks of don't fall into the gender category.

Another male prosecutor, when talking about the types of bias crimes that he sees in his county, reinforced the idea that the majority of hate crimes are viewed by law enforcement officials as lower-level offenses, often committed by juveniles:

> When we got a synagogue graffitied with swastikas, or whatever, or somebody goes after the gravestones in a Jewish cemetery with swastikas, there's almost always some idiot kid, either trying to get attention, or he's toying with the neo-Nazi concepts in one way or the other.

Finally, when trying to explain why there had not been any gender-bias cases in New Jersey, one male interest group member surmised:

> I think the difference is that you don't see the underlying crime and the gender bias co-mingled. You know, how often do you see somebody, "I beat her up because she's a woman; I hate women." You know, you just don't have that hate component, and I think that's the big difference. I mean, there are people, as you well know, that they literally hate, they hate all blacks. Not 99 percent, they hate all of them. They hate all gays. Hell, I know people that hate all Italian Americans, okay? That's an absolute, 100 percent hate. Nobody, no man hates all women, unless he's crazy.

Since gender-bias offenses do not fit the notion of a "typical" hate crime, investigators and prosecutors are reluctant to use the gender category to pursue such offenses. As demonstrated by the above quote, and as discussed in the previous chapter, legal actors do not move beyond the surface definition of "hate," and thus they perceive the motivation of a gender-bias crime to be different from the motivation of a "typical" bias crime. Rather than recognizing that bias crimes involve a discriminatory selection of a victim in order to enforce a particular social order, law enforcement officials superficially view such acts as being committed solely because of an intense dislike for the victim's group.

According to Lawrence, there are "two analytically distinct, albeit somewhat overlapping, models of bias crimes" (1999, 29–30). These models shape the formation of hate crime laws and influence how bias crime cases are viewed within the legal system. Lawrence's two models are the "discriminatory selection" approach and the "racial animus" approach. Whereas the animus model requires proof that the crime was committed due to the defendant's bias or hatred of the victim's characteristics (Bonner 2002), the discriminatory selection model does not focus on the specific motivation or intention of the perpetrator. Instead, the focus of this approach is on proving that the victim was selected because of a particular characteristic (Steen and Cohen 2004). Although animus is often present in bias crimes, the use of the racial animus approach does not accurately describe the real intent behind bias-motivated crimes. As Weisburd and Levin explain: "The key to bias crime categorization is not really the hateful 'specific intent' of the offender, but rather the offender's discriminatory use of violence to enforce a particular social hierarchy that is biased against the targeted status category" (1993–94, 36). In other words, by using the discriminatory selection approach, legal actors can move beyond the surface definition of a hate crime and, in effect, more readily accept how gender-bias offenses fit in the hate crime framework. Although gender-motivated violence can contain an animus against the victim's gender, since legal actors have a difficult time conceptualizing how to prove this hatred of another gender, it would be advantageous for the gender category (and, arguably, other types of bias crimes as well) if proving animus were no longer required. As Wang explains: "The discriminatory victim selection model better accomplishes the asserted goals of bias crimes legislation. That model does not exclude crimes motivated by 'pure' animus, yet unlike the 'racial animus' model it has the potential to cover all crimes that produce the harmful effects associated with bias crimes" (1999, 899).

In spite of the fact that research has shown gender-motivated violence is often committed because of a dislike or hate of the victim's gender (for example, see Scully and Marolla 1985), such crimes are still not considered gender-bias offenses. The analysis of the interviews conducted for this study revealed several reasons why the gender category poses a distinct challenge under the hate crime law, and why legal actors continue to be uncertain about this category. As the discussion to follow will show, investigators, prosecutors, and interest group members explained the difficulty of proving the bias element in gender-bias cases, explained how the larger society affects their perceptions of gender-motivated violence, and maintained that gender-bias cases fall under the jurisdiction of the civil court, not the criminal justice system. Because of these reasons, a consistent theme throughout the interviews was that gender-bias offenses—including domestic violence and sexual assaults—would be difficult to pursue as gender-motivated hate crimes.

Difficult to Prove Gender Bias

When discussing what sorts of evidence are used to prove the bias element in a case, both investigators and prosecutors stated that symbols, confessions, and statements from the victim or a witness are the most common. Seven interviewees specifically mentioned that words spoken during the offense were the most effective type of evidence used to prove that a crime was motivated by bias. One male prosecutor said:

> [You show bias] usually by things that the defendant himself had said or says. It's difficult because you're proving motive. You're proving what was going on inside the defendant's brain at the time he committed the act. So you have to be able to show what he's thinking in some way. The only real way—the best way to show what he's thinking is by the words that come out of his mouth. So if you get conversation into evidence about him saying stuff about being biased, or if there were conversations between the defendant and the victim themselves, himself, herself, it will come into evidence. But that's the way to prove, by stuff that the defendant himself had said with other people listening, or in the situation where he cusses or gives us a culpatory statement.

As discussed in chapter 2, police and prosecutors often do not pursue offenses as hate crimes because of the additional burden of proving the bias element. In hate crime cases, not only do the legal actors have to gather sufficient evidence to prove that a crime was committed, but there must also be sufficient evidence to prove that the offense was motivated by a particular bias. As one male prosecutor explained, even if there is a sense that a crime was motivated by a specific bias, proving that can be difficult, and the extra work affects the number of cases that are pursued under the hate crime statute:

> There must've been something in the case, some facts, somewhere in the case, that led people to believe that it was biased. But having to prove it as a factual element beyond a reasonable doubt greatly narrows the scope of cases that are going to be considered as bias cases.

The majority of interviewees—including investigators, prosecutors, and interest group members—expressed this concern about the difficulty of proving the bias element, and they agreed that most cases are not pursued as hate crimes unless the evidence clearly demonstrates that the crime was motivated by a specific bias. This concern was particularly evident when discussing how one might attempt to prove gender bias in a case. As these cases are not conceptualized as "traditional" hate crimes, the interviewees had a difficult time coming up with scenarios in which the gender category could be utilized. One male interest group member—who, notably, works with bias crimes on a daily basis—confessed that gender is not on the forefront of his mind when he reads about someone being attacked: "I don't think of gender as a motivating factor. 'I hate women' is about as obvious as it gets." Two interviewees argued that in order for a gender-bias case to be considered a hate crime, it would have to be an especially horrific case.

> I think it has to be one of those really, you know, egregious, almost viscerally reactive type of cases, where it is in the forefront of the media, where it really gets people churned up. (male interest group member)

> Law enforcement officers tend not to perceive gender bias very readily at all. It would only be in the extreme case, usually. That is, you have a sociopath who has a documented hate for women, then it would really get on the law enforcement radar screen. (male county prosecutor)

Thus, in order for law enforcement officials to perceive gender bias in a case, not only would the evidence have to be blatant, but the case would also have to be an atrocious incident that created significant media attention and public concern. Since violence against women is so much a part of our daily lives, it would not be recognized by law enforcement officials as gender-motivated violence unless it moved beyond what is considered normal or routine. However, as demonstrated by the Sodini case mentioned in chapter 1, even when a horrific crime does occur—such as when a man goes on a murder spree in order to seek revenge against women—very little attention is given to the gender bias involved in the case (Herbert 2009). In other words, even horrific cases such as Sodini's killing spree are not labeled as gender-motivated hate crimes by most of the news media or by law enforcement officials, further demonstrating how "normalized" violence against women is in our society, and consequently, the low probability of prosecuting an act as gender-bias hate crime.

Although several of the interviewees brought up hallmark cases such as the racially motivated murder of James Byrd Jr. in Texas or the murder of Matthew Shepard, a gay college student in Wyoming, none of the investigators or prosecutors mentioned a comparable case for gender. This was surprising because, as discussed in chapter 3, the Montreal massacre had been cited by one of the legislative actors as a reason for including the gender category in New Jersey's hate crime law. (As a reminder, the case involved a male college student who murdered fourteen women at the University of Montreal, blaming the women for being both "feminists" and the cause of his personal failures.) Although this case generated a large amount of media attention throughout the United States as well as Canada and was considered a triggering event during the developmental phase of the gender category in New Jersey, it was apparent that the investigators and prosecutors were not aware of the incident. Evidently, the case had little influence on New Jersey law enforcement since the legislative phase.

Hate crimes were defined by the law enforcement officials as criminal acts committed with the purpose of intimidating another individual based on one of the protected characteristics. Therefore, to pursue a gender-bias case as a hate crime, it is not just a matter of a crime's being committed against a member of the opposite sex; there must be evidence showing that the crime was committed with the purpose of intimidating the victim because of his or her gender. Therefore, it was difficult for these legal actors to place crimes committed against the opposite sex within the same context as other types of hate crimes. In a race-based crime, for example, the racial difference between the perpetrator and the victim is a starting point for categorizing the crime as a bias offense. Although the racial difference is not sufficient evidence to prove that the crime was motivated by bias, the difference alerts law enforcement officials to the possibility of that motivation.

In contrast, a gender difference between the victim and the perpetrator does not alert law enforcement officials to the possibility of a gender-bias crime. Because women make up over half of the population, the gender component of a crime is often disregarded. As one female prosecutor explained: "Every crime has a 50 percent chance of being perpetrated against the opposite sex." However, what legal actors seem to ignore when thinking about gender-bias crimes is the disproportionate rate in which women are victims of gender-motivated violence.

Rarely are men selected as victims because they are men, yet women are often selected as victims for the sole reason that they are women. This is evident in the fact that women are disproportionately victims of sexual assaults and domestic violence, and the perpetrators of such crimes are predominantly male. For example, according to the 2006 New Jersey crime report, women were victims in 77 percent of all domestic violence offenses. Although the report does not reveal the gender of the offender, if one assumes that the "spouse" listed as the offender is of the opposite sex,[3] then according to these statistics, females are victimized by males at a significantly greater rate than males are victimized by females. Indeed, the report shows that forty-one women were sexually assaulted by their spouses in 2006, yet there were no such incidences reported for men (New Jersey State Police 2006). Therefore, by arguing that both males and females have an equal chance of being victimized overlooks the gender dynamic associated with gender-motivated violence; and as a result, gender-based crimes are not considered to be possible bias crimes in the same way as crimes based on one of the other enumerated categories, such as race or religion. This was evident when the interviewees discussed the uneasy fit of domestic assaults and sexual assaults in the hate crime framework.

Domestic Violence and Sexual Assaults: An Uneasy Fit

Prosecutors and investigators already had a difficult time trying to fit gender-bias cases in the same framework as other types of hate crimes, and domestic violence and sexual assault cases presented an additional challenge. Despite the fact that victims of domestic violence and sexual assaults are predominantly women and perpetrators of such crimes are predominantly men, the majority of the interviewees—including investigators, prosecutors, and interest group members—expressed concerns about pursuing such crimes as gender-bias offenses.

As discussed in the preceding chapter, gender-motivated sexual assaults are exempted from the bias crime statute; as a result, none of the investigators or prosecutors had pursued such cases under the hate crime law. Furthermore, none of the subjects had investigated or prosecuted a sexual assault utilizing one of the other enumerated categories, which is permitted under the statute. When asked whether such crimes could be considered bias crimes were they not exempted from the statute, half of the interviewees—again, including prosecutors, investigators, and interest group members—explained that since sexual assaults are already difficult to prove, it would be even more difficult under the bias crime statute.

> Well, I think the sense of a lot of prosecutors is that if you have a sexual assault, that alone is difficult enough to prove. And on top of that, [more] levels of proof . . . are necessary to show that, in addition to being a sexual assault, the case was motivated by bias . . . especially in crimes where the very essence of the crime, I think, incorporates that. (female county prosecutor)

> Right now, all you have to do is prove the act that someone was purposely or knowingly sexually assaulted. It doesn't matter what other kinds of motive they had. Now you have to very specifically prove a gender motive, which would be interesting, especially if you do not have any other proof, a confession of some kind, some prior acts to prove. If all you have is the identification of the victim, [it] might be difficult to actually prove that the crime happened because of a very specific dislike towards women ... It simply can't be that a crime happened. It would have to be something which would tend to show that this person was sexually assaulted because of gender. So the question becomes, well, what is it that the law enforcement officer is going to come forth with in [the] way of proof? It's those kinds of questions that present real difficulties and issues that the prosecution and law enforcement would have to confront. (male county prosecutor)

This difficulty of proof was also mentioned in cases in which there was an additional motive present. For instance, one female prosecutor explained:

> If somebody was committing a sexual assault and their intent was to commit a sexual assault upon someone because they are an Orthodox Jew, for example, as opposed to, you know, just the first female they come upon ... that would be considered a bias crime. But in most cases, the crime itself, you know, the motivation, the intent that has to be shown in connection to the crime itself is ... difficult enough to prove. And it's not likely that we would proceed with that.

Thus, even if given the opportunity to attach the bias charge to a gender-motivated sexual assault, prosecutors might still be reluctant to do so because of the difficulty of proving the bias element in such cases. Another female prosecutor said:

> I would charge both sexual assault and the bias statutes, but, if it came to trial, I'd probably dismiss the bias charge because it is too hairsplitting to prove, if possible at all.

Half of the interviewees also felt that because there are already severe penalties for sexual assaults, it would be redundant to use the enhanced penalty statute to address such crimes, especially because of the difficulty of proving sexual assaults.

> If you were a prosecutor, why in the world would you prosecute rape as a hate crime if you didn't have to? Rape is already a felony in every state in America, and serious crime should be treated seriously. And sometimes you would get more penalty if it was a hate crime, but you would have to prove the bias motivation that

[the rapist] intentionally selected the victim on the basis of this immutable characteristic, gender, and that is the reason the crime was committed. And no prosecutor would ever try and prove that . . . rape is a felony, and a really serious crime. And if you could get them on that, without having to prove the additional bias motivation, then that's the way you would do it. So you can't be surprised that there's not that many gender-based hate crimes. It's because rape is already really, really serious. (male interest group member)

The problem with the bias crime category, and the bias crime statute to a certain extent, is that it requires a prosecutor to prove something else, an additional element to the underlying offense. And there are certain categories of crimes for which the penalties are so severe already, that proving that something else doesn't give you anything else . . . Proving that it's a bias-related aggravated sexual assault doesn't get you anything more than a first-degree crime. So why should you have to worry about proving that? (male county prosecutor)

Criminal statutes consider sex offenses to be serious crimes. For instance, in New Jersey, an aggravated sexual assault is a first-degree crime, and sexual assault is a second-degree crime (N.J. Stat. section 2C:14-2). However, research has shown that only a small number of sexual assaults reported to the police actually go to trial, and of those cases, very few result in a conviction. For instance, LaFree (1989) found that only 37 percent of rape cases reported to the police resulted in an arrest, 6 percent went to trial, and of those convicted, less than 5 percent received a prison sentence (cited in Belknap 2007, 303). So the argument that sexual assaults are not considered bias crimes because there are already laws and severe penalties associated with such crimes is worthy of further exploration.

Although the investigators and prosecutors in this study did not mention the victim-offender relationship in regard to sexual assaults, research has shown that this dynamic plays a significant role in how rape cases are perceived by criminal justice professionals. Studies have consistently found that law enforcement officials consider stranger rapes more serious than acquaintance rapes, and that convictions are less likely to occur in cases where the victim knew the offender (O'Toole, Schiffman, and Edwards 2007, 199). Since the majority of sexual assaults occur between acquaintances,[4] the manner in which these cases are handled in the criminal justice system is not only troubling for rape victims, but also raises questions about how such cases fit in the hate crime framework. As discussed below, the interviewees in this study did not bring up the victim-offender relationship as a reason why sexual assaults are not considered bias crimes. Nonetheless, this dynamic was consistently mentioned as a reason why domestic violence does not fit the hate crime rationale. Thus, it seems that the relationship between the victim and the offender would also come into play with sexual assaults, causing legal actors not to find such crimes as serious as other forms of bias crimes.

However, as prosecutors are known to overcharge in cases in order to secure convictions, it is interesting that these individuals would not want to attach the bias charge to sexual assaults. It would seem that attaching the bias charge to a sexual assault would make it easier to get a guilty plea to a lesser charge. Indeed, almost half of the interviewees discussed the frequent use of plea bargaining in bias-related cases. One male prosecutor explained:

> Ninety-five percent plead in one way or another. You know, whether or not they plead to the bias offense or not, I don't know. We often plead around it. We plead them to something that is equally as serious under the law, [but] which does not have the stamp on it as a bias crime. People don't like to stand up in open court, you know, and admit that they're a racist. So we make arrangements for them to plead guilty to just beating the guy with a hammer. Something that goes down easier to them in court. Those are purely practical considerations. If the penalties are the same, we don't really care.

Furthermore, one female interest group member noted:

> I think they charge [bias] to force plea bargains, actually. That's my informal knowledge. I don't work with criminal law, but people I've talked to about it have said that's how it's used. It's just used to make the possible penalties so heavy that the person will plea bargain to the original crime.

If attaching a bias charge to an offense encourages defendants to plead guilty, then it would seem advantageous to do the same in sexual assault cases. In fact, two interviewees, one male investigator and one female investigator, discussed the benefit of attaching the bias charge to sexual assaults. Not only would it increase the penalty, as the female investigator explained, "it would give even more strength if you could charge . . . more power, it would just give you more teeth."

However, it is not surprising that the bias charge is not utilized with sexual assaults. Gender-motivated violence, particularly rape, has a controversial place in the criminal justice system. Unfortunately, rape myths and victim blaming continue to permeate the legal system. For instance, victims are often blamed for the assaults (Pollard 1992; Whatley 2005), especially if they knew the offender and if alcohol or drugs were involved. Victims of sexual assaults are thus often discredited within the legal system, and the authenticity of their victimization is often challenged (Frohmann 1991; O'Toole, Schiffman, and Edwards 2007, 199; Taslitz 1999). This hinders victims from obtaining justice in rape cases. For example, in what was probably the most prominent court case examining rape as a gender-motivated offense— *U.S. v. Morrison*—the Supreme Court denied the civil action, claiming that Congress lacked the authority to enact the specific provision within the Violence Against Women Act that provided legal remedy to victims of gender-based offenses (as discussed in chapter 2). As long as legal actors continue to disregard the seriousness of sexual assaults, particularly acquaintance rapes, such crimes will fail to become a part of the hate crime framework.

Unlike gender-motivated sexual assault cases, domestic assaults are not exempted from New Jersey's bias crime statute; nevertheless, the majority of the interviewees in this study did not consider domestic assaults to be gender-bias offenses. Almost half of the interviewees—including both prosecutors and investigators—said that domestic violence, like sexual assaults, was not considered a bias offense as there were separate statutes for such cases. For example, when asked whether domestic violence could be considered a gender-bias offense, one male bias crime investigator stated matter-of-factly: "Nope. They're different statutes. They're close, but the statutes don't apply." Even recognizing that domestic assaults are primarily offenses against women, investigators and prosecutors were reluctant to view domestic violence as a gender-bias hate crime. One male prosecutor said:

> We're not considering domestic violence as gender biased crimes . . . I don't even know if they're intended to be—I mean, by the perpetrator. I don't see it. I see it as an act of violence against another human being, and generally the acts of violence or intimidation are acts against women, true, but I mean, I think we should be prosecuting [them] under domestic violence.

It is interesting to note that seven interviewees used this argument to explain why domestic violence cases are not considered bias offenses, and all of the seven were male. As discussed in the previous chapter, the majority of interviewees who made the "redundancy argument"—laws to address sexual assaults already existed, and that explained the exemption within the bias crime statute—were also male. While the legal system remains a male-dominated environment, the laws pertaining to gender-motivated violence are believed to be sufficient. Law enforcement officials tend not to view domestic violence in the context of a patriarchal society, and thus they perceive domestic assault statutes to be gender-neutral and adequate for addressing such violence.

In contrast to interviewees' comments on sexual assaults (as discussed in the previous chapter), the motivation of power and control was not mentioned by any of the investigators or prosecutors to explain why domestic violence occurs. Indeed, the only individual to bring up power and control in the context of domestic violence was the female advocate who worked on such cases. The fact that these issues were not brought up by the law enforcement officials was somewhat surprising, as advocates for the victims of domestic violence have worked hard to educate law enforcement officials about the primary role of power and control as motivation for domestic violence. For instance, as McPhail notes, the Power and Control Wheel has been "widely circulated" and is "a standard teaching tool" in law enforcement training programs (2002a, 192).[5]

Instead, investigators and prosecutors, both male and female, explained that the motivation for domestic assaults was due to issues within the relationship between the two parties. More specifically, five prosecutors and two investigators argued that domestic assaults were the result of problems within the intimate relationship, not because of a hatred of or bias against the victim. The following quotes demonstrate that these interviewees did not see domestic assaults as fitting the hate crime rationale because of the personal relationship between the two individuals.

> But I'm not exactly sure if they're being victimized because they're women, when they don't beat up anybody else but household members. So you're not targeting an entire class there, you're more targeting the person that you're living with. (female county prosecutor)

> I don't know why, but my gut reaction is that if it's a husband and wife, I can't see where it would necessarily be a biased crime. I don't know how in the world you would marry someone and then somehow be responsible, be guilty of a biased crime against your own spouse. I mean, it just doesn't make sense to me. (male county prosecutor)

> I think that the definition of a bias crime is one [in] which the purpose, one of the main motivating purposes or intents by the actor, the criminal actor is to intimidate based upon, you know, a protected classification . . . and in most of the domestic violence cases, it rises out of the relationships between the parties. (female county prosecutor)

> You know, it's just something that, at least the way some people are raised. You know, that it becomes a family affair. That's what I can see, and that's what we're taught in school when we go to college, that you perpetuate what you were brought

up with, okay? And if your mom and dad slapped one another around after they had a few drinks, well when you have a few drinks, you're going to slap your wife around and she's going to slap you around. I don't see how you could equate that to being a gender-biased crime in either event. You know what I'm saying? Because that's domestic problems that the courts deal with and the police deal with on a daily basis. I don't see how you could make that a biased crime. (male bias crime investigator)

Because of the personal relationship between the two individuals involved in domestic assaults, the cases did not fit these interviewees' definition of a hate crime. It is surprising that the issues of power and control were not mentioned by the law enforcement officials, but not surprising that the personal relationship between the two parties explained why such crimes were not bias offenses. Historically, domestic violence has been treated by the criminal justice system as a minor offense, if it is considered a crime at all.[6] Even with relatively new policies such as mandatory arrest practices, domestic assault cases are often treated as trivial offenses in the criminal justice system.[7] Furthermore, domestic violence continues to be viewed as a private matter between two parties; this perception was evident in the responses of the investigators and prosecutors shown above. Because domestic assaults were considered a family affair, or because the perpetrator did not "beat up anybody else but household members," the parallels between domestic violence and other forms of bias crimes were ignored.

Although research has shown that hate crimes do not always involve complete strangers, the fact that the parties in a domestic assault are involved in an intimate relationship made it impossible for the legal actors to consider such cases as bias-motivated offenses. Since the victims were not viewed as being targeted because of their membership in a particular group, such as women, the crimes did not conform to the interviewees' conception of a hate crime. Failing to recognize domestic assaults as bias crimes ignores the fact that such crimes are a way for men to maintain a male-dominated social hierarchy. Indeed, domestic violence is one of the most obvious examples of a crime motivated by an offender's desire to exert power and to intimidate another individual.

It is interesting to note that even the one prosecutor who used the word "intimidation" to describe a domestic assault did not view such crimes as gender-motivated bias offenses, even though the statutory definition of a bias crime in New Jersey includes the phrase "with a purpose to intimidate." Furthermore, although the interviewees explained that words spoken during an offense were the most effective way to prove the bias element, only one female interest group member acknowledged that domestic assaults are filled with verbal abuse targeting the victim's gender. This lack of recognition demonstrates that words used to demean women are considered commonplace and do not signify a bias against the female victim. This is further evident in a discussion to follow, regarding the lack of media attention to gender-motivated crimes.

Despite the fact that only male interviewees offered the conclusion that domestic violence is not considered a bias crime because there are already laws to address such offenses, there were surprisingly no other gender differences between the subjects' responses, or any real differences between the responses of investigators and prosecutors. The prevailing opinion among the investigators and prosecutors, both male and female, was that domestic violence cases are separate from hate crimes cases. Interestingly, not only law enforcement officials held this view: an advocate for victims of domestic violence who has worked with such cases for many years agreed that such offenses should not be pursued under the hate crime law. While she believed that domestic violence theoretically fit in the hate crime framework, she expressed pragmatic concerns for prosecuting domestic assaults as gender-motivated bias crimes.

Because of the prevalence of domestic violence, if these cases were to be prosecuted as gender-motivated hate crimes, she explained that there would be "just too many of them" and "we wouldn't get anything done." She also explained that most victims of domestic violence do not want to pursue legal action; they just want the abuse to stop. Furthermore, she was very concerned about the unintended consequences of pursuing domestic violence as a hate crime, particularly for the victims:

> You have no idea how often we are, like, we hold back from initiatives that would make sanctions, you know, more severe for batterers, because we understand that victims would get caught up in that. And then they're going to suffer; they're going to suffer for that. And, you know, if we declare domestic violence a bias crime against women, then you can be sure within three years we'll have a whole movement about how women hate men.

It is not surprising that this advocate expressed concerns about pursuing domestic violence as gender-bias offenses. Angelari notes that when discussion arose in Connecticut about including gender in that state's hate crime legislation, the Connecticut Coalition against Domestic Violence chose not to advocate for the gender category as it was concerned that law enforcement officials would become confused, and thus less effective, if they were required to treat domestic assaults as bias crimes (1994, 97). Furthermore, it is not surprising that the advocate interviewed for this study expressed concern for the victims. Research has shown that policies intended to benefit women, such as mandatory arrest policies, have caused an increasing number of women to be arrested for defending themselves from their violent partners (Renzetti 1998, 188).

However, claiming that treating domestic assaults as gender-bias crimes would negatively affect all victims is a broad statement worthy of further consideration. Just as there have been women who have benefited from mandatory arrest policies, many women would benefit if domestic violence were pursued as a bias crime. Hate crime laws in most states are enhanced penalty statutes that typically elevate the underlying crime one degree above its original status, so if a bias charge were attached to a domestic assault, the defendant would be likely to receive a more severe punishment. Because domestic assault cases are often ignored as minor offenses, attaching the hate crime label to the case would benefit those women who want legal action taken against their abuser. Furthermore, failing to recognize domestic assaults as gender-bias crimes ignores the reality that such violence not only affects the individual victim, but society as well. In the congressional hearings leading up to the Violence Against Women Act, for example, employers testified about the economic burden that domestic violence placed on their companies due to insurance costs and absenteeism, and representatives of medical and health associations testified that such violence contributes to the enormous medical and mental health costs throughout the country. Therefore, not only would the victim benefit if the abuser received an enhanced penalty, but the larger society would also benefit.

However, even considering the possible benefits that could arise from prosecuting domestic violence as a bias crime, the domestic violence advocate explained that it would be difficult for the larger society to understand the connection between domestic violence and hate crimes because of the extent to which much of society still enables violence against women:

> It really is supported by the larger society that values men and devalues women to the extent that it's more difficult for a woman to make it, if you will, in our society. First of all, by many, it's still considered that a male partner has some rights over his female partner, or a husband has some rights over his wife. And among men who use violence against or abuse women, among some men it is considered normative, it's normal. They will support each other in that effort, if you will, whereas that is not the case for women. Women don't support women in being abusive to their husbands or their partners. So, I mean, it's just something that we still haven't

cleansed, if you will, from our mentality from long time ago when, you know, men abused their wives and their children and were legally allowed to physically justify that. So we have these societal underpinnings that support this, you know, this abuse in the direction from men to women.

Although the argument that the larger society does not view domestic violence as a hate crime is valid, so is the counterargument that attaching the label of hate crime to such violence could educate the larger society about the gender-bias element inherent in domestic assaults. Attaching the bias charge to domestic assaults could also serve a deterrent function. Research shows that domestic assaults, even if first charged as a felony, rarely result in significant criminal sanctions; if there is a punishment, most often it is probation (Ferraro 1993). Therefore, attaching the bias charge would enhance the penalty, thus potentially making offenders, and arguably the larger society, finally recognize the severity of the crime. Interestingly, the concern about whether society could view gender-bias offenses as hate crimes was not unique to this interviewee. Both investigators and prosecutors also mentioned the larger social environment as an impediment to successfully pursuing gender-motivated offenses as hate crimes.

The Larger Societal Context

Almost half of the interviewees expressed concern that even if gender-bias cases were actively pursued by law enforcement officials, successfully prosecuting such cases would be difficult because the larger society does not recognize gender bias as easily as other forms of bias. This issue was often brought up in discussions of whether domestic assaults and sexual assaults could be considered gender-motivated violence. As the bias element in these crimes is often not as straightforward as in more "traditional" hate crimes (like painting a swastika on a synagogue), these interviewees did not believe that the public would see domestic violence or sexual assaults as gender-motivated bias crimes.

As the result of the 2000 U.S. Supreme Court decision in *Apprendi v. New Jersey* (530 U.S. 466), the bias element must be charged as a separate offense from the underlying crime and must be proven beyond a reasonable doubt. For example, if an individual were charged with a gender-motivated domestic assault, the bias charge would be added to the original charge of assault, yet the charges would be prosecuted as separate offenses. The state would have to prove both charges beyond a reasonable doubt, and if the individual was convicted, the jury would determine whether the sentence should be enhanced due to the bias element. Arguing that the larger society does not identify gender bias as clearly as other forms of bias, five interviewees—two prosecutors, one investigator, and two interest group members—expressed doubt about the ability to prove the gender bias element to a jury. One male prosecutor said:

> Keep in mind that the jury is composed of the same people who are out there in the community, and although they will—even if they believe the facts, they may have a difficult time being able to connect gender bias to the crime.

Consequently, these interviewees were averse to pursuing offenses as gender-bias crimes because they did not believe that a jury would convict in such cases. And as one male interest group member explained, prosecutors typically do not try a case unless it is a strong one that will probably result in a conviction:

> A prosecutor does not bring a case to indictment and trial unless the crime is handed to them on a silver platter and they can get a conviction. And I don't say that lightly. But I see it more than once a day, every day. And it's usually in sexual assault cases, you know, against females.

It is not surprising that many of these individuals doubted the ability of the public, specifically a jury, to comprehend gender-motivated violence as hate crimes. Since the majority of the interviewees were uncertain about the gender category themselves, it seems logical for them to argue that the larger society would also have difficulty understanding how gender fits in the hate crime framework. That may be a valid argument, but it is somewhat presumptuous due to the fact that none of the investigators or prosecutors had experience with investigating or prosecuting a gender-bias crime. If legal actors used the gender category, they might find that a jury would be able to connect the bias element to a gender-based case. In fact, the category has been used successfully in the past. For example, a California jury convicted a man of a gender-bias crime for randomly assaulting a woman on the street (T. Perry 2000).

Furthermore, as discussed earlier in this chapter, plea bargains are as common in bias-related cases as they are in other cases (Grattet and Jenness 2003, 403). If plea bargaining is used so frequently, then the argument about juries' affecting the outcome in gender-bias cases is somewhat tenuous. Indeed, it is discouraging that these interviewees blamed the larger society for why gender-motivated violence is not pursued as bias crimes within the legal system and for not recognizing the ability of the law to challenge public attitudes and beliefs. The public certainly plays a role in jury trials, yet until legal actors use the gender category, gender will remain on the fringe of the hate crime domain. By not using the category, or not even attempting to use it, legal actors perpetuate the lack of knowledge surrounding gender-motivated crimes.

Falls within Civil Arena

Another explanation offered by the interviewees for why they themselves have not encountered a gender-bias crime was because such offenses fall under the jurisdiction of the civil court, not the criminal court. Three of the investigators and three of the prosecutors argued that they had not been involved in a gender-bias crime because the offenses were often civil problems; thus, such cases were not handled within the criminal justice system. As one female prosecutor explained:

> There's plenty of civil bias cases that are brought into the courts and elsewhere, but, a criminal case that's infected with bias based upon gender? You know, I don't think that approach has ever been taken, at least in this office.

These interviewees believed, for example, that the majority of these cases involved harassment or discrimination within the workplace and that, as a result, the problems were addressed by human resources departments or through civil action. One female bias crime investigator said:

> I think that most people don't report them. And if they do decide to do something about it, I think they'd rather do it civilly . . . I think they pursue it civilly because often something happened at work, and they may have a person there that, they may have a personnel person . . . or some sort of person that does that sort of documentation.

In cases where action could be taken in the criminal court, the interviewees did not believe that people were aware that they could pursue charges in the criminal justice system. In fact, seven subjects doubted that the public even knew about the gender category in the hate crime law. As one male prosecutor said: "I don't think there is a general awareness in the public's eye of that type of crime." Another male prosecutor even argued that civil attorneys would not recommend that a client pursue criminal action, because these attorneys are more concerned with the monetary awards within the civil court:

> Attorneys, let's say, who represent women in these, in the workplace environment, will be more concerned about filing a civil action rather than a criminal action, because that's where they're going to make their money, quite frankly . . . Even if

you lined up ten attorneys that do that type of work, and they all knew about the crime, the possibility of the crime, I don't think that they would refer that person to a police department or a prosecutor, because they would be more interested in pursuing a monetary reward.

It is noteworthy that half of the investigators and one-third of the prosecutors used the argument that gender-bias offenses fall within the civil arena as an explanation for why they have not encountered a gender-bias crime. Although gender-bias cases may be handled civilly, the idea that cases fell within the jurisdiction of the civil court was not brought up in discussions of offenses based on the other six enumerated categories. For instance, none of the interviewees talked about how the civil court handles race-based harassment cases in order to explain why they believed gender-based harassment charges were processed in this way. Instead, the subjects just assumed that gender-bias harassment charges were handled civilly in order to explain why they had not experienced a gender-bias criminal case.

The perception that the civil court handles gender-bias cases demonstrates two common problems with the gender category. First, legal actors perceive gender-based harassment as limited to sexual harassment in the workplace; thus, when it occurs outside of the work setting—for instance, in the home—it is not recognized as a bias crime. The common perception of the limited context in which the sexual harassment of women occurs is in stark contrast to perceptions of the victims of other categories of bias crimes. Interviewees in this study considered criminal harassment to be synonymous with racial or religious harassment. For instance, when subjects talked about a bias harassment case, the most common examples included using the N-word or the swastika symbol. When one interviewee attempted to describe a scenario in which gender-bias might occur outside of the workplace, he created a hypothetical situation, as he could not draw from his professional experience. This male investigator said a gender-bias harassment case could be made if "fuck you, bitch" was written on the side of a woman's house. However, as gender-bias harassment is not recognized as similar to other forms of bias-related harassment, this investigator admitted that police would probably report such an incident as malicious mischief, not a gender-bias crime. In fact, gender-bias harassment is not limited to the workplace setting; the investigator's belief that this situation would not be perceived as a bias crime not only demonstrates the lack of knowledge surrounding the gender category, it also reveals how little consideration is given to gender-bias offenses.

A second problem with the gender category in hate crime law is the concern of gender essentialism. In basic terms, gender essentialism ignores the reality that women's experiences are dependent on the connections between their race, class, and sexual orientation. Put simply, all women do not share a single "female experience": the life experience of a white lesbian is markedly different from that of a Hispanic heterosexual woman. Hate crime policies require incidents to be classified under one category, and gender essentialism is a concern within the hate crime discourse because individuals are often targeted due to one or more group characteristics. As McPhail explains:

> Status categories are spoken of as if they were discrete and separate categories. Such notions not only create divisions between categories of people, they fail to recognize that people occupy multiple categories. By ignoring people who fall within multiple targeted status categories, it is often women who are made invisible. (2002b, 137)

In this study, gender-bias cases were assumed to be under the jurisdiction of the civil court, yet it is unclear whether incidents involving multiple categories, such as the harassment of an African American woman, would be classified by law enforcement officials as a racial or a gender case. Although interviewees explained that it would depend on the words said during the offense, the reality is that derogatory comments are rarely limited to one status category. For example, Martin described an incident in which a white man yelled at an African American woman: "Move, you Black nigger bitch mother fucker!!" (1995, 321). The police recorded the case as racial harassment (cited in McPhail 2002b, 138). The fact that none of the interviewees in this study had encountered a gender-bias crime demonstrates that the gender component is usually overlooked in hate crime incidents.

As previously discussed in this chapter, it was easier for law enforcement officials to recognize the bias element in cases based on race, religion, or sexual orientation. These categories have been present in the hate crime law since its origination, and legal actors have had experience investigating and prosecuting such crimes. However, as law enforcement officials are uncertain about how gender bias fits in the hate crime framework, the gender category poses a challenge, especially in situations where the officials must decipher the motive when multiple categories could apply. Since the gender category confuses legal actors, rather than identifying a bias incident as a gender offense, law enforcement officials will automatically gravitate to one of the other categories. This practice keeps the gender category marginalized within the hate crime domain.

Lack of Media Attention

Another reason why the gender category is not used by law enforcement officials is the lack of media attention to gender-motivated violence. Research has shown that the media play an important role in constructing social problems (Best 1999); if the media do not pay attention to possible gender-bias incidents, such crimes remain isolated from both the public and the legal discourse. One male interest group member explained how the lack of media attention affects the public debate on gender-bias hate crimes:

> Yeah, I don't really see that many articles that say "this should've been charged as a hate crime" and "this never should've been charged as a hate crime." I think it's not part of the public debate. I can never remember seeing an article that says "this rape should've been charged as a hate crime." I cannot remember ever seeing an article like that . . . But I see things all the time that say "hey, this was obviously a race-based hate crime and why isn't the sheriff looking at it?" or, you know, "this person was attacked because they're, you know, a Muslim and law enforcement is trying to hide that fact." . . . I think it's just not part of the public debate. I don't think people really think much about it.

This lack of media attention was substantiated through the content analysis of newspaper articles written after the gender category was included in New Jersey's hate crime law. Out of the 1,009 articles written about hate crimes between January 1995 and January 2007, only 68 articles contained the word "gender" in the text, and 16 of those 68 articles were duplicates.[8] Notably, none of these articles specifically mentioned a gender-bias offense; rather, they mentioned the gender category as part of the state bias crime statute (in 22 of the 52 original articles), as part of pending federal legislation (10 articles), or as part of another state's hate crime law (5 articles).

The gender category was also mentioned in articles discussing bias incidents motivated by one of the other enumerated categories. For instance, out of the 52 original articles, 27 were written about a bias incident that had occurred on either the local or national level. Race-bias incidents were the most common (12), followed by cases of religious bias (8) and sexual orientation bias (7). The gender category was mentioned in 11 of these articles, primarily by political actors discussing the importance of enforcing the hate crime law.

For example, on July 17, 2003, an article about an alleged bias attack on a white homeless man by a group of black teenagers quoted Attorney General Peter Harvey as saying: "We simply cannot tolerate people attacking other people based on race, religion, ethnicity, or gender" ("Reward Offered for Leads in Paintball Gun Assault" 2003). And on May 6, 2004, an article discussing the investigation of a group of firefighters who had been harassing a gay couple living next door to the fire station quoted an attorney as saying: "We don't condone harassment of anyone who lives in town, whether based on race, creed, color, or gender" ("Gay Couple Say Secaucus, N.J. Firefighters Flung Rocks and Insults" 2004).

Although the appearance of the gender category was minimal, the fact that it was mentioned at all demonstrates that claims-makers such as politicians, legal actors, and the media were at least aware of the category. Moreover, the gender category was mentioned alongside the more "traditional" categories of race, religion, and ethnicity, a significant feat given that these categories were included in the law much earlier than gender. But a series of three articles written two years after gender was included in the state bias crime statute make it clear that the gender category was not in fact on the radar of groups such as the media and politicians and, consequently, on the radar of law enforcement officials.

The articles appeared in the Bergen County *Record*, a major New Jersey newspaper, and addressed a bias incident (Uris 1997a, 1997b, 1997c). The incident involved a female clerk working at the Division of Motor Vehicles and an African male client, Dr. Christopher Okechukwu, who had recently immigrated to the United States from Nigeria. According to the first newspaper article, Okechukwu had waited in line for two hours before being helped by Pia Veggian. The article reported that after a tense encounter in which Veggian was "rude" to Okechukwu, he asked to speak with her supervisor, causing Veggian to become "even more angry." After the supervisor assisted Okechukwu and he was about to leave, Veggian "came up behind him" and called him "a stupid nigger." He then called the police, and Veggian was charged with harassment under the bias crime statute. Veggian was suspended from her job, and the director of the Division of Motor Vehicles drove up from Trenton to personally apologize to Okechukwu (Uris 1997a).

The second article reported that the sixty-year-old Veggian, who had worked at the Division of Motor Vehicles for nine years, apologized to Okechukwu but was fired from her job (Uris 1997b). In this article, Veggian explained that she "never meant to scare" Okechukwu, but he was "screaming at her and calling her a 'stupid woman.'" The article quoted Veggian as saying: "I felt humiliated. He was jumping up and down and saying, stupid woman, you did this wrong, and I went over the boiling point." Okechukwu responded: "She had been yelling and cursing me and my mother so, yes, I called her stupid. She seems to take a condescending tone with blacks and immigrants." Veggian explained that she was an Italian immigrant herself and thus would not treat immigrants any differently from other people. The article mentioned that Veggian had been charged with bias-related harassment.

The final article reported that Veggian had filed a counter complaint, saying that she "was provoked . . . after [Okechukwu] repeatedly called her a 'stupid woman'" (Uris 1997c). Her husband said: "She was trying to uphold the rules . . . He told her five times that she was a stupid woman. That's harassment too." The relatively brief third article explained that the harassment charge against Okechukwu was a petty disorderly persons offense while the charge against Veggian was more serious. However, it did not explain why that was so. Nor did it explain whether the charge against Okechukwu was for gender-bias harassment, even though the article listed gender along with the other enumerated categories in New Jersey's bias crime statute.

Although this incident happened only two years after the inclusion of the gender category, the lack of any mention of that category except as part of the bias crime statute is a telling example of how the media has failed to cover gender-bias incidents. The author of the three articles was quick to report that Veggian had used a racial slur but missed the opportunity to point out that the female slur was a form of gender-bias harassment. Furthermore, even though Veggian's husband explained that the counter complaint was due to the female slur by Okechukwu, the reporter did not discuss why this harassment charge would be considered less serious than the harassment charge of racial bias. In fact, words are commonly used to demean women. For example, the B-word is frequently used in popular culture with little or no consideration of the consequences (Moore 2007); some individuals even claim free speech protection for such degrading terms when they are used as musical lyrics (Boyd 2007). However, similar racially charged terms, such as the N-word, are not thrown around as lightly; indeed, such words spark controversy when used in public discourse.

Like words used to degrade women, words used to demean blacks—such as the N-word—are common in certain genres of music, particularly rap (Moore 2007). However, the reaction to demeaning language is very different when the target is women. For instance, the radio personality Don Imus caused quite a controversy (and was ultimately fired) for his use of derogatory terms to describe the women on the Rutgers University basketball team in 2007 (Faber 2007). However, it was not the degradation of the basketball players' gender that caused concern; it was the racial slur that fueled the controversy in this incident. Similar outcomes have occurred even when individuals have used the N-word in less public settings.[9] Yet it is virtually impossible to find an individual who was fired solely for using the B-word. This is another reason why law enforcement officials do not recognize gender-bias terms as evidence of a hate crime, particularly in the context of sexual assault and domestic violence cases. If the same standards were applied to such terms as derogatory comments about racial or religious groups, the public and law enforcement officials would more easily identify the bias element within gender-bias crimes.

Unfortunately, no further information appeared in the press about the case involving Veggian and Okechukwu. It is disconcerting, however, that the media failed to recognize how this incident could have been a case of gender-bias harassment. The media could have used the opportunity to include gender-bias crimes in the discourse about hate crimes and to educate the public about the relatively new gender category. Instead, by failing to recognize the gender-bias component of this incident, the media perpetuated the lack of knowledge about such crimes.

The lack of attention is even more troubling because of the influence that the media has on the investigation and prosecution of hate crimes. Over half of the subjects interviewed for this study agreed that the media does play a role in these matters. If an incident draws significant media attention, investigators and prosecutors will examine the case more closely to determine whether there is sufficient evidence to raise the incident to the level of a bias crime. For instance, a female bias crime investigator said she has gotten phone calls from media representatives asking about bias incidences within her jurisdiction. If the local police do not report possible bias offenses to her, as the designated bias crime investigator in her county, she will not usually know she should investigate the cases. However, if the media draw attention to a particular case, she can then ask the police why the case was not reported as a bias incident. Sometimes in this way, cases that would otherwise have fallen through the cracks are accurately investigated as bias crimes.

A male prosecutor provided another example of how the media can influence the investigation and prosecution of cases:

> We move a lot of cases, and sometimes we miss stuff, and sometimes we don't know stuff. And sometimes the media is [sic] able to bring things to our attention that we didn't see it at first . . . nobody likes to be told "you screwed up," or "you're wrong," or "you have to go back . . . and look at something again," but it's a healthy exercise

to do that kind of work. And we try hard to keep ourselves open-minded about it ... We don't have a monopoly on the truth or on the reality of the situation, and because we have so many cases, we often make decisions on small amounts of information. So yeah, sometimes the media does [sic] influence the way we handle it.

Because the media play a major role in how the public perceives a social issue, it is significant that so little attention is given to the gender category. Members of the public receive much of their information on social issues from the media, so if gender-bias cases are not reported, the public generally does not know that these types of crimes exist. This is troubling, particular because victims of gender-bias crimes may not be aware of the assistance available to them within the criminal justice system.

Perhaps even more disconcerting is the influence the media has on whether cases are thoroughly examined as possible bias crimes. By bringing attention to a possible bias incident, the media can not only inform the public, but can also bring the case to the attention of key people in the criminal justice system. This is important because some cases may not be investigated as bias crimes unless the media identify them as such or pay particular attention to them. Therefore, by failing to cover gender-bias crimes, especially in comparison to the coverage of other enumerated categories, the media perpetuate the idea that the gender category is not a viable part of the state's hate crime law. In sum, this lack of coverage affects how the public and law enforcement officials perceive the gender category and its fit in the hate crime framework.

The Utility of the Gender Category

As shown above, the majority of the investigators and prosecutors interviewed for this study were uncertain about the gender category. In fact, many of them questioned how they might use it in the state's hate crime statute, particularly because of the difficulty in proving gender bias in hate crimes. Therefore, it is not surprising that almost half of the interviewees questioned the utility of the gender category. One male interest group member even expressed doubt that gender-bias crimes would ever be actively pursued in the criminal justice system:

Unfortunately, good ideas and the reality of the justice system are two different things ... Should there be bias crimes? In my opinion, absolutely. Should they be properly investigated and prosecuted? Definitely. Will they be? No, and I don't think that's going to change.

Notably, it was prosecutors who predominantly challenged the utility of the bias crime statute; specifically, five out of the nine prosecutors expressly stated that the law was not effective. They argued that the law was ineffective because the underlying offense is usually sufficient for prosecution in bias crimes. The wording of the statute was also an issue for three prosecutors. As one female prosecutor explained:

> The statute is poorly worded, and because it is victim driven, it creates problems in trying to prosecute, and in dealing practically with the victim who thinks he or she should win because he or she was intimidated without more [evidence].

The statute's requirement that the offense must have been committed with a "purpose to intimidate" can create problems for the prosecution, as the charge relies heavily on the victim's perspective of the crime. This is a particular problem with sexual assaults. Rape victims face considerable challenges within the legal system, especially the legitimacy of their victimization. Due to prevailing rape myths—such as the incorrect assumption that women commonly "cry rape" or make false accusations—victims of sexual assaults must continuously prove to legal actors that they were indeed victims of a crime. This does not occur with other types of crimes. As Taslitz explains in his analysis of rape and the culture of the courtroom, "for no other crime were jurors told to distrust the victim" (1999, 152).

Since it was mainly prosecutors who challenged the effectiveness of the law, it was to be expected that interviewees mentioned the fact that bias cases are rarely prosecuted in New Jersey.[10] Prosecutors determine whether to attach the bias charge to a case, and naturally they will not do so if they do not believe the bias crime statute is effective. Hate crimes require additional proof, and it seems futile from the prosecutor's perspective to add the bias charge if he or she can obtain a conviction without it. The next logical step is to question the purpose of having a bias crime statute if law enforcement officials are not utilizing it. More specifically, what is the purpose of having the gender category in the state hate crime law if it is not used? Interestingly, although bias crimes are rarely referred for prosecution, and gender-bias crimes are not even reported, more than half of the interviewees maintained that the law was valuable as it made a statement about acceptable conduct, was a tool that law enforcement officials could use when necessary, and served deterrent and educational functions.

Makes a Statement

One of the primary functions of the law, according to five interviewees, was the symbolic statement it makes about hate crimes. Although these investigators, prosecutors, and interest group members recognized that the gender category, in particular, was not being utilized, they still believed that the law was important. One male interest group member explained:

> You know, as we're talking, and I'm thinking about that case . . . where the gay male was beaten up. You know, there is just something so fundamentally wrong about what was done to that man—I mean, that kind of hatred that still exists, you know, that I'm going to punch the living hell out of you just because, you know, you're different than me. Whether it's a gay male or an African American man, it's just *so wrong*. And the statement that we prosecute those wrongs, even if we don't do it very often—I think that's significant. I think it's significant and important to have because it does make a statement, you know, in our society about what we will tolerate and what we won't.

Moreover, three of the five prosecutors who had previously questioned the effectiveness of the law argued that the law was successful in the sense that it represented the values of society. One of these prosecutors, a man, even mentioned that the law was necessary as it informs both the public and law enforcement officials about the importance of treating people equally:

> I think the principal success of statutes like that is for making this statement, this sort of governmental statement, that these people have to be treated the same. And that's as important for public consumption as for consumption inside the government itself . . . cops need to be told, you got to treat these people the same . . . Law enforcement in general, judges . . . You got to treat these people the same. They need to be told that. There needs to be an explicit policy, and passing a criminal statute makes it an explicit policy in certain ways. And I think that's very good.

As these interviewees observed, hate crime laws make a statement about the moral values of society; however, the fact that the gender category has not been used in the bias crime statute supports the claim that this category is merely symbolic and does not serve a practical purpose. Critics of hate crime laws often argue that hate crime legislation is merely symbolic, as it gives politicians the opportunity to pay lip service to the cause but does not involve any budgetary constraints (Jacobs and Potter 1998, 78). This appears to be the case with the gender category. By including the category in the hate crime law, politicians made a symbolic statement about the intolerance of gender-motivated violence; yet there has been no follow-through, as such crimes are not pursued under the hate crime statute. The symbolic nature of the law is further demonstrated through the discussion of its deterrent and educational functions.

Functions as a Deterrent and Education

Half of the interviewees argued that the law was valuable for its deterrent and educational functions. For example, both specific and general deterrence were mentioned as reasons for the existence of the gender category. One male interest group member stated: "Well, if it deters one hundred people in New Jersey a year, is the law worth having? Sure." A male prosecutor argued that the law could potentially serve as a specific deterrent:

> Whether or not it's successful in terms of suppressing that type of activity, through prosecutions, through general deterrence theory, I'm not sure. Because I'm not sure there are enough of those prosecutions to make a difference . . . in terms of specific deterrence, in terms of hurting the people, or punishing the people that do those types of offenses . . . it works in the cases that are brought.

Even considering that the gender category has not been used since its inclusion in the bias crime statute, five interviewees argued that the law was necessary for when that first case presents itself. One female prosecutor explained:

> I mean, I think the [reason] that it's there is to protect the people who have been victimized. I mean, we have an antiterrorism statute, but we don't have any terrorists that we're prosecuting in [our city]. So the fact that the statute is there doesn't mean we should take it off the books because we don't get to use it. I think it's there for when it's needed.

Also, as a male bias crime investigator discussed, having the gender category in the bias crime statute but not using it does not change the effectiveness of the law. Instead, he argued that it is effective as it provides law enforcement officials with a tool to use when they do want to pursue gender-bias crimes: "I think it's effective because it sits there and it gives law enforcement the chance if they want to pursue the matter further." Finally, two interviewees claimed that the existence of the gender category in the bias crime statute serves an educational purpose. One male prosecutor commented: "I think that it raises the profile, raises the issue's profile. It publicly raises the issue and puts it out there."

Although none of the investigators or prosecutors had used the gender category, they continued to believe that the law served a necessary purpose. Although it is encouraging that these legal actors believed this, their opinion is also perplexing as the majority of them were not even sure how gender fit in the hate crime framework. In fact, many of these same people had previously discussed how difficult it was to prove gender bias and get a conviction, and how they would therefore be reluctant to bring such cases to trial. It seems contradictory that the interviewees would question the practical value of the law, yet simultaneously argue that it serves a needed purpose.

Moreover, almost half of the subjects had argued that the public was not aware that they could pursue gender-bias criminal charges. If the public is unaware of the gender category, the argument that the law has served a deterrent or educational function seems illogical. In order for a law to be an effective general deterrent, the public must be aware of the law and the punishment associated with violating it; for a law to be effective as a specific deterrent, legal actors have to actually prosecute and administer punishment for such crimes. Again, it seems contradictory to argue that the law serves a deterrent and educational function if the gender category is not being used.

Hence, the gender category has served a symbolic function at most in New Jersey's bias crime statute. The category has received limited coverage in the media since it became part of the law. If the gender category was mentioned in the media, it was primarily as an enumerated category within the bias crime statute; there were no discussions of gender-bias crimes or even alleged gender-bias incidents. The purely symbolic function of the category is further demonstrated by the facts that no gender-bias crimes had been recorded in the state's annual crime reports, and that many of the interviewees in this study questioned the practical utility of the category. Indeed, thus far, the category's primary function appears to have been a means of appeasing the people involved in the developmental phase of the legislation.

Perhaps it was understood by the legislative actors that the gender category would maintain this symbolic function and remain off the radar of investigators and prosecutors. The lack of attention given to the category by both legal actors and the media certainly facilitates this outcome. The gender category remains absent from the hate crime discourse, despite having been included in the state's bias crime statute for over a decade. However, just as it was encouraging that the interviewees in this study believed that the law served a needed symbolic purpose, it was also promising that many of them suggested changes that would give the category practical utility as well. These suggestions are incorporated into the policy implications discussed in the final chapter.

5 | Where Do We Go from Here?
Policy Implications and Directions for Future Research

A woman standing outside a downtown nightclub is knocked to the ground by a man she does not know. Without saying a word to her, he assaults her and fractures her skull. This man had also verbally and physically assaulted four other women after they had rejected his advances. In the incident above, a jury in California found Billy Dean McCall guilty of one felony assault and four misdemeanor assaults. He was convicted of a gender-bias hate crime for the felony assault in which the woman suffered a fractured skull (T. Perry 2000). Such violence by men against women is not rare. Women are victims of violence every day for the sole reason that they are women. Although problems of inadequate data collection and underreporting continue to plague statistical estimates, experts agree that gender-based crimes occur at staggering rates—especially domestic violence and rape (Carney 2001; Ciraco 2001).

Despite the extent of male violence against women, very rarely are acts of such violence considered gender-bias crimes. The gender category of hate crime legislation is seldom utilized; consequently, gender-motivated violence remains marginalized within the hate crime domain. Hate crime legislation has been institutionalized on the federal and state levels, and the gender category—although still contentious—has for the most part been accepted within such legislation. This is demonstrated by the inclusion of the gender category in federal hate crime legislation and the increasing number of states that include gender in their own bias crime statutes. However, despite the growing acceptance of this category, its implementation remains notably rare.

Although policymakers have utilized the category as a way to recognize the extent of gender-motivated violence in this country, it continues to face resistance on the enforcement level; consequently, the category has failed as an instrument of social change. Policymakers may have anticipated that the inclusion of the gender category would highlight the inherent biases within gender-based crimes, effectively changing how such crimes are handled within the criminal justice system. But because the gender category is rarely used, violence against women is not recognized for what it is—discriminatory acts of violence against women because of their gender.

Vago observes that "the extent to which law can provide an effective impetus for social change varies according to the conditions present in a particular situation" (2003 312). Such conditions include the amount of information available about a piece of legislation, a precise statement of the law so as to prevent multiple interpretations of it, and the responsiveness of enforcement agencies in implementing the law (ibid., 312–13). The case study presented in this book demonstrates that these particular conditions were not present in New Jersey. For instance, despite the fact that gender had been a part of the state's bias crime statute for over ten years, interviewees were still unsure of how the category fit in the hate crime framework. Investigators and prosecutors were also reluctant to conceptualize gender-based offenses as hate crimes, much less enforce the gender category within the bias crime statute. Thus, the gender category has not been effective in changing the status of gender-motivated violence within the state's legal system.

Moreover, there is often resistance to a law, which affects its ability to serve as an instrument for social change (Vago 2003, 325). This resistance can take many forms and occurs for a variety of reasons. For instance, ideological resistance occurs if the law challenges a prevailing set of beliefs. In addition, a law is resisted if it runs counter to habitual behaviors. Both forms of resistance were apparent in the current study. Interviewees argued that gender-based crimes such as domestic violence and sexual assaults were already addressed by other statutes. Legal actors accustomed to dealing with such crimes through these laws were reluctant to conceptualize gender-based offenses as hate crimes. Perhaps most important, the gender category encountered resistance because the conceptualization of such crimes as bias-motivated offenses contradicts the dominant patriarchal ideology of society. In particular, sexual assaults and domestic violence were not viewed as discriminatory acts of violence against women; thus, they were excluded from the purview of the bias crime statute. Instead, law enforcement officials viewed such violence as motivated by something besides a bias against the female victim. Because our society is dominated by a patriarchal ideology, gender-motivated offenses are not considered to be criminal acts committed by some male offenders in order to maintain a dominant position within the social hierarchy: "While not every man beats his female partner or rapes women . . . society's acceptance of patriarchal assumptions and structures also accepts and condones these violations of women's autonomy" (Center for Women Policy Studies 1991, 3). Consequently, violence against women is regulated to a second-tier status within the hate crime domain.

The purpose of this research was to shed light on the place of gender within state hate crime legislation. This study fills a gap in the empirical research by moving beyond conceptual arguments. In doing so, the book accomplishes two goals: it helps criminal justice professionals understand the complexities of the gender category, and it informs policymakers and others interested in combating gender-motivated violence.

Recap: The Gender Category of New Jersey's Hate Crime Law

Employing qualitative methods that included interviews with bias crime investigators, county prosecutors, interest group members, and key legislative personnel, and through an analysis of the contents of legislative records and media accounts, this research explored what factors were involved in including the gender category in New Jersey's bias crime statute and how the category has been used since its addition to the law. The study revealed that the gender category in the statute has been relegated to a symbolic piece of legislation.

Despite the controversy surrounding the gender category in past federal lawmaking and scholarly discussions, there was surprisingly little debate about including it in New Jersey's bias crime statute. There was no overt opposition to the gender category, from either political actors or interest group members. Indeed, the only opposition to the proposed bill was due to the questionable constitutionality of hate crime laws in general, and even this opposition was minimal. Although the lack of extensive debate on the state level was unexpected, Jenness (1999) found similar results when analyzing the discussions about the national Violence Against Women Act (VAWA) compared to the narrative surrounding gender during the federal hearings on the Hate Crime Statistics Act (HCSA).

As discussed in chapter 2, the gender category was hotly debated and ultimately excluded during the developmental phase of the HCSA; however, a few years later, there was no such opposition to conceptualizing gender-motivated violence as a bias crime during the developmental phase of VAWA. Moreover, there was little participation during the developmental phase from women's groups and other groups concerned about combating violence against women. In fact, it was not until three years after VAWA had been conceived that nationally known feminist organizations provided testimony in support of the act (Jenness 1999, 564). Put simply, although gender had been excluded from the hate crime framework on the national level, the category received recognition as a legitimate category after the implementation of the federal HCSA. This process is what Jenness and Grattet refer to as domain expansion: "Domain expansion occurs when claims-makers offer new definitions for and thus extend the boundaries of the phenomenon under discussion" (2001, 54). As hate crime policy was institutionalized on the federal and state levels, and the domain of hate crime law expanded to include additional categories, the gender category increasingly gained legitimacy within federal hate crime legislation. And this study demonstrates, the legitimacy of the gender category began to filter down to state legislatures as well.

However, not all states include gender in their hate crime laws, so it is apparent that other factors were also involved in the inclusion of the category in New Jersey's bias crime statute. Like past research (see Becker 1999; Jenness and Grattet 2001; Soule and Earl 2001), this study shows that factors such as the political and legal contexts, interest group activities, triggering events, and the media all played a role in the development of the hate crime law. However, the most significant factor for the inclusion of gender was the political context in New Jersey. The importance of a receptive political environment has also been noted in research on general law creation (Berry and Berry 1990) and hate crime law specifically (Becker 1999; Grattet, Jenness, and Curry 1998; Haider-Markel 1998; Jenness and Grattet 2001; Soule and Earl 2001). At the time the bill adding gender was signed into law, New Jersey had already proven itself to be a receptive and innovative state in regard to hate crime legislation. This was evident in the facts that the legislature had previously enacted a civil remedy law that included the gender category, and that New Jersey was the first state to establish a statewide office, the Office of Bias Crimes and Community Relations (OBCCR), focused on the prevention, investigation, and prosecution of hate crimes.

Moreover, research has found that state legislatures will enact policies in order to conform to other states' or federal legislation (Jenness and Grattet 2001). During the period when the bill to include gender was proposed and then signed into law, Congress held hearings regarding the Violence Against Women Act. The testimony and data accumulated at these hearings reinforced the importance of recognizing and combating gender-motivated violence, and the New Jersey legislature was certainly aware of this federal legislation. Also during this time, the U.S. Supreme Court had validated and shaped the future of hate crime legislation in two significant court cases.

In the first case, *R.A.V. v. City of St. Paul* (1992), the Court declared it unconstitutional for state statutes to include value-laden words aimed at prohibiting certain types of conduct; yet in the second case, *Wisconsin v. Mitchell* (1993), the Court upheld the constitutionality of penalty-enhancement statutes because they addressed particularly harmful conduct and did not punish types of expressions protected by the First Amendment. Although New Jersey's hate crime law was a penalty-enhancement statute, it was still subject to constitutional challenges as it included value-laden words such as "ill will" and "hatred." As political actors in the state had already established the importance of hate crime law—as shown by their emotional statements to the media and the creation of the OBCCR—it was necessary for them to revise the statute so that it would pass constitutional muster. Therefore, as the result of the decision in *R.A.V.* and the existence of a political environment supportive of hate crime law, the time was opportune for revising the bias crime statute, while expanding it to include gender.

The ease with which the hate crime law was passed demonstrates how bias crime legislation, and the gender category specifically, are institutionalized within the political domain. There was very little opposition to the proposed hate crime law, and no explicit opposition to the gender category. Moreover, the hate crime law was a bipartisan issue, supported by both Republicans and Democrats; as a result, there was legislative consensus regarding the importance of passing the law. Also, newspaper accounts revealed that politicians viewed such legislation as a significant tool to combat hate-motivated violence. The law served both educational and deterrent purposes, and it emphasized to the public the view that hate crimes are serious and deserve particular attention.

Although there was minimal fanfare regarding the inclusion of gender, there has been even less consideration of the gender category since the passage of the law. In fact, the symbolic nature of the gender category was clearly evident in the analysis of how little the category has been utilized. Although the category had been on the books for over ten years at the time this study was conducted, there had been no reports of a gender-bias crime in New Jersey, nor did any of the legal actors involved in this research have experience with investigating or prosecuting a gender-based hate crime. Therefore the focus of the study became: why is the gender category not used by legal actors, and how do gender-bias crimes, such as domestic violence and rape, fit within the hate crime framework?

This analysis revealed several factors that influenced how law enforcement officials and prosecutors perceived bias crime statutes and the gender category in particular. Similar to past research (see Bell 2002; McVeigh, Welch, and Bjarnason 2003), this study showed that the political context played a significant role in how hate crime laws were enforced in New Jersey. For instance, in contrast to when the bias crime statute was first enacted in 1995, hate crime legislation no longer benefits from significant political and financial support. Although political actors continued to express in the media the importance of combating hate-motivated violence, the resources dedicated to the issue have decreased. This was particularly evident in the recent disbandment of the OBCCR. When first established, this office had benefited from the considerable political support it received from the top administration; as a result, the office became a prominent fixture in the investigation and prosecution of bias crimes throughout the state. However, the office's role has been greatly reduced.

The office used to maintain a director, staff, and approximately ten investigators who were responsible for supervising bias crime investigations throughout the state. The office was also responsible for training law enforcement personnel and providing educational sessions about bias crime in schools. At the time of this study, only two state employees, one supervisor and one investigator, were left in the office. When asked what had happened to the office, two interviewees said the cause was a change in the administration. One of them considered it "a shame" because New Jersey used to be considered a role model throughout the country in regard to the enforcement of hate crime laws. The reason for the change in the administrative focus is not clear, but there are two possible explanations.

First, the gender category was first included in the hate crime legislation during the administration of Governor Christine Todd Whitman. She might have been more concerned about gender-bias crimes than were her male predecessor in the governor's office, Jim Florio, and her two male successors, Donald DiFrancesco and James McGreevey. However, Jim Florio was governor when the bill to include gender in the bias crime statute was introduced, and it was under his leadership that the civil remedy law (which included gender) was passed. Besides, as the state's annual crime reports show, the gender category was not utilized during Governor Whitman's term of office, from 1994 to 2001.

The second possible explanation seems more likely: the change in the state-level focus on hate crimes mirrored a similar change on the national level. During the 1990s, when the OBCCR was established, hate crime legislation enjoyed significant political support both in New Jersey and on the federal level. As explained in chapter 2, during this time, federal hate crime laws were enacted—such as the Hate Crime Statistics Act of 1990 and the Hate Crimes Sentencing

Act of 1994. However, in the years that followed, the topic of hate crimes no longer received the same consideration and support on the federal level. For instance, President George W. Bush's administration warned that he would veto any new hate crimes legislation that reached his desk (Conyers 2007). And despite the encouragement from various advocacy groups and key legislative actors, it took over a decade for Congress to pass the Matthew Shepard and James Byrd, Jr. Hate Crimes Prevention Act (HCPA), which finally became law in October 2009.

As other priorities arose on the federal level and different issues came to the forefront of the national agenda, changes on the state level also affected state and local governments. The change is demonstrated by the current national focus on homeland security. One of the primary focuses of police now is on increasing national security; as a result, money and personnel have been redirected from other areas of law enforcement (International Association of Chiefs of Police 2008). Yearwood and Freeman explain:

> The terror attacks of September 11, 2001, the subsequent war on terrorism, and the war in Iraq all continue to affect recruitment and retention by police agencies. The current focus on homeland security and additional requirements placed on local and state agencies without adequate funding will affect not only the current budgets but also future budgets of law enforcement agencies. (2004)

In sum, due to a change in law enforcement resources and budgetary constraints, the enforcement of hate crime law is no longer a top priority for those state and local governments that at one time had worked hard to combat a form of domestic terrorism: hate crime.

This study also discovered that investigators and prosecutors did not utilize bias crime statutes because they found it difficult to prove the bias element, which confirms the results of previous studies of hate crime law (for example, see Bell 2002; Finn 1988; McPhail and DiNitto 2005). This was particularly true for the investigation and prosecution of gender-bias crimes. Because those crimes—particularly domestic violence and sexual assaults—did not fit the idea that these legal actors had of a "typical" hate crime, they were reluctant to consider the bias crime statute as relevant in these cases. Rape was thought to be motivated by issues of power and control or by sexual gratification, and domestic assaults by problems within an intimate relationship.

Perhaps even more telling is that many of the interviewees, when trying to explain why they did not have experience with the gender category, believed that such offenses fell within the jurisdiction of the civil court, not the criminal justice system. Because these interviewees were reluctant to conceptualize gender-bias offenses as hate crimes, they asserted that such cases were outside of their jurisdiction. They also considered the gender category irrelevant in cases of domestic assaults and rape because there were already laws to address such crimes, and the punishment associated with such laws seemed sufficient. However, as the next section will show, these gender-bias offenses are not pursued aggressively within the legal system.

The analysis also revealed that the gender category received little consideration by the media. Although the media were favorable to hate crime laws in general, as evidenced by the supportive statements and extensive coverage of bias incidents in newspaper articles, the gender category was mentioned only as part of the bias crime statute or in a list of all the enumerated categories. Indeed, as discussed in chapter 4, in an incident in New Jersey in which gender bias was evident, press coverage did not mention that the misogynist slurs present in the offense could have been construed as gender-bias harassment, focusing instead on the racial bias aspect of the case. The fact that little attention was generally paid to the gender category meant that there was no incentive for law enforcement officials to pursue gender-motivated offenses as hate crimes. The interviews for this study revealed that the media often influence whether cases are thoroughly investigated as bias crimes. Thus, when there is no coverage of gender-motivated violence, or when the media fail to identify a crime as a gender-bias offense, the gender-motivated violence continues to be overlooked by law enforcement officials.

Gusfield notes that "a law weak in its instrumental functions may nevertheless perform significant symbolic functions" (1967, 179), and social scientists and legal scholars have recognized the potential symbolic effects of hate crime legislation (Gerstenfeld 2004, 21; see also Beale 2000; Jenness and Grattet 2001; Lawrence 2000). Hate crime laws send a message to society that such crimes are abhorred, not only because of the underlying offense, but also because of what the offense itself symbolizes. As hate crimes are prejudicial acts against a particular group identity, bias crime legislation emphasizes the importance of treating all individuals equally. The label of hate crime reinforces throughout society the idea that this type of conduct is condemned, fully acknowledges the harm done to both the victim and the victim's community, and opens up a dialogue on how to eradicate such biases. Moreover, as Jenness and Grattet explain:

> Criminal justice policies are seldom justified purely by their instrumental value, especially their deterrent effects. In addition to the oft-cited goals of incapacitation

and retribution, they also must be seen, in Durkheimian terms, as expressions of collective sentiments. Hate crime laws, in this regard, have a function similar to that of laws enhancing penalties for attacks on teachers or police officers. In addition to punishment, they seek to use state authority to reinforce prosocial values of tolerance and respect. More broadly, criminal laws always express symbolic valuations; thus to oppose hate crime law [because of its symbolic nature] is dubious at best. (2001, 179)

Put simply, hate crime legislation serves a purpose by reinforcing community values and norms. Even if few cases are prosecuted as bias crimes, when the legal system and the media recognize the existence of such crimes, the symbolic functions of these laws become apparent. For example, in California, a gay male eighth-grade student was murdered by one of his male classmates because he had asked this classmate to be his valentine. The tragic incident was appropriately labeled a hate crime, and it generated dialogue within the local community and garnered national attention as well. As a result of this case, state and national advocacy groups are pushing legislatures to review antibias policies and outreach efforts in California schools (Cathcart 2008).

Unfortunately, no known study demonstrates whether the enforcement of hate crime legislation decreases the number of bias-motivated acts committed locally or nationally. In other words, whether the laws achieve a specific or general deterrent effect is unknown. Although empirical work has not examined the effectiveness of bias crime laws in reducing prejudicial attitudes, past research has illustrated how other legislative acts can influence substantial attitude changes (Cogan 2003, 471). Moreover, studies have demonstrated that litigation can bring social change and that, even if unsuccessful, legal action raises expectations among citizens, serves as an educational tool, and forces those in power to be held accountable for their actions (Klarman 2002; McCann 1994; Polletta 2000). Therefore, in regard to hate crime law, one might argue that the recognition of cases by the legal system and the media as bias crimes, can cause a segment of society to rethink its prejudicial beliefs.[1]

Nonetheless, the symbolic function of the gender category is debatable and a cause for concern. Although political actors asserted the importance of the gender category during the developmental phase of the New Jersey hate crime law, the category has not been enforced by the legal system and is rarely mentioned by the media. And as Gerstenfeld observes: "If hate crime laws do have symbolic effects, there are corollaries that should not be overlooked. If prosecuting hate crimes sends a message that such behavior is unacceptable, then *failing* to prosecute might convey the idea that the society approves of the behavior" (2004, 22).

Therefore, the absence of prosecutions under the gender category demonstrates just how little consideration gender-motivated violence receives within both the public and legal arenas. Because society is dominated by patriarchal ideologies and the legal profession continues to be dominated by men (Martin and Jurik 1996), violence against women is not given the same status as more "traditional" hate crimes, the majority of which are committed against male victims by male offenders.[2] As Jenness puts it, "gender has found a home in legal discourse on hate crime legislation, but it remains in the guest house of that home" (2003, 86; cited in McPhail and DiNitto 2005, 1179). Indeed, the current treatment of gender-motivated violence portrays such crimes as not deserving the same recognition as other forms of discriminatory violence. Continuing to disregard gender-motivated violence in this way speaks volumes not only to the millions of women who are victims of such violence, but also to the millions of women who fear victimization.

One of the justifications for hate crime laws is that bias-motivated crimes affect not only the victims, but the targeted community as well. However, by not recognizing domestic violence and sexual assaults as gender-bias crimes, the effects of such crimes are considered to be unrelated to the consequences of other types of bias crimes. This is despite the fact that the community effects are similar to those created by other forms of hate crimes. For instance, the fear and vulnerability that women feel after hearing about a rape is analogous to the fear and vulnerability that African Americans feel after hearing about a cross burning. Just as African Americans understand how easily it could have been their lawn on which the cross was found, women understand how easily they could have been the victim of a sexual assault. This is also true for domestic violence. As explained in the first chapter, many women fear that they or someone they know will be a victim of domestic violence (Harutyunyan 2008). Thus, by not acknowledging the communal affects of gender-motivated violence or how such crimes affect women collectively, we perpetuate the fear that half the population experiences. It is unfortunate when laws, such as those regarding gender-bias hate crimes, are kept on the margins or in the "guest house," when they could be effective tools for finally recognizing and combating gender-motivated violence.

Policy Implications

One goal of this project was to offer recommendations to policymakers interested in the gender category of hate crime policy. Past studies have recognized that state legislatures often look to other states when determining whether to develop similar policies (Berry and Berry 1990; Walker 1969), and this has been particularly true for hate crime law (Grattet, Jenness, and Curry 1998; Soule and Earl 2001). Therefore, the present study examined the factors that led to the development of the gender category within New Jersey's bias crime statute, with the goal of explaining the process for legislators whose states have not yet included the category in their own bias crime statutes. By explicating the process in New Jersey, this research assists legislators who are contemplating adding gender to their states' hate crime law. And with the inclusion of the gender category in the recently enacted HCPA on the federal level, a window of opportunity has once again opened to expand the inclusion of gender on the state level as well.

Although the political and legal contexts, the media, interest group activities, and triggering events all played a role in the inclusion of the gender category in New Jersey, ultimately the category was added with minimal fanfare as the result of opportune circumstances. Although other states contemplating the inclusion of the category may not have such ideal circumstances in which to work, several encouraging conclusions may still be derived from this analysis.

First, this study discovered that the gender category was included in New Jersey's hate crime law without any opposition from legal actors or interest groups. Moreover, the inclusion served a symbolic purpose for politicians. Not only did the inclusion give them an opportunity to garner support from interest groups and constituents concerned with combating gender-motivated violence, it also provided them with an opportunity to denounce bigotry without expending significant political capital. Indeed, hate crime legislation enjoyed support on both ends of the political continuum; it was considered a means of reinforcing civil rights and intolerance for discriminatory violence, yet it was also a way to get tough on crime by increasing penalties for offenders. Therefore, by supporting hate crime legislation, politicians can appeal to both liberal and conservative constituents. And because the inclusion of the gender category generates little controversy on the political landscape, legislators can include it without expending significant political and financial capital. Thus, this study's first policy recommendation is for the states that have not already done so to incorporate the gender category into existing bias crime statutes.

Policy Recommendation #1: Include the gender category in hate crime laws. Because the category can be added without expending significant political capital, state legislators and other politicians should acknowledge the importance of addressing gender-motivated violence by expanding bias crime statutes to include this category.

When New Jersey included the gender category in its bias crime statute, as discussed in chapter 3, the bill excluded gender-motivated sexual assaults from the category of hate crimes. New Jersey is not the only state to have such an exemption, and—like many of the interviewees in this study—opponents to the gender category often argue that including sexual assault in hate crime legislation is unnecessary as there are already laws to address such crimes, and the penalties associated with such laws are severe. However, research consistently demonstrates that sexual assaults are often not treated seriously within the legal system; for example, Carney (2001) explains that one-fourth of convicted rapists are sentenced solely to probation, spending no time in jail or prison, and the average length of probation is just over three years. Weisburd and Levin (1993–94), citing statistics from the Department of Justice, show that 13 percent of convicted rapists are never given jail or prison sentences, and for those who are incarcerated, the median time served is less than four years.

Moreover, research has demonstrated the parallels between rape and other forms of bias crimes; this literature is discussed at length in chapter 1. To summarize, research has shown that many rapes are committed to seek revenge against women as a class (Scully and Marolla. 1985). Scholars have also explained that women alter their lifestyles in order to avoid victimization (Carney 2001; Miller 1994, 232), and that incidents of rape and the fear of victimization affect women as a collective group, just as more traditional forms of bias crimes affect other communities as a whole (Center for Women Policy Studies 1991; Pendo 1994). Furthermore, scholars have demonstrated that increased penalties are justified, as they would have specific and general deterrent effects, validate women's victimization within the criminal justice system, and help eradicate rape myths within society (Carney 2001).

By excluding gender-motivated sexual assaults, legislatures essentially disregard the connections between rape and bias crimes. The exemption basically removes any possibility that a sexual assault could be pursued as a bias offense within the criminal justice system. Thus, legislatures perpetuate the notion that sexual assaults are not as serious as other forms of bias crimes and do not deserve the label of hate crime. With the exemption, legislatures also eliminate a tool for law enforcement officials that could prove beneficial for both victims and the larger society. As women's life experiences are not universal, having multiple methods with which to address sexual violence is necessary (Hopkins and Koss 2005).[3] Furthermore, pursuing such cases as bias-motivated offenses would not only increase the penalties for offenders, but having this avenue available would also benefit the plea-bargaining process. In fact, five interviewees in this study, including investigators and prosecutors, expressly stated that gender-bias sexual assaults should be considered hate crimes. They believed that sexual assaults were inherently gender biased and felt that pursuing rapes as gender-bias crimes would be advantageous since it would provide "more teeth" to the case.

This approach was recently applied in a rape case in New Hampshire ("Judge Upholds Hate-crime Law But Dismisses Charges" 2004). The prosecutor attempted to show that the defendant, because of his hostility toward women, kidnapped and raped one woman and attempted to do the same to another woman one week later. Assistant County Attorney Roger Chadwick argued that the various things the defendant did and said during the alleged assaults showed his hatred toward women in general. Although the judge did not find the evidence sufficient to prove gender bias, the case shows that this approach can be used in future sexual assault cases. Therefore, it is important for these exemptions to be removed from existing hate crime policies and not to include them in future bias crime statutes.

> *Policy Recommendation #2:* Do not exempt gender-motivated sexual assaults from bias crime statutes. Instead, give law enforcement officials the opportunity to pursue gender-motivated sexual assaults as hate crimes. This approach could be particularly useful in the plea-bargaining process, and it would provide another means with which to address sexual violence in the legal system.

Prior studies have shown that law enforcement officials often do not utilize hate crime legislation because they believe it to be merely symbolic (Bell 2002; Nolan and Akiyama 2004), or because they believe that proving the bias element in such cases is too difficult (Bell 2002; Boyd, Hammer, and Berk 1996; Finn 1988). Research has also found that prosecutors are unsure of how to fit gender-motivated crimes into the hate crime paradigm (McPhail and DiNitto 2005). This study confirmed these conclusions. Therefore, a second goal of this research was to assist criminal justice professionals in dealing with the complexities of the gender category.

However, before these professionals can begin to use the gender category, it is imperative to address the disparate views of advocacy groups focused on gender-based crimes such as sexual assault and domestic violence. As mentioned in chapter 2, the National Coalition against Domestic Violence supported the inclusion of gender in federal hate crime legislation, yet both sexual assault and domestic violence advocates in New Jersey were uncertain about connecting the gender category to such crimes. If the legal community is to utilize the gender category, advocacy groups at the local, state, and national levels focused on combating gender-motivated violence must disseminate a consistent message. Therefore, women's groups and other advocacy groups need to be educated on how the gender category can be used to fight gender-based crimes such as domestic violence and sexual assaults, in order for this category to become a viable piece of hate crime legislation.

> *Policy Recommendation #3:* Educate advocacy groups on how gender-based crimes, such as domestic violence and sexual assaults, fit within the hate crime framework. This education should include examples of cases of domestic violence and sexual assaults that have been pursued as gender-bias crimes and should show how using bias crime statutes in this manner can increase penalties and conviction rates.

In addition to advocacy groups, law enforcement officials also need to be educated on how gender-motivated violence can be successfully investigated and prosecuted under bias crime statutes. Both investigators and prosecutors interviewed for this study did not know how they could establish gender bias in a potential hate crime case. They claimed that proving the bias element would be too difficult, particularly in cases of domestic violence and sexual assaults.

Representatives of the National Organization for Women met with officials from the FBI to discuss the inclusion of gender in the HCPA that was passed in October 2009 ("Hate Crimes Expansion Covers Gender, Orientation, Disability" 2010). With the inclusion of gender in the HCPA, the FBI must now collect data on the gender category and, therefore, its personnel must be trained on what constitutes a gender-based hate crime. As an article in a publication from the National Organization for Women explains: "The most important challenge now is to train local and state law enforcement officials to recognize when a hate crime has been committed" (ibid.).

This study shows that the training needs to provide law enforcement officials with concrete examples of the evidence required to establish gender bias and of how the gender category has been successfully utilized in past court cases. One example of the successful application of the gender category in a domestic violence incident is *State of Massachusetts v. Aboulez*, No. 94-0985H. In this case, the court issued an injunction under the state's bias crime law (Goldscheid and Kaufman 2001). The court determined that there was sufficient evidence of gender bias as a motivation because there was an established pattern of verbal and physical abuse (including female slurs) by the offender, and threats to kill his partner if she ever left him or sought a restraining order against him.[4]

Another example is a New Hampshire case in which the judge determined that the defendant had a documented history of physically and mentally abusing women and thus sentenced him under the state's bias crime statute (Jordan 1994). The New Hampshire case is also a good example of how using the gender category to prosecute domestic violence cases benefits both the victim and the larger society. The defendant had five previous convictions of domestic assault, yet he had not served any time in jail. Because he was convicted under the hate crime statute, the judge sentenced him to two to five years in state prison. By using the gender category, the judge gave the defendant an appropriate sentence, one that would not have occurred without the penalty-enhancement statute.

It is important for training on gender bias to be provided at police academies. However, such training also must be provided on a regular basis to seasoned police officers, prosecutors, and judges because the individuals in charge of bias crime investigations are often veteran officers and prosecutors. Furthermore, research has demonstrated that regular training sessions reinforce the importance of actively pursuing hate crimes, and without such sessions, police officers do not perceive hate crimes as a priority within the justice system (Nolan and Akiyama 2004).

Interviewees in this study also commented on the importance of education and training for law enforcement personnel; in fact, a few of them said they would like more opportunities to attend training on hate crimes. Educated advocacy groups could provide this information at the police academy and during regular training sessions. In addition, as judges and lawyers attend professional conferences on a regular basis, panel discussions or keynote presentations at those meetings could provide them with this information. It would also be worthwhile for organizations such as the OBCCR to be established, as they can be a resource for educating law enforcement officials on how to effectively use bias crime statutes.

Policy Recommendation #4: Educate law enforcement officials on how to utilize the gender category to investigate and prosecute gender-bias crimes. This education needs to include examples of the criteria used to establish the gender-bias element, such as derogatory comments specific to the victim's gender and a defendant's pattern of abuse directed at one or more female victims.

Not only is it important to educate advocacy groups and legal professionals, it is also imperative to educate the public about the gender category in hate crime law. As noted in chapter 4, many of the interviewees in this study argued that victims of gender-based crimes were not aware that they could pursue such cases within the criminal legal system. Therefore, advocacy groups and law enforcement officials need to implement education campaigns on how gender-motivated violence will not be tolerated and will be punished to the full extent. These campaigns would educate victims of the avenue available to them within the criminal legal system and would also serve as a general deterrent to potential offenders. Law enforcement officials often use similar tactics in regard to offenses such as drinking and driving, and there is no reason why this method could not also be used in regard to domestic violence, sexual assaults, and other gender-bias crimes.

Public education campaigns would also help change the larger societal context for gender-bias crimes. Victims of gender-motivated violence continue to face distinct challenges within both the public and legal contexts. Rape myths are still prevalent, and many individuals continue to believe that domestic violence is a private matter not worthy of legal intervention. Indeed, violence against women is so much a part of our daily lives that it is often considered normal and overlooked. Thus, if public education campaigns explained that gender-motivated violence is a hate crime, the larger society would begin to see such violence as equivalent to other types of bias crimes.

Furthermore, as many of the interviewees in this study expressed concerns about utilizing the gender category because the larger social environment does not perceive such offenses as "typical" hate crimes, it is necessary to address this issue so that the gender category does not remain simply a symbolic piece of legislation. Conducting education campaigns in the media would encourage greater coverage of gender-motivated violence as the media would be forced to acknowledge the issue. Such campaigns could come from the various grass-roots organizations focused on combating violence against women, or from state and national coalitions interested in the welfare of women. These campaigns could include public service announcements on television and the radio, billboards in high traffic areas, and opinion pieces in major newspapers.

Policy Recommendation #5: Use education campaigns in the media to teach the public about the gender category. This would not only serve as a general deterrent of gender-bias crimes, but it would also inform victims of the recourses available to them within the criminal legal system.

These policy recommendations are an attempt to help policymakers and legal actors understand the complexities of the gender category. However, as this area of research is relatively new, and this study was not without its own limitations (which are discussed at length in Appendix A), the following section offers suggestions for future research.

Directions for Future Research

Because of the paucity of research on the gender category, particularly in regard to how law enforcement officials conceptualize and enforce this category, future research must continue to investigate the lack of attention gender-motivated violence receives in the legal arena and the media. Not only would this research continue to highlight the lack of consideration given to the gender category, it would also serve to increase the practical value of the category within hate crime law.

Due to the limitations of the current study, this research needs to be replicated in other states that include the gender category. Although the legal actors in New Jersey were very informative about how the gender category is perceived within that state, the interviewees in this study had not investigated or prosecuted a gender-bias offense. Therefore, law enforcement officials still lack knowledge about how to successfully pursue a gender-bias offense. For example, this study could not provide concrete examples of the type of evidence that investigators and prosecutors have used to decide whether a crime rises to the level of a gender-bias offense, or how prosecutors have connected the bias element to a case of domestic violence or rape to obtain a gender-bias conviction. Therefore, it would be beneficial if future studies explored how law enforcement officials have actually utilized the category within the criminal justice system. As previously noted, legal action has been taken in New Hampshire and California, and although it is not clear whether a gender-bias case has been prosecuted in Minnesota, such crimes have been documented in that state's annual crime reports. Therefore, a replication of this study would not only inform the hate crime literature, it would also inform the legal actors interested in making the gender category a viable piece of hate crime legislation.

As previously discussed, both legal actors and advocacy groups questioned the effectiveness of using the gender category to prosecute domestic violence and sexual assaults under New Jersey's hate crime statute. However, it is unclear whether victims of domestic violence and sexual assaults would even be interested in pursuing their cases as gender-bias offenses. If the public is unaware of the category, then victims are not aware that this avenue is available to them.

Advocacy groups and law enforcement officials should not merely assume that victims of such crimes would not be interested in pursuing their cases as hate crimes. Instead, victims of gender-bias crimes need to be informed of this approach and given the opportunity to make their own decisions. As women are the experts on their own experience, future research should empower them and allow them to be heard on the issue.

Future research also needs to explore how relatively new categories, such as "gender identity or expression," affect the enforcement of the gender category. On January 13, 2008, the New Jersey state legislature passed a bill to include "gender identity or expression" in the state bias crime statute. It is interesting that some states (such as California) include antitransgender crimes under the umbrella of "gender," yet New Jersey chose to include crimes motivated by this particular bias in a separate category. The category has been added to the Bias Incident Offense Report form,[5] yet there is still no column for such crimes in the state's annual bias crime reports. It would be informative if future research explored how law enforcement officials utilize the relatively new category of "gender identity," and whether that category poses as much difficulty as "gender" for the officials.

Finally, future research should continue to explore the gender essentialism concerns regarding bias crime legislation. As explained in chapter 4, gender cases often reflect other biases as well; for instance, an African American woman might be harassed because of her gender and race, or a Hispanic lesbian woman might be assaulted because of her gender, ethnicity, and sexual orientation. The requirement that law enforcement officials choose one category is misleading, and gender bias is often not acknowledged because law enforcement officials are uncertain of how it fits within the hate crime framework. In cases where a victim fits in multiple identity categories, research should examine how law enforcement officials designate an incident as bias-related, and what types of evidence they use to determine the specific motive. Unfortunately, this study did not fully explore these questions. It seems important for hate crime policy to recognize that multiple categories are often present in a bias incident, but before policies are changed, research should inform the debate about reform so that hate crime laws are accurately and effectively enforced.

The gender category is a relatively new category in a relatively novel law. Thus it is not suprising that scholars, policymakers, and law enforcement officials continue to question how gender-motivated violence fits within the hate crime framework. However, as violence against women remains a serious problem in our society, it is imperative that we continue to search for the most effective means with which to combat this violence. If hate crime laws are to be an additional tool for law enforcement officials to use in order to achieve justice for victims and the community at large, then it is essential that we make this tool as effective as possible.

Appendix A

Methodology

This appendix presents details about the methodological approach used in this research. First I discuss the data collection process for both the content analysis and the interviews. Next I explain the coding and analysis strategy of the study, as well as provide a brief discussion of the software used to organize and analyze the interview data. The appendix concludes with an examination of the limitations of this research.

A qualitative methodological approach is the ideal way to capture the nuances of the legislative process, as well as the perceptions of the actors involved. To address reliability and validity issues, I utilized a triangulated design of content analysis and semistructured interviews to fully explore the development and enforcement of the gender category in New Jersey's bias crime statute. Triangulation involves using multiple data-gathering techniques and multiple theories to investigate the same phenomenon (Berg 2001, 5). Because of the exploratory nature of this work, it was essential to use multiple methods in order to fully understand the development and enforcement of this contentious category. As Bachman and Lanier note: "The use of multiple research methods to study one research question . . . suggests that a researcher can get a clearer picture of the social reality being studied by viewing it from several different perspectives" (2006, 49). Moreover, as this was a case study of New Jersey's bias crime statute, it was necessary to use multiple sources of data in order to provide an in-depth description of the inclusion process and the implementation process of the gender category (Creswell 2007, 75; Kohlbacher 2006).

The first phase of the data collection entailed gathering legislative histories and newspaper articles to explore the development of the gender category in New Jersey. I analyzed the content of this material, with context provided by communications (including interviews and e-mail correspondence) with significant key players. Next, to examine how the gender category has been implemented and enforced since the passage of the law, I analyzed the content of major New Jersey newspapers and interviews with bias crime investigators, county prosecutors, and members of special interest groups. The following sections discuss these methods and the study's subjects.

Content Analysis

The first component of this study was to examine the process by which gender was included as a protected status in New Jersey's hate crime statute. As discussed in the text, jurisdictions have enacted hate crime legislation for a variety of reasons. For example, Becker (1999) found that Ohio's ethnic intimidation law developed as the result of interest group activity, media campaigns, and a specific triggering event. Jenness and Grattet (2001) claim that hate crime legislation stems from larger social movements throughout history, such as the women's rights and civil rights movements. Stolz (1999) argues that hate crime legislation is often enacted in order to perform one or more symbolic functions—to educate, reassure, or threaten—and that it is often a response to public concern about a crime problem. I explored these themes in the current work through the content analysis.

To explore the creation of hate crime legislation in New Jersey, specifically in regard to the inclusion of gender as a status group, I analyzed the content of various public records pertaining to the development of this legislation. Because the earliest available session on the New Jersey State Legislature website is the 1996–97 legislative session, I used the Lexis-Nexis Academic database to find the relevant bills prior to 1996. A search of this database using the keywords "bias crime" and "gender" resulted in two pertinent matches (see Appendix B for the text of the bills). I also conducted a search using the keywords "hate crime" and "gender," but this search yielded no matches.

The material obtained from the database contained only the text of each bill. However, the New Jersey State Library maintains legislative histories, including secondary sources showing legislative intent for enacted laws. A librarian there provided hard copies of the materials for each of the bills mentioned above. However, the legislative histories were limited, containing no transcripts of hearings. Indeed, only one of the histories included any secondary information (two newspaper articles and a press release from the governor's office); and the legislative history of the bill that added gender to the bias crime statute contained only the text of the bill.

The next step was to gather newspaper articles pertaining to gender and bias crimes. A search of the New Jersey news sources in the Lexis-Nexis Academic database[1] within the relevant period (January 1995 through January 2007) using the keyword "hate crime" yielded 858 articles. A similar search using the keyword "bias crime" resulted in 151 articles. A search using "gender" as a keyword and "hate crime" as a general term produced 53 articles, and a search using "gender" as a keyword and "bias crime" as a general term yielded 15 articles. Of those 68 articles, 16 were duplicates. Hence, 52 articles comprised the final sample of newspaper accounts pertaining to gender and bias crimes that had been written after the passage of the law.

Because the Lexis-Nexis Academic database contained only articles published since 1995, I also searched the archives of two leading New Jersey newspapers—the Newark *Star-Ledger* and the Trenton *Times*—to find articles written about gender and bias crimes prior to the passage of the law. I utilized the website NJ.com as it contained archived newspaper articles for the *Star-Ledger* dating back to May 1989 and for the *Times* dating back to March 1993.[2] Using the same keywords as in the Lexis-Nexis search, the *Star-Ledger* archives produced 22 articles specific to gender and bias crimes, and the *Times* archives yielded 5 articles. Seven articles were duplicates; thus the final sample consisted of 20 articles.

Interviews

Previous research on bias crimes suggested that there would be a variety of definitions and opinions regarding such offenses throughout New Jersey, and that the specific practices in each jurisdiction would vary depending upon the organizational and community contexts. Thus, it was imperative that the sample include subjects from around the state of New Jersey, representing different counties and municipal agencies. I used two types of sampling techniques to select the interview respondents: the purposive sampling technique, and the snowball sampling technique. The first technique is used when a researcher has knowledge about a group or population and selects subjects who represent it (Berg 2001, 32). The second technique involves first surveying or interviewing people with characteristics relevant to the research, and then asking these individuals for names of potential additional subjects who also possess the characteristics (ibid., 33).

This study used purposive sampling with the list of county prosecutors and bias crime investigators then available from the website of the Office of Bias Crime and Community Relations.[3] The list contained addresses and telephone numbers for twenty-three prosecutors and twenty-eight investigators. There are twenty-one counties in New Jersey, and typically one prosecutor and one investigator are assigned to bias crimes in each county.

I sent open-ended surveys to the prosecutors listed, but only three completed surveys were returned, for a response rate of 13 percent.[4] Both prosecutors and investigators received phone calls requesting their participation, but most individuals initially declined. The most common reason offered by the prosecutors was that they had little experience with hate crime cases and thus did not feel they could offer much assistance. Investigators expressed concerns regarding confidentiality issues with their cases, and many investigators maintained that they had to seek approval from their supervisor in order to participate.

Because of the initial difficulty in obtaining participants, I made an appeal for assistance to two organizations, the New Jersey Bias Crime Officers Association and the New Jersey County Prosecutors Association. Individuals in both associations were very helpful, granting permission to attend a monthly meeting in order to introduce the research and request participation. I was also granted permission to attend the annual training administered by the New Jersey Bias Crime Officers Association. Attending these meetings proved beneficial, as I obtained participants at all three meetings. In addition, the New Jersey County Prosecutors Association provided an updated address list for all the chief county prosecutors in the state. E-mail messages were sent to the chief prosecutors, requesting either their participation or their assistance in getting the prosecutors and investigators within their jurisdiction to participate. This method was also successful, as several individuals agreed to participate.

During this process, I also contacted members of special interest groups and key legislative players. The sponsors of the two relevant bills were contacted through the New Jersey State Legislature website. Senator Jack Sinagra, one of the original sponsors of the bill to include gender, was no longer listed on this website, but a Google search revealed his contact information. One respondent provided the e-mail address for a key member of the Assembly, and the content analysis of newspaper accounts produced the name of another individual key to the inclusion of gender. I also obtained this person's contact information by a Google search. The websites of the special interest groups provided contact information for their members.

I created separate interview guides for the investigators, the prosecutors, and other interviewees, including elected representatives and members of special interest groups. The interview guides are provided in Appendix E. As all of the interviews took place over the phone, most subjects were unable to read and sign the informed consent form before the actual interview.[5] (Several respondents did request a form and the list of interview questions be faxed to them before being interviewed.) The subjects who did not sign the consent form before the interview received detailed explanations of the confidential nature of the study and the rationale behind recording the conversation, and then were asked permission to audiotape the interview. All but two of the subjects agreed to be audiotaped. I took copious handwritten notes during all of the interviews.

The interviews ranged from approximately sixteen minutes to an hour, with an average length of forty minutes. Members of each group varied on their willingness to answer questions; however, the shortest interviews tended to be with the bias crime investigators. I conducted interviews until the point of saturation—when no new information was emerging from the subjects as a group (Corbin and Strauss 2008, 145).[6] This point was reached fairly quickly, as individuals in each group seemed to think similarly about bias crime laws in general, and the gender category specifically. I completed a total of nineteen interviews.

The nineteen interviewees included six bias crime investigators, six county prosecutors, six special interest group representatives, and one key legislative player. Additional material included three completed surveys (consisting of both open- and close-ended questions) from county prosecutors, e-mail correspondence with a member of the state Assembly, and telephone communications with a former member of the staff of Senator Jack Sinagra—as noted above, one of the original sponsors of the bill to include gender in the bias crime statute. Overall, there were twenty-four informants, thirteen males and eleven females. The breakdown by gender is as follows: nine prosecutors (six male, three female); six investigators (four male, two female); six special interest group members (three male, three female); and three legislative actors (all female). As previously mentioned, it was imperative that the subjects—especially the prosecutors and bias crime investigators—represented a variety of counties within the state in order to accurately examine the different organizational and community contexts involved in the enforcement of the law. Eight of the state's twenty-one counties were represented.

Analytical Strategy

Because this area of research is relatively new, it was important to explore whatever themes arose during data collection; thus, both the collection and analysis of data needed to remain flexible so as to accurately capture the full story. As a result, this study incorporated both inductive and deductive methods when developing analytical categories. As Kondracki, Wellman, and Amundson explain: "Inductive and deductive approaches are not mutually exclusive, and it is often useful to apply both ... [as] the results can be used to refine categories and, if necessary, create new variables to capture new aspects of message content or form" (2002, 225).[7]

Previous studies on bias crime legislation provided a list of potential categories to be used in the analysis (for example, see Becker 1999; Bell 2002; Finn 1988; Grattet, Jenness, and Curry 1998; Haider-Markel 2004; Jacobs and Potter 1998; Jenness and Grattet 2001; McPhail and DiNitto 2005; Soule and Earl 2001). This was the deductive approach. However, additional themes emerged during the coding process, and these new themes were explored until saturation was reached with the data. This was the inductive approach. These themes are discussed in the following section.

I used the open coding method, as described by Strauss and Corbin (1998), in order to code the data for both the content analysis and the interviews. As the authors explain, open coding can be accomplished in several different ways, and three specific techniques can be used during the initial process: line-by-line analysis, paragraph analysis, and document analysis (ibid., 119–20). Although this coding method is generally utilized with the grounded theory approach in order to allow theory to emerge from the data (Creswell 2007, 160), employing all three techniques during the coding process in this study ensured a thorough and systematic examination of the data.

Content Analysis

Although content analysis is often considered a quantitative analytical technique, this strategy can also be used to systematically code and analyze qualitative data (Bernard and Ryan 2010, 287). A quantitative content analysis analyzes textual data by counting the frequencies with which explicit themes occur; a qualitative content analysis goes beyond merely counting words to examining language and inferred meanings of the communication under study (Hsieh and Shannon, 2005; Kondracki, Wellman, and Amundson 2002). The latter approach is often referred to as latent content analysis (Hsieh and Shannon 2005) and has been utilized in a variety of disciplines.

I used content analysis to reveal the formal steps involved in the inclusion of the gender category. First, I analyzed the legislative records and media accounts. Next, I analyzed newspaper articles written after the passage of the law to examine how the gender category has been portrayed in the media. A color-coding scheme was utilized to manually code the data. This method was necessary as two of the legislative histories retrieved from the New Jersey State Library contained documents not available through the Lexis-Nexis database, and these documents could not be imported into the qualitative software program used to code the interview data.

At the start of the analytical process, broad themes such as political environment, interest group activities, triggering events, educational purpose, symbolic purpose, and deterrent effect received particular attention. Previous research on hate crime legislation had found all these themes to be significant. However, as the coding process continued, more specific codes began to emerge. For example, in the sample of articles published prior to the passage of the law, I used the broad code "legal discussion" for articles that contained a discussion about the constitutionality of New Jersey's hate crime law. Within this broad theme, I utilized the subcode "law is too selective" for occurrences of the argument that the law protected only certain classes of people; I used the subcode "law violates First Amendment rights" for occurrences of the argument that the law was unconstitutional because of free speech issues.

I also used this approach with the sample of articles published after the passage of the law. All of the articles in this sample contained the word "gender," but more specific codes emerged during the content analysis, differentiating between factual statements and substantive discussions. For example, subcodes such as "mentioned as part of pending federal legislation," "mentioned as part of another state's legislation," and "only mentioned as part of state statute" emerged from the data to explain why the gender category was mentioned in an article. Finally, I took notes of any observations or ideas that transpired during the coding process.

Interview Analytical Strategy

I transcribed all of the audiotaped phone interviews, surveys, and written notes and then imported the transcriptions into the software program Atlas.ti, in order to properly organize and analyze the data. This program not only allows researchers to systematically organize transcripts; as Seale states, programs like it—"encourages rigor" in data analysis because it "creates an auditable trail that ought to enhance the credibility of findings" (2003, 294).

At the start of the coding process, I paid particular attention to themes identified in prior research concerning the enforcement of hate crime laws. These themes consisted of broad categories such as "political context" and "organizational context." However, as the coding progressed, specific codes began to emerge within these broad thematic categories. For example, within the broad code "organizational context," specific subcodes such as "lack of time or resources" or "poor police work" emerged as codes to identify why bias crimes are not reported or thoroughly investigated. To explain why gender-bias cases are not reported, I utilized the broad code "uncertainty of gender"; within this broad theme, the specific subcodes "falls under civil case" and "difficulty of proof" emerged.

As new codes emerged throughout the process, it was important to go back and recode earlier documents. In the end, the coding process consisted of three steps: (1) initial coding of half of the documents; (2) recoding the first half of the documents, along with initial coding of the second half of the documents; (3) recoding all of the documents. The three-step process ensured a systematic and thorough analysis of the data.

Study Limitations

With any research, there are always limitations that may or may not affect the quality of the findings. I was aware of these limitations throughout the research process, and attempted to rectify them whenever possible. This section discusses the limitations of this study.

One of the limitations is the lack of generalizability of the findings, which is often the case with qualitative research (Auerbach and Silverstein 2003, 82). As this research was conducted only in New Jersey, the findings cannot be generalized to other states. Nevertheless, the findings can provide a base line with which to examine other states' processes. Because the sample only represented eight of the twenty-one counties in the state, it is also difficult to generalize the findings to the experiences of bias crime investigators and county prosecutors throughout the entire state of New Jersey. However, the eight counties were scattered throughout the state and included some of the larger and smaller counties. Moreover, as the interviews with county prosecutors and bias crime investigators made clear, the way in which bias crimes were investigated varied within the represented counties. For instance, one investigator was assigned solely to bias crimes; an investigator in another county was responsible for a wide range of duties. Therefore, despite the issue of generalizability, the findings presented in this study may be transferable, as it seems logical that the more abstract patterns emerging from the data would be found in other locations (ibid., 87).

The sample of interviewees was not created by random methods, so there may also be an issue of selection bias. In other words, the sample could have been skewed to provide a more favorable impression of hate crime laws, since individuals who chose to participate in the research may be more dedicated to the topic. To overcome these issues, future research might utilize random sampling techniques to gather the necessary interviewees, rather than the purposive and snowball sampling techniques used in this study. Another limitation of the sample may be its relatively small size when compared to sample sizes in other types of research. However, as McPhail explains: "Sample size is viewed differently within qualitative rather than quantitative studies. Ending the study has less to do with how many individuals participated and more to do with achieving saturation" (2002a, 282–83). In this study, I relied on the respondents' experiences and perspectives to inform the data collection process and finished conducting interviews when the point of saturation was reached. Furthermore, similar to Becker's (1999) study of Ohio's ethnic intimidation law, the purpose of this research was to gather an authentic understanding of people's experiences in regard to the development and enforcement of the gender category. Therefore, the focus was on the authenticity of the respondents' narratives, not necessarily the reliability of the data.

Qualitative research is often criticized for the subjectivity or personal influence that the researcher brings to the research; this is another limitation of the study. Because qualitative research does not utilize a set of standardized procedures similar to what is found in quantitative studies, the data analysis is subject to the researcher's personal experience. Others may interpret the data differently as the result of divergent perspectives. Therefore, in order to maintain objectivity, Strauss and Corbin offer the qualitative researcher a few tips: (1) think comparatively, or turn to the literature to find examples of similar phenomena; (2) obtain multiple viewpoints of an event; (3) periodically step back and question what is happening within the data; (4) maintain an attitude of skepticism; and (5) follow the research procedures (1998, 43–46).

In order to maintain a level of objectivity with the data in this study, I followed these suggestions throughout the research and writing process. For example, I used past research not only to develop research questions, but also to see if the findings of this study were comparable. I utilized a triangulated research design to observe both the development and the enforcement of the gender category from a variety of perspectives. Furthermore, when a new idea emerged in the data, it would be validated with data obtained in subsequent interviews before I considered the idea to be legitimate.

Finally, this study is limited because none of the interviewees had ever investigated or prosecuted a gender-bias crime. As explained in chapter 4, many of the respondents were uncertain about how gender even fit within the bias crime domain. Consequently, this research cannot examine the enforcement of the gender category in its entirety. The interviewees offered their perspectives on the gender category, but it is unknown how they would handle a gender-bias case if one presented itself. Future research would benefit from replicating this study in a jurisdiction that has fully investigated and prosecuted gender-bias crimes.

Appendix B

New Jersey Bias Crime Statutes

N.J.S. section 2C:16-1. Bias intimidation [approved January 11, 2002].

a. Bias Intimidation. A person is guilty of the crime of bias intimidation if he commits, attempts to commit, conspires with another to commit, or threatens the immediate commission of an offense specified in chapters 11 through 18 of Title 2C of the New Jersey Statutes; N.J.S. 2C:33-4; N.J.S. 2C:39-3; N.J.S.2C:39-4 or N.J.S. 2C:39-5,

(1) with a purpose to intimidate an individual or group of individuals because of race, color, religion, gender, handicap, sexual orientation, or ethnicity; or

(2) knowing that the conduct constituting the offense would cause an individual or group of individuals to be intimidated because of race, color, religion, gender, handicap, sexual orientation, or ethnicity; or

(3) under circumstances that caused any victim of the underlying offense to be intimidated and the victim, considering the manner in which the offense was committed, reasonably believed either that (a) the offense was committed with a purpose to intimidate the victim or any person or entity in whose welfare the victim is interested because of race, color, religion, gender, handicap, sexual orientation, or ethnicity, or (b) the victim or the victim's property was selected to be the target of the offense because of the victim's race, color, religion, gender, handicap, sexual orientation, or ethnicity.

b. Permissive inference concerning selection of targeted person or property. Proof that the target of the underlying offense was selected by the defendant, or by another acting in concert with the defendant, because of race, color, religion, gender, handicap, sexual orientation, or ethnicity shall give rise to a permissive inference by the trier of fact that the defendant acted with a purpose to intimidate an individual or group of individuals because of race, color, religion, gender, handicap, sexual orientation, or ethnicity.

c. Grading. Bias intimidation is a crime of the fourth degree if the underlying offense referred to in subsection a. is a disorderly persons offense or petty disorderly persons offense. Otherwise, bias intimidation is a crime one degree higher than the most serious underlying crime referred to in subsection a., except that where the underlying crime is a crime of the first degree, bias intimidation is a first-degree crime and the defendant upon conviction thereof may, notwithstanding the provisions of paragraph (1) of subsection a. of N.J.S. 2C:43-6, be sentenced to an ordinary term of imprisonment between 15 years and 30 years, with a presumptive term of 20 years.
d. Gender exemption in sexual offense prosecutions. It shall not be a violation of subsection a. if the underlying criminal offense is a violation of chapter 14 of Title 2C of the New Jersey Statutes and the circumstance specified in paragraph (1), (2) or (3) of subsection a. of this section is based solely upon the gender of the victim.
e. Merger. Notwithstanding the provisions of N.J.S. 2C:1-8 or any other provision of law, a conviction for bias intimidation shall not merge with a conviction of any of the underlying offenses referred to in subsection a. of this section, nor shall any conviction for such underlying offense merge with a conviction for bias intimidation. The court shall impose separate sentences upon a conviction for bias intimidation and a conviction of any underlying offense.

N.J.S. section 2A:53A-21. Civil cause of action for bias crime victims [approved June 11, 1993].

1. a. A person, acting with purpose to intimidate an individual or group of individuals because of race, color, religion, gender, handicap, sexual orientation or ethnicity, who engages in conduct that is an offense under the provisions of the "New Jersey Code of Criminal Justice," Title 2C of the New Jersey Statutes, commits a civil offense.
    b. Any person who sustains injury to person or property as a result of a violation of subsection a. shall have a cause of action against the person or persons who committed the civil offense resulting in the injury. In the case of a homicide committed in violation of subsection a., the estate of the deceased shall have a cause of action. Nothing in this subsection shall be construed to preclude the parent

or legal guardian of a person who has sustained injury as a result of a violation of subsection a. from initiating a civil action on behalf of a minor child or ward.

c. The Attorney General, as parens patriae, may initiate a cause of action against any person who violates subsection a. of this section on behalf of any person or persons who have sustained injury to person or property as a result of the commission of the civil offense.

d. Upon proof, by a preponderance of the evidence, of a defendant's violation of subsection a. of this section and of resulting damages, the defendant shall be liable as follows:

(1) To the person or persons injured, for an award in the amount of damages incurred as a result of the commission of the civil offense, including damages for any emotional distress suffered as a result of the civil offense, such punitive damages as may be assessed, and any reasonable attorney's fees and costs of suit incurred;

(2) To the State, in any case in which the Attorney General has participated, reasonable attorney's fees and costs of investigation and suit;

(3) Such injunctive relief as the court may deem necessary to avoid the defendant's continued violation of subsection a.; and

(4) Any additional appropriate equitable relief, including restraints to avoid repeated violation.

e. An award entered pursuant to paragraph (1) of subsection d. of this section shall be reduced by the amount of any restitution that has been awarded for the same injury following criminal conviction or juvenile adjudication, and, notwithstanding the provisions of paragraph (1) of subsection d., damages awarded for injuries that have previously been compensated by the Violent Crimes Compensation Board shall be paid to the board for deposit in the Violent Crimes Compensation Board Account.

f. All fees and costs assessed for the benefit of the State pursuant to paragraph (2) of subsection d. of this section shall be paid to the State Treasurer for deposit in the Civil Rights Enforcement Fund established pursuant to section 2 of this act.

g. The parent or guardian of a juvenile against whom an award has been entered pursuant to paragraph (1) of subsection d. of this section shall be liable for payment only if the parent has been named as a defendant and it has been established, by a preponderance of the evidence, that the parent or guardian's conduct was a significant contributing factor in the juvenile's commission of the offense.

2. There shall be established in the State Treasury a separate, nonlapsing fund designated the Civil Rights Enforcement Fund. Amounts credited to the fund shall be used by the Attorney General for the payment of expenses and costs incurred by the Attorney General in enforcement of the laws of this State protecting civil rights, in the development and delivery of training for public employees, including law enforcement officers, responsible for enforcement of these law [sic] and in the development and delivery of related public education programs.

3. The provisions of this act are intended to provide remedies independent of and in addition to those that may apply under the provisions of the "New Jersey Code of Criminal Justice." The civil actions authorized by this act are available whether or not the conduct has been prosecuted as an offense under provisions of Title 2C of the New Jersey Statutes and whether or not any such prosecution has resulted in a conviction.

Appendix C

Senate Bills 1146 and 402

1992 Bill Text NJ S.B. 1146

VERSION: Enacted
VERSION-DATE: June 11, 1993
SYNOPSIS: AN ACT to provide a civil cause of action for the benefit of victims of bias crime and supplementing Title 2A of the New Jersey Statutes.
DIGEST:
STATEMENT:
This bill would provide a civil remedy independent of and in addition to those available under the criminal provisions of the New Jersey Statutes for victims of bias crimes. The bill provides that a person, acting with the purpose to intimidate an individual or group of individuals because of race, color, religion, gender, handicap, sexual orientation or ethnicity, who engages in conduct that is an offense under the provisions of the criminal code commits a civil offense. Under the provisions of this bill, any person who commits this civil offense would be civilly liable for any injury or property damage resulting from his actions. The bill would also provide that the Attorney General, as parents [sic] patriae, would be authorized to bring an action against any person who commits this civil offense.

In addition, the bill provides that any party seeking recovery under the provisions of this bill would be entitled to damages including punitive damages, reasonable attorney's fees and costs, damages for emotional distress or any other appropriate equitable relief. The bill also provides that any award received under the act would be reduced by the amount of any restitution that has been awarded for the same injury following a criminal conviction.

Finally, under the provisions of the bill the Attorney General may be awarded reasonable attorney's fees and cost for any case in which he has participated. These monies would be deposited in a Civil Rights Enforcement Fund established under the provisions of the bill.

Establishes a civil cause of action for victims of bias crimes.

TEXT: BE IT ENACTED by the Senate and General Assembly of the State of New Jersey:

1. a. A person, acting with purpose to intimidate an individual or group of individuals because of race, color, religion, gender, handicap, sexual orientation or ethnicity, who engages in conduct that is an offense under the provisions of the "New Jersey Code of Criminal Justice," Title 2C of the New Jersey Statutes, commits a civil offense.
b. Any person who sustains injury to person or property as a result of a violation of section a. shall have a cause of action against the person or persons who committed the civil offense resulting in the injury. In the case of a homicide committed in violation of section a., the estate of the deceased shall have a cause of action. Nothing in this subsection shall be construed to preclude the parent or legal guardian of a person who has sustained injury as a result of a violation of subsection a. from initiating a civil action on behalf of a minor child or ward.
c. The Attorney General, as parents [sic] patriae, may initiate a cause of action against any person who violates subsection a. of this section on behalf of any person or persons who have sustained injury to person or property as a result of the commission of the civil offense.
d. Upon proof, by a preponderance of the evidence, of a defendant's violation of subsection a. of this section and of resulting damages, the defendant shall be liable as follows:
   (1) To the person or persons injured, for an award in the amount of damages incurred as a result of the commission of the civil offense, including damages for any emotional distress suffered as a result of the civil offense, such punitive damages as may be assessed, and any reasonable attorney's fees and costs of suit incurred;
   (2) To the State, in any case in which the Attorney General has participated, reasonable attorney's fees and costs of investigation and suit;
   (3) Such injunctive relief as the Court may deem necessary to avoid the defendant's continued violation of subsection a.; and,
   (4) Any additional appropriate equitable relief, including restraints to avoid repeated violation.
e. An award entered pursuant to paragraph (1) of subsection d. of this section shall be reduced by the amount of any restitution that has been awarded for the same injury following criminal conviction or juvenile adjudication, and, notwithstanding the provisions of paragraph (1.) of subsection d., damages awarded for injuries that

have previously been compensated by the Violent Crimes Compensation Board shall be paid to the Board for deposit in the Violent Crimes Compensation Board Account.

f. All fees and costs assessed for the benefit of the State pursuant to paragraph (2) of subsection d. of this section shall be paid to the State Treasurer for deposit in the Civil Rights Enforcement Fund established pursuant to section 2 of this act.

g. The parent or guardian of a juvenile against whom an award has been entered pursuant to paragraph (1) of subsection d. of this section shall be liable for payment only if the parent has been named as a defendant and it has been established, by a preponderance of the evidence, that the parent or guardian's conduct was a significant contributing factor in the juvenile's commission of the offense.

2. There shall be established in the State Treasury a separate, nonlapsing fund designated the Civil Rights Enforcement Fund. Amounts credited to the fund shall be used by the Attorney General for the payment of expenses and costs incurred by the Attorney General in enforcement of the laws of this State protecting civil rights, in the development and delivery of training for public employees, including law enforcement officers, responsible for enforcement of these law [sic] and in the development and delivery of related public education programs.

3. The provisions of this act are intended to provide remedies independent of and in addition to those that may apply under the provisions of the "New Jersey Code of Criminal Justice." The civil actions authorized by this act are available whether or not the conduct has been prosecuted as an offense under the provisions of Title 2C of the New Jersey Statutes and whether or not any such prosecution has resulted in a conviction.

4. The terms "conduct" and "offense" shall have the meaning provided in N.J.S.2C:1-14. The term "juvenile" shall have the meaning provided in section 24 of P.L.1982, c.77 (2A:4A-43).

5. This act shall take effect immediately.

SPONSOR: Gormley

1994 Bill Text NJ S.B. 402

VERSION: Enacted
VERSION-DATE: August 14, 1995

SYNOPSIS: AN ACT concerning bias crimes and amending N.J.S.2C:12-1, 2C:33-4, 2C:44-3 and P.L.1981, c.282.

STATEMENT:

New Jersey's Code of Criminal Justice presently prohibits crimes committed with the purpose to intimidate an individual or group of individuals because of race, color, religion, sexual orientation or ethnicity. This bill would amend these sections to expand the Code to include crimes committed with a purpose to intimidate because of gender or handicap.

The bill would also amend the criminal sentencing enhancement provisions of the Code to permit applications for enhanced penalties in two cases: (1) where the defendant has been found guilty of putting another in fear of bodily violence by placing on private property a symbol or object that exposes the other to threats of violence, N.J.S.A.2C:33-10; and (2) where the defendant has been found guilty of purposely defacing or damaging private property or property primarily used for religious, educational, residential, memorial, charitable or cemetery purposes by placing a symbol or object that exposes another person to threats of violence, N.J.S.A2C:33-11.

Furthermore, the bill would amend N.J.S.A.2C:33-10 and 2C:33-11 to delete reference to particular forms of speech and thereby eliminate the potential for constitutional challenge on the basis of R.A.V. Petition v. City of St. Paul, Minnesota, U.S. (No. 90-7675, decided June 22, 1992), 60 U.S.L.W 4667. In R.A.V. the Supreme Court held that while a state may not single out particular "fighting words" for punishment based on the message those words convey, a state may continue to prohibit all "fighting words" and words that convey threats of violence.

Extends bias crime to include crimes intended to intimidate because of gender and handicap.

TEXT: BE IT ENACTED by the Senate and General Assembly of the State of New Jersey:

1. N.J.S.2C:12-1 is amended to read as follows:
2. 2C:12-1. Assault.
   a. Simple assault. A person is guilty of assault if he:
      (1) Attempts to cause or purposely, knowingly or recklessly causes bodily injury to another; or
      (2) Negligently causes bodily injury to another with a deadly weapon; or
      (3) Attempts by physical menace to put another in fear of imminent serious bodily injury.

Simple assault is a disorderly persons offense unless committed in a fight or scuffle entered into by mutual consent, in which case it is a petty disorderly persons offense.

> b. Aggravated assault. A person is guilty of aggravated assault if he:
>
> (1) Attempts to cause serious bodily injury to another, or causes such injury purposely or knowingly or under circumstances manifesting extreme indifference to the value of human life recklessly causes such injury; or
>
> (2) Attempts to cause or purposely or knowingly causes bodily injury to another with a deadly weapon; or
>
> (3) Recklessly causes bodily injury to another with a deadly weapon; or
>
> (4) Knowingly under circumstances manifesting extreme indifference to the value of human life points a firearm, as defined in section 2C:39-1f., at or in the direction of another, whether or not the actor believes it to be loaded; or
>
> (5) Commits a simple assault as defined in subsection a. (1) and (2) of this section upon:
>
>> (a) Any law enforcement officer acting in the performance of his duties while in uniform or exhibiting evidence of his authority; or
>>
>> (b) Any paid or volunteer fireman acting in the performance of his duties while in uniform or otherwise clearly identifiable as being engaged in the performance of the duties of a fireman; or
>>
>> (c) Any person engaged in emergency first-aid or medical services acting in the performance of his duties while in uniform or otherwise clearly identifiable as being engaged in the performance of emergency first-aid or medical services; or
>>
>> (d) Any school board member or school administrator, teacher or other employee of a school board while clearly identifiable as being engaged in the performance of his duties or because of his status as a member or employee of a school board; or
>
> (6) Causes serious bodily injury to another person while fleeing or attempting to elude a law enforcement officer in violation of subsection b. of N.J.S.2C:209-2. Notwithstanding any other

provision of law to the contrary, a person shall be strictly liable for a violation of this subsection upon proof of a violation of subsection b. of N.J.S.2C:29-2 which resulted in serious bodily injury to another person; or

(7) Causes bodily injury to another person while fleeing or attempting to elude a law enforcement officer in violation of subsection b. of N.J.S.2C:29-2. Notwithstanding any other provision of law to the contrary, a person shall be strictly liable for a violation of this subsection upon proof of a violation of subsection b. of N.J.S.2C:29-2 which resulted in bodily injury to another person.

Aggravated assault under subsection b. (1) and b. (6) is a crime of the second degree; under subsection b. (2) and b. (7) is a crime of the third degree; under subsection b. (3) and b. (4) is a crime of the fourth degree; and under subsection b. (5) is a crime of the third degree if the victim suffers bodily injury, otherwise it is a crime of the fourth degree.

c. A person is guilty of assault by auto or vessel when the person drives a vehicle or vessel recklessly and causes either serious bodily injury or bodily injury to another. Assault by auto or vessel is a crime of the fourth degree if serious bodily injury results and is a disorderly persons offense if bodily injury results.

As used in this section, "auto or vessel" means of [sic] conveyance propelled otherwise than by muscular power.

d. A person who is employed by a facility as defined in section 2 of P.L.1977, c.239 (C.52:27G-2) who commits a simple assault as defined in paragraph (1) or (2) of subsection a. of this section upon an institutionalized elderly person as defined in section 2 of P.L.1977, c.239 (C.52:27G-2) is guilty of a crime of the fourth degree.

e. A person who commits a simple assault as defined in subsection a. of this section is guilty of a crime of the fourth degree if the person acted [D> , at least in part, with ill will, hatred or bias toward, and <D] with a purpose to intimidate [D> , <D] an individual or group of individuals because of race, color, religion, [A> GENDER, HANDICAP, <A] sexual orientation, or ethnicity. (cf: P.L.1991, c.341, s.2.)[1]

2. N.J.S.2C:33-4 is amended to read as follows:

2C:33-4. Harassment.

Except as provided in subsection d., a person commits a petty disorderly persons offense if, with purpose to harass another, he:

a. Makes, or causes to be made, a communication or communications anonymously or at extremely inconvenient hours, or in offensively coarse language, or any other manner likely to cause annoyance or alarm;

b. Subjects another to striking, kicking, shoving, or other offensive touching, or threatens to do so; or

c. Engages in any other course of alarming conduct or of repeatedly committed acts with purpose to alarm or seriously annoy such other person.

A communication under subsection a. may be deemed to have been made either at the place where it originated or at the place where it was received.

d. A person commits a crime of the fourth degree if in committing an offense under this section, he acted [D>, at least in part, with ill will, hatred or bias toward, and <D] with a purpose to intimidate [D>, <D] an individual or group of individuals because of race, color, religion, [A> GENDER, HANDICAP, <A] sexual orientation or ethnicity. (cf: P.L.1990, c.87, s.2.)

3. N.J.S.2C:44-3 is amended to read as follows:

2C:44-3. Criteria for Sentence of Extended Term of Imprisonment.

The court may, upon application of the prosecuting attorney, sentence a person who has been convicted of a crime of the first, second or third degree to an extended term of imprisonment if it finds one or more of the grounds specified in this section. The court shall, upon application of the prosecuting attorney, sentence a person who has been convicted of a crime, other than a violation of N.J.S.2C:12-1a., N.J.S.2C:33-4, [D> or a violation of section 1 or 2 of P.L.1981, c.282 (C.2C:33-10 or 2C:33-11), <D] [A> OR A VIOLATION OF N.J.S.2C:14-2 OR 2C:14-3 IF THE GROUNDS FOR THE APPLICATION IS PURPOSE TO INTIMIDATE BECAUSE OF GENDER, <A] to an extended term if it finds, by a preponderance of the evidence, the grounds in subsection e. If the grounds specified in subsection d. are found, and the person is being sentenced for commission of any of the offenses enumerated in N.J.S.2C:-3-6c. or N.J.S.2C:43-6g., the court shall sentence the defendant to an extended term as required by N.J.S.2C:43-6c. or N.J.S.2C:43-6g., and application by the prosecutor shall not be required. The finding of the court shall be incorporated in the record.

a. The defendant is a persistent offender. A persistent offender is a person who at the time of the commission of the crime is 21 years of age or over, who has been previously convicted on at least two separate occasions of two crimes, committed at different times, when he was at least 18 years of age, if the latest in time of these crimes or the date of the defendant's last release from confinement, whichever is later, is within 10 years of the date of the crime for which the defendant is being sentenced.

b. The defendant is a professional criminal. A professional criminal is a person who committed a crime as part of a continuing criminal activity in concert with two or more persons, and the circumstances of the crime show he has knowingly devoted himself to criminal activity as a major source of livelihood.

c. The defendant committed the crime as consideration for the receipt, or in expectation of the receipt, of anything of pecuniary value the amount of which was unrelated to the proceeds of the crime or he procured the commission of the offense by payment or promise of payment of anything of pecuniary value.

d. Second offender with a firearm. The defendant is at least 18 years of age and has been previously convicted of any of the following crimes: 2C:11-3, 2C:11-4, 2C:12-1b., 2C:13-1, 2C:14-2a., 2C:14-3a., 2C:15-1, 2C:18-2, 2C:29-5, 2C:39-4a., or has been previously convicted of an offense under Title 2A of the New Jersey Statutes which is equivalent of the offenses enumerated in this subsection and he used or possessed a firearm, as defined in 2C:39-1f., in the course of committing or attempting to commit any of these crimes, including the immediate flight therefrom.

e. The defendant in committing the crime acted [D> , at least in part, with ill will, hatred or bias toward, and <D] with a purpose to intimidate [D> , <D] an individual or group of individuals because of race, color, [A> GENDER, HANDICAP, <A] religion, sexual orientation or ethnicity. (cf: P.L.1990, c.87, s.4)

4. Section 1 of P.L.1981, c.282 (C.2C:33-10) is amended to read as follows:

1. A person is guilty of [A> A <A] crime of the third degree if he purposely, knowingly or recklessly puts or attempts to put another in fear of bodily violence by placing on [D> public or <D] private property [A> OF ANOTHER <A] a symbol, an object, a characterization, an appellation or graffiti that exposes another to threats of violence [D> , contempt or hatred on the basis of race, color, creed or religion, including, but not limited to a burning cross or Nazi swastika <D] . A person shall not be

guilty of an attempt unless his actions cause a serious and imminent likelihood of causing fear of unlawful bodily violence. (cf: P.L.1981, c.282, s.1)

5. Section 2 of P.L.1981, c.282 (C.2C:33-11) is amended to read as follows:

2. A person is guilty of a crime of the fourth degree if he purposely defaces or damages, without authorization of the owner or tenant, any private premises or property primarily used for religious, educational, residential, memorial, charitable, or cemetery purposes, or for assembly by persons [D> of a particular race, color, creed or religion <D] [A> FOR PURPOSE OF EXERCISING ANY RIGHT GUARANTEED BY LAW OR BY THE CONSTITUTION OF THIS STATE OR OF THE UNITED STATES <A] by placing thereon a symbol, an object, a characterization, an appellation, or graffiti that exposes another to threat of violence [D> , contempt or hatred on the basis of race, color, creed or religion, including, but not limited to, a burning cross or Nazi swastika <D] . (cf: P.L.1981, c.282, s.2)

6. This act shall take effect immediately.

SPONSOR: Sinagra

Appendix D

New Jersey Bias Crime Legislation Effective as of March 13, 2008 [after the period studied in the book]

SYNOPSIS: AN ACT concerning hate crimes and bullying, establishing a commission, amending various parts of the statutory law, and supplementing Title 52 of the Revised Statutes.
BE IT ENACTED by the Senate and General Assembly of the State of New Jersey:
1. N.J.S.2C:16-1 is amended to read as follows:
2C:16-1. *Bias Intimidation.*

> a. Bias Intimidation. A person is guilty of the crime of bias intimidation if he commits, attempts to commit, conspires with another to commit, or threatens the immediate commission of an offense specified in chapters 11 through 18 of Title 2C of the New Jersey Statutes; N.J.S.2C:33-4; N.J.S.2C:39-3; N.J.S.2C:39-4 or N.J.S.2C:39-5,
>> (1) with a purpose to intimidate an individual or group of individuals because of race, color, religion, gender, disability, sexual orientation, gender identity or expression, national origin, or ethnicity; or
>> (2) knowing that the conduct constituting the offense would cause an individual or group of individuals to be intimidated because of race, color, religion, gender, disability, sexual orientation, gender identity or expression, national origin, or ethnicity; or
>> (3) under circumstances that caused any victim of the underlying offense to be intimidated and the victim, considering the manner in which the offense was committed, reasonably believed either that (a) the offense was committed with a purpose to intimidate the victim or any person or entity in whose welfare the victim is interested because of race, color, religion, gender, disability, sexual orientation, gender identity or expression, national origin, or ethnicity, or (b) the victim or the victim's property was selected to be the target of the offense because of the victim's race, color, religion, gender, disability, sexual orientation, gender identity or expression, national origin, or ethnicity.

b. Permissive inference concerning selection of targeted person or property. Proof that the target of the underlying offense was selected by the defendant, or by another acting in concert with the defendant, because of race, color, religion, gender, disability, sexual orientation, gender identity or expression, national origin, or ethnicity shall give rise to a permissive inference by the trier of fact that the defendant acted with a purpose to intimidate an individual or group of individuals because of race, color, religion, gender, disability, sexual orientation, gender identity or expression, national origin, or ethnicity.

c. Grading. Bias intimidation is a crime of the fourth degree if the underlying offense referred to in subsection a. is a disorderly persons offense or petty disorderly persons offense. Otherwise, bias intimidation is a crime one degree higher than the most serious underlying crime referred to in subsection a., except that where the underlying crime is a crime of the first degree, bias intimidation is a first-degree crime and the defendant upon conviction thereof may, notwithstanding the provisions of paragraph (1) of subsection a. of N.J.S.2C:43-6, be sentenced to an ordinary term of imprisonment between 15 years and 30 years, with a presumptive term of 20 years.

d. Gender exemption in sexual offense prosecutions. It shall not be a violation of subsection a. if the underlying criminal offense is a violation of chapter 14 of Title 2C of the New Jersey Statutes and the circumstance specified in paragraph (1), (2) or (3) of subsection a. of this section is based solely upon the gender of the victim.

e. Merger. Notwithstanding the provisions of N.J.S.2C:1-8 or any other provision of law, a conviction for bias intimidation shall not merge with a conviction of any of the underlying offenses referred to in subsection a. of this section, nor shall any conviction for such underlying offense merge with a conviction for bias intimidation. The court shall impose separate sentences upon a conviction for bias intimidation and a conviction of any underlying offense.

f. Additional Penalties. In addition to any fine imposed pursuant to N.J.S.2C:43-3 or any term of imprisonment imposed pursuant to N.J.S.2C:43-6, a court may order a person convicted of bias intimidation to one or more of the following:

    (1) complete a class or program on sensitivity to diverse communities, or other similar training in the area of civil rights;

(2) complete a counseling program intended to reduce the tendency toward violent and antisocial behavior; and

(3) make payments or other compensation to a community-based program or local agency that provides services to victims of bias intimidation.

g. As used in this section "gender identity or expression" means having or being perceived as having a gender related identity or expression whether or not stereotypically associated with a person's assigned sex at birth.

h. It shall not be a defense to a prosecution for a crime under this section that the defendant was mistaken as to the race, color, religion, gender, disability, sexual orientation, gender identity or expression, national origin, or ethnicity of the victim.

2. Section 1 of P.L.1993, c.137 (C.2A:53A-21) is amended to read as follows:

C. 2A:53A-21 *Civil cause of action for bias crime victims.*

1. a. A person, acting with purpose to intimidate an individual or group of individuals because of race, color, religion, gender, disability, sexual orientation, gender identity or expression, national origin, or ethnicity, who engages in conduct that is an offense under the provisions of the "New Jersey Code of Criminal Justice," Title 2C of the New Jersey Statutes, commits a civil offense.

b. Any person who sustains injury to person or property as a result of a violation of subsection a. shall have a cause of action against the person or persons who committed the civil offense resulting in the injury. In the case of a homicide committed in violation of subsection a., the estate of the deceased shall have a cause of action. Nothing in this subsection shall be construed to preclude the parent or legal guardian of a person who has sustained injury as a result of a violation of subsection a. from initiating a civil action on behalf of a minor child or ward.

c. The Attorney General, as parens patriae, may initiate a cause of action against any person who violates subsection a. of this section on behalf of any person or persons who have sustained injury to person or property as a result of the commission of the civil offense.

d. Upon proof, by a preponderance of the evidence, of a defendant's violation of subsection a. of this section and of resulting damages, the defendant shall be liable as follows:

(1) To the person or persons injured, for an award in the amount of damages incurred as a result of the commission of the civil offense, including damages for any emotional distress suffered as a result of the civil offense, such punitive damages as may be assessed, and any reasonable attorney's fees and costs of suit incurred;

(2) To the State, in any case in which the Attorney General has participated, reasonable attorney's fees and costs of investigation and suit;

(3) Such injunctive relief as the court may deem necessary to avoid the defendant's continued violation of subsection a.; and

(4) Any additional appropriate equitable relief, including restraints to avoid repeated violation.

e. An award entered pursuant to paragraph (1) of subsection d. of this section shall be reduced by the amount of any restitution that has been awarded for the same injury following criminal conviction or juvenile adjudication, and, notwithstanding the provisions of paragraph (1) of subsection d., damages awarded for injuries that have previously been compensated by the Victims of Crime Compensation Agency shall be paid to the agency for deposit in the Violent Crimes Compensation Board Account.

f. All fees and costs assessed for the benefit of the State pursuant to paragraph (2) of subsection d. of this section shall be paid to the State Treasurer for deposit in the Civil Rights Enforcement Fund established pursuant to section 2 of P.L.1993, c.137 (C.2A:53A-22).

g. The parent or guardian of a juvenile against whom an award has been entered pursuant to paragraph (1) of subsection d. of this section shall be liable for payment only if the parent has been named as a defendant and it has been established, by a preponderance of the evidence, that the parent or guardian's conduct was a significant contributing factor in the juvenile's commission of the offense.

3. Section 11 of P.L.1971, c.317 (C.52:4B-11) is amended to read as follows:

C.52:4B-11 Victim compensation.

11. The agency may order the payment of compensation in accordance with the provisions of P.L.1971, c.317 for personal injury or death which resulted from:

a. an attempt to prevent the commission of crime or to arrest a suspected criminal or in aiding or attempting to aid a police officer so to do; or

b. the commission or attempt to commit any of the following offenses:
  (1) aggravated assault;
  (2) (Deleted by amendment, P.L.1995, c.135);
  (3) threats to do bodily harm;
  (4) lewd, indecent, or obscene acts;
  (5) indecent acts with children;
  (6) kidnapping;
  (7) murder;
  (8) manslaughter;
  (9) aggravated sexual assault, sexual assault, aggravated criminal sexual contact, criminal sexual contact;
  (10) any other crime involving violence including domestic violence as defined by section 3 of P.L.1981, c.426 (C.2C:25-3) or section 3 of P.L.1991, c.261 (C.2C:25-19);
  (11) burglary;
  (12) tampering with a cosmetic, drug or food product;
  (1 3) a violation of human trafficking, section 1 of P.L.2005, c.77 (C.2C:13-8); or
 c. the commission of a violation of R.S.39:4-50, section 5 of P.L.1990, c.103 (C.39:3-10.13), section 19 of P.L.1954, c.236 (C.12:7-34.19) or section 3 of P.L.1952, c.157 (C.12:7-46); or
 d. theft of an automobile pursuant to N.J.S.2C:20-2, eluding a law enforcement officer pursuant to subsection b. of N.J.S.2C:29-2 or unlawful taking of a motor vehicle pursuant to subsection b., c. or d. of N.J.S.2C:20-10 where injuries to the victim occur in the course of operating an automobile in furtherance of the offense; or
 e. the commission of a violation of N.J.S. 2C:16-1, bias intimidation.
4. Section 3 of P.L.1966, c.37 (C.52:17B-5.3) is amended to read as follows:
C.52:17B-5.3 Quarterly crime report by local and county police; contents, incidence of street gang activity, bias crime.
3.   a. All local and county police authorities shall submit a quarterly report to the Attorney General, on forms prescribed by the Attorney General, which report shall contain the number and nature of offenses committed within their respective jurisdictions, the disposition of such matters, information relating to criminal street gang activities within their respective jurisdictions, information relating to any offense directed against a person or group, or their property, by reason of their race, color, religion, gender, disability, sexual

orientation, gender identity or expression, national origin, or ethnicity and such other information as the Attorney General may require, respecting information relating to the cause and prevention of crime, recidivism, the rehabilitation of criminals and the proper administration of criminal justice.

C. 52:17B-5.4a Collection, analysis of information, central repository.

5. The Attorney General shall maintain a central repository for the collection and analysis of information collected pursuant to section 3 of P.L.1966, c.37 (C.52:17B-5.3). Information in the repository shall be made available to the public. The Attorney General may designate the Division of State Police in the Department of Law and Public Safety to be the agency to maintain the repository and provide information from the repository to the public.

C. 52:17B-77.12 Required training concerning bias intimidation crimes for police officers.

6. The Police Training Commission shall require all new police officers to complete two hours of training, which may include interactive training, in identifying, responding to, and reporting bias intimidation crimes. The Police Training Commission shall develop or revise the training course in consultation with the New Jersey Human Relations Council established pursuant to section 1 of P.L.1997, c.257 (C.52:9DD-8). The training course shall include the following topics:

    a. features that identify or could identify a bias intimidation crime;

    b. laws dealing with bias intimidation crimes;

    c. law enforcement procedures, reporting, and documentation of bias intimidation crimes; and

    d. techniques and methods to handle incidents of bias intimidation crimes, including training on how to deal sensitively with victims and referring victims of bias intimidation crimes to organizations that provide assistance and compensation to victims.

7. Section 3 of P.L.2002, c.83 (C.18A:37-15) is amended to read as follows:

C.18A:37-15 Adoption of policy concerning intimidation or bullying by each school district.

3.   a. Each school district shall adopt a policy prohibiting harassment, intimidation or bullying on school property, at a school-sponsored function or on a school bus. The school district shall attempt to adopt the policy through a process that includes representation of parents or guardians, school employees, volunteers, students, administrators, and community representatives.

b. A school district shall have local control over the content of the policy, except that the policy shall contain, at a minimum, the following components:

(1) a statement prohibiting harassment, intimidation or bullying of a student;

(2) a definition of harassment, intimidation or bullying no less inclusive than that set forth in section 2 of P.L.2002, c.83 (C.18A:37-14);

(3) a description of the type of behavior expected from each student;

(4) consequences and appropriate remedial action for a person who commits an act of harassment, intimidation or bullying;

(5) a procedure for reporting an act of harassment, intimidation or bullying, including a provision that permits a person to report an act of harassment, intimidation or bullying anonymously; however, this shall not be construed to permit formal disciplinary action solely on the basis of an anonymous report;

(6) a procedure for prompt investigation of reports of violations and complaints, identifying either the principal or the principal's designee as the person responsible for the investigation;

(7) the range of ways in which a school will respond once an incident of harassment, intimidation or bullying is identified;

(8) a statement that prohibits reprisal or retaliation against any person who reports an act of harassment, intimidation or bullying and the consequence and appropriate remedial action for a person who engages in reprisal or retaliation;

(9) consequences and appropriate remedial action for a person found to have falsely accused another as a means of retaliation or as a means of harassment, intimidation or bullying;

(10) a statement of how the policy is to be publicized, including notice that the policy applies to participation in school-sponsored functions; and

(11) a requirement that the policy be posted on the school district's website and distributed annually to parents and guardians who have children enrolled in a school in the school district.

c. A school district shall adopt a policy and transmit a copy of its policy to the appropriate county superintendent of schools by September 1, 2003.

d. To assist school districts in developing policies for the prevention of harassment, intimidation or bullying, the Commissioner of Education shall develop a model policy applicable to grades kindergarten through 12. This model policy shall be issued no later than December 1, 2002.

e. Notice of the school district's policy shall appear in any publication of the school district that sets forth the comprehensive rules, procedures and standards of conduct for schools within the school district, and in any student handbook.

C. 18A:37-15.2 *Actions required relative to bullying policy.*

8. Within 60 days of the effective date of this section each school district shall amend its bullying policy in accordance with section 3 of P.L.2002, c.83 (C.18A:37-15) as amended by section 7 of P.L.2007, c.303, make the policy available on the district's website, and notify students and parents that the policy is available on the district's website.

9.   a. There is hereby established the Commission on Bullying in Schools.

b. The commission shall consist of 14 members as follows:

(1) the Commissioner of the Department of Education, or his designee;

(2) the Director of the Division on Civil Rights in the Department of Law and Public Safety, or his designee;

(3) the Governor shall appoint eight public members: one representative of the New Jersey Education Association, one representative of the New Jersey School Boards Association, one representative of the Anti-Defamation League, one representative of the New Jersey Principals and Supervisors Association, and four public members with a background in, or special knowledge of, the legal, policy, educational, social or psychological aspects of bullying in schools;

(4) the President of the Senate shall appoint two public members with a background in, or special knowledge of, the legal, policy, educational, social or psychological aspects of bullying in schools; and

(5) the Speaker of the General Assembly shall appoint two public members with a background in, or special knowledge of, the legal, policy, educational, social or psychological aspects of bullying in schools.

c. The commission shall study and make recommendations regarding:
   (1) the implementation and effectiveness of school bullying laws and regulations;
   (2) the adequacy of legal remedies available to students who are victims of bullying and their parents and guardians;
   (3) the adequacy of legal protections available to teachers who are in compliance with school bullying policies;
   (4) training of teachers, school administrators, and law enforcement personnel in responding to, investigating and reporting incidents of bullying;
   (5) funding issues related to the implementation of the State school bullying laws and regulations; and
   (6) the implementation of a possible collaboration between the Department of Education and the Division on Civil Rights in the Department of Law and Public Safety on a Statewide initiative against school bullying.

d. The members shall be appointed within 30 days of enactment.

e. The members shall serve without compensation, but may be reimbursed for necessary expenses incurred in the performance of their duties, within the limits of funds appropriated or otherwise made available to the commission for its purposes.

f. The commission shall choose a chairperson from among its members.

g. Any vacancy in the membership shall be filled in the same manner as the original appointment.

h. The commission is entitled to the assistance and service of the employees of any State, county or municipal department, board, bureau, commission or agency as it may require and as may be available to it for its purposes, and to employ stenographic and clerical assistance and to incur traveling or other miscellaneous expenses as may be necessary in order to perform its duties, within the limits of funds appropriated or otherwise made available to the commission for its purposes.

i. The commission shall conduct a minimum of three public hearings: one in the northern portion of the State; one in the central portion of the State; and one in the southern portion of the State.

j. The commission shall report its findings and recommendations, along with any legislation it desires to recommend for adoption by the Legislature, to the Governor and the Legislature in accordance with section 2 of P.L.1991, c.164 (C.52:14-19.1). The commission shall issue its final report no later than nine months after final appointment of its members.

k. The commission shall expire upon submission of its final report to the Governor and the Legislature.

10. Section 9 of this act shall take effect immediately. Sections 1 through 8 shall take effect on the 60 [sic] day after enactment, but the Attorney General and the Commissioner of the Department of Education shall take such anticipatory administrative action in advance thereof as shall be necessary for the implementation of this act.

HISTORY: Approved January 13, 2008
SPONSOR: Buono

Appendix E

Interview Guides

Interview Guide for Prosecutors

What is your official title?
How long have you been a prosecutor?
What type of cases do you most frequently deal with? What experiences have you had with bias crime cases?
What is your working definition of a bias crime?
What resources are available to you as a prosecutor for bias crime cases? Are the resources sufficient for properly prosecuting such cases?
Have there been special trainings on the inclusion of gender? If so, have you attended any?
What do you think is the purpose of including gender in the bias crime statutes?
What is your own position on the inclusion of gender?
What offenses are classified as gender-bias? How easy or difficult is it to define gender-motivated crimes?
Are domestic assault cases considered gender-bias offenses? Why or why not?
What is your position on the exemption stated in the statute regarding the exclusion of sexual assault and criminal sexual contact (N.J.S. 2C:14-2 and N.J.S. 2C:14-3)?
Would including crimes such as sexual assault change how you prosecute gender-bias crimes? If so, how?
What kind of evidence is needed to classify a crime as gender-motivated bias?
In order to successfully prosecute a case, does a crime have to be motivated by gender bias or does there only need to be evidence that gender bias existed during the commission of a crime?
Do you think this is an effective law even though there have been so few cases of a gender-bias crime? Why or why not?
What kind of reaction (positive or negative) have you encountered in trying to prosecute gender-bias crimes?
Does the political climate of New Jersey influence whether gender-motivated bias cases are investigated and/or prosecuted? If yes, how?

Do the media influence whether gender-motivated bias cases are investigated and/or prosecuted? If yes, how?

In your opinion, is there a status category included in the bias crime statute that should not be? If yes, which one and why?

In your opinion, is there a category still missing from the current statute? If so, which one and why?

What are the most common underreported bias-motivated offenses? Why do you think this is so?

What are the most common reported bias-motivated crimes? Why do you think this is so?

What affects whether or not a victim reports a bias crime? What would encourage or discourage victims from reporting a bias crime?

What affects whether an officer identifies a crime as bias motivated?

What affects whether the state decides to pursue charges against alleged offenders?

Is there anything else you would like to add in regard to the gender category?

Interview Guide for Bias Investigators

What is your official title?

How long have you been an investigator?

What is your working definition of a bias crime?

What kind of experiences have you had with bias crimes?

What resources are available to you as an investigator for bias crime cases? Are the resources sufficient for properly investigating such cases?

What do you think is the purpose of including gender in the bias crime statutes?

What is your own position on the inclusion of gender?

What kind of training have you had specifically on bias crime incidences? Have there been special trainings on the inclusion of gender?

What offenses are classified as gender biased? How easy or difficult is it to define gender-motivated crimes?

What kind of evidence is needed to classify a crime as gender-motivated bias? Are domestic assault cases considered gender-bias offenses? Why or why not?

What is your position on the exemption stated in the statute regarding the exclusion of sexual assault and criminal sexual contact (N.J.S. 2C:14-2 and N.J.S. 2C:14-3)?

Would including crimes such as sexual assault change how you investigate gender-bias crimes? If so, how?

What kind of reaction (positive or negative) have you encountered in trying to investigate gender-bias crimes?

Do you think this is an effective law even though there have been so few cases of a gender-bias crime? Why or why not?

Does the political climate of New Jersey influence whether gender-motivated bias cases are investigated and/or prosecuted? If yes, how?

Do the media influence whether gender-motivated bias cases are investigated and/or prosecuted? If yes, how?

In your opinion, is there a status category included in the bias crime statute that should not be? If yes, which one and why?

In your opinion, is there a category still missing from the current statute? If so, which one and why?

What are the most common underreported bias-motivated offenses? Why do you think this is so?

What are the most common reported bias-motivated crimes? Why do you think this is so?

What affects whether or not a victim reports a bias crime? What would encourage or discourage victims from reporting a bias crime?

What affects whether an officer identifies a crime as bias motivated?

What affects whether the state decides to pursue charges against alleged offenders?

Is there anything else you would like to add in regard to the gender category?

Interview Guide for Elected Representatives
and Members of Special Interest Groups

How long have you been in your current position?

What experience have you had with bias crime cases?

What is your position regarding the inclusion of gender as a status group?

What are your arguments for (or against) the inclusion of gender?

How easy or difficult is it to define gender bias and to include these crimes in bias crime legislation?

What role did the political climate of New Jersey have in creating this legislation?

What role did the media have in encouraging or discouraging the inclusion of gender?

What role did interest groups have in the creation of this legislation? Which organizations were the most influential?

Was there a particular incident or situation that facilitated the enactment of this legislation? (I.e., was there a triggering event?)

Why do you think New Jersey included gender as a protected group within bias crime laws? What is the purpose of this specific piece of legislation?

Why do you think there have been so few cases of gender-bias crimes in New Jersey since the enactment of this law?

Do you think this is an effective law even though there have been so few cases of a gender-bias crime? Why or why not?

What is your position on the exemption stated in the statute regarding the exclusion of sexual offenses (N.J.S. 2C:14-2 and N.J.S. 2C:14-3)? How would including crimes such as sexual assault change how these cases are investigated and prosecuted?

What kind of reaction (positive or negative) have you encountered in supporting (or opposing) gender-bias legislation?

What is the purpose of bias crime legislation in general?

Why do you think bias crime legislation developed in New Jersey?

What factors are involved in deciding which groups are included in the statutes?

Who or what organizations have been the strongest supporters of the bias crime legislation? Who are what organizations have been the strongest critics?

In your opinion, is there a status category included in the bias crime statute that should not be? If yes, which one and why?

In your opinion, is there a category still missing from the current statute? If so, which one and why?

What are the most common underreported bias-motivated offenses? Why do you think this is so?

What are the most common reported bias-motivated crimes? Why do you think this is so?

What affects whether or not a victim reports a bias crime? What would encourage or discourage victims from reporting a bias crime?

What affects whether an officer identifies a crime as bias motivated?

What affects whether the state decides to pursue charges against alleged offenders?

In your opinion, for something to be a bias-motivated crime, does bias have to be the sole motive or can there be a mixed motive?

In your opinion, does law enforcement have the necessary resources to properly investigate bias crimes? Do prosecutors have sufficient resources? If no to either, what resources are needed?

Notes

1. Why Does Gender Matter?

1. VAWA provides several strategies to address the flaws and deficiencies of state laws in regard to violence against women, and to provide assistance for victims of gender-motivated violence. The law has been reauthorized in 2000 and then again in 2005. It will be discussed at greater length in chapter 2.

2. The terms "bias crime" and "hate crime" are often used interchangeably within the literature due to the similarity of the concepts. Thus, I have chosen to use the terms interchangeably throughout the book.

3. According to the Anti-Defamation League (2008), forty-five states and the District of Columbia have enacted penalty-enhancement statutes. For a more thorough discussion of the different types of hate crime provisions, see the report on hate crime legislation written by the Center for Women Policy Studies (2001).

4. Haider-Markel (1998) discovered through interviews with local activists that sexual orientation had originally been included in Oklahoma's hate crime legislation but was deleted in order to get the bill passed.

5. Although some women may blame rape victims by questioning the victim's behavior prior to the offense (for example, blame may be placed on the victim due to her choice of clothing or whether she had been using drugs or alcohol), research consistently demonstrates that women indicate greater sympathy than men do for rape victims, and that men are more likely than women to blame rape victims for the offense (Anderson, Cooper, and Okamura 1997; Black and Gold 2008; Pollard 1992; Whatley 2005). Moreover, research has shown that although women may blame the victim in order to deny their personal vulnerability, men may blame the victim in order to justify the behavior of the rapist (Lonsway and Fitzgerald 1995; cited in Melton 2010).

6. The states that, in addition to Washington, D.C., include gender in their hate crime legislation are: Alaska, Arizona, California, Connecticut, Hawaii, Illinois, Iowa, Louisiana, Maine, Michigan, Minnesota, Mississippi, Missouri, Nebraska, New Hampshire, New Jersey, New Mexico, New York, North Carolina, North Dakota, Rhode Island, Tennessee, Texas, Vermont, Washington, and West Virginia (Anti-Defamation League 2008).

7. Often the gender category is misunderstood as including only crimes against women. Although this book focuses on crimes against women, I agree that the gender category could also include crimes against men if they are selected as victims because of their gender, and the category could also include transgendered individuals (and other gender identities) in situations in which there is not a separate "gender identity" category in the bias crime statute.

8. The feminist approach is one of the main perspectives used in studying violence between intimate partners; the other main perspective is often called "the family violence approach" (Kurz 1993, 253) or the "gender symmetry" argument (Belknap and Melton 2005). This second perspective asserts that men and women are equally violent within intimate relationships (Johnson 2008, 3) and thus challenges the feminist perspective. According to the gender symmetry argument, women commit violent acts against their male partners just as often as men commit acts of violence against their female partners. These findings are generally based upon survey research utilizing the Conflict Tactics Scale (Belknap and Melton 2005). Despite the growing acceptance of the family violence approach within certain circles, feminist scholars continue to challenge this perspective on several grounds (Belknap and Melton 2005; Miller 2005, 22). For instance, studies relying on the Conflict Tactics Scale are criticized because they fail to consider the context of the violent incident. Specifically, these studies do not examine why the offender was violent—whether the violent act was triggered by past abuse or used as self-defense, or whether it was used to dominate or terrorize one's partner (Miller 2005, 18–19). Ignoring the context of the incident makes it difficult to accurately assess the degree of harm (both physical and mental) associated with the violent act. Moreover, as Miller explains, even if feminist studies of intimate partner violence are challenged by proponents of the family violence perspective, two of the most well-respected national victimization surveys (the National Crime Victimization Survey and the National Violence Against Women Survey) consistently "reveal dramatic differences in rates of intimate violence, lending strong support that the gender distribution is asymmetrical" (2005, 21). For further discussion of the debate between the feminist approach and the family violence perspective, see Belknap and Melton 2005; Kurz 1993; and Miller 2005.

9. In her study of a twelve-week female offender's treatment program in two counties, Miller found that the majority of the women (sixty-two out of ninety-five) used violence as a defensive tactic to get away from a violent incident or were trying to leave in order to avoid violence (2005, 120); whereas only five of the women used preemptive, aggressive violence (125). Moreover, Miller discovered that the women typically used violence after the male partner had used violence, especially when the women perceived their children were in danger (120). In a separate study examining the differences between male and female intimate partner homicides, Swatt (2006) discovered that, unlike homicides of male intimate partners, female intimate homicides were linked to defensive reactions resulting from prior abuse.

10. In the report, the distinct type of gender bias is not shown. Thus it is unknown whether these crimes were committed against groups such as women, men, and transgendered people.

11. Out of the twenty-five gender-bias crimes reported in California during this period, two were antifemale and twenty-three were antitransgender.

12. Unlike the state of California, New Jersey did not include a category for antitransgender crimes. However, as discussed in chapter 5, the New Jersey legislature passed a bill on January 13, 2008, to amend the state's bias crime statutes to include "gender identity or expression" as one of the protected groups. See Appendix D for the text of this bill. As the law became effective as of March 13, 2008, while this book relies on data collected before that date, the law is refererred to as pending and the previous law is referred to as current.

13. These reports are available on the New Jersey State Police website (http://www.njsp.org/info/stats.html).

14. During 2007, 13,241 law enforcement agencies participated in the FBI's Uniform Crime Report Program's hate crime data collection, and of those agencies, 2,025 (15.3 percent) reported 7,624 incidents. The remaining 84.7 percent of the participating agencies reported that no hate crimes occurred in their jurisdictions (Federal Bureau of Investigation 2008).

15. For more information regarding the programs and services once offered by this office, see its website (http://www.nj.gov/oag/dcj/obccr/). Although there is no single definitive answer as to why the office was closed a few years ago, interviewees in this study suggested that it was due to funding issues and a shift of priorities within the higher ranks of state government. The office's closing is discussed at greater length in chapter 5.

16. As explained in Appendix A, the prosecutors were initially asked to complete a survey, but it became apparent that this method was not successful in obtaining respondents. As a result, it was discontinued, and the focus shifted to obtaining interview subjects.

2. Hate Crime Legislation

1. According to FBI guidelines, investigators should consider the following factors when assessing whether crimes are motivated by bias: whether bias-related comments, written statements, or gestures were made by the offender; whether bias-related drawings, markings, symbols, or graffiti were left at the crime scene; whether objects, items, or things indicating bias were used; whether the victim was in a neighborhood where previous hate crimes had been committed; whether a substantial portion of the community believes that the offense was motivated by bias; whether the victim participated in activities that proclaimed his or her membership in a protected group; whether the incident coincided with a holiday relating to a significant date for a protected group;

whether the offender was previously involved in similar hate crimes or was a member of a hate group; whether a hate group was involved in the incident; whether animosity has historically existed between the victim's and the offender's groups; and whether the victim was not a member of a protected class, but a member of a group advocating support for the protected class (Goldscheid 1999, 133–34).

2. Congress has the authority to enact legislation under the Commerce Clause if the law falls in one of three categories: (1) regulation of the use of the channels of interstate commerce; (2) regulation or protection of the instrumentalities of interstate commerce, or persons or things in interstate commerce, even though the threat may come only from intrastate activities; and (3) regulation of an activity that substantially affects interstate commerce. According to Section Five of the Fourteenth Amendment, Congress may enforce by appropriate legislation the constitutional guarantee that no state shall deprive any person of life, liberty, or property without due process of law, nor deny any person equal protection of the laws (see *United States v. Morrison*, 529 U.S. 598).

3. In order to file a civil suit under that section of VAWA, the victim has to prove that the crime of violence was an act that would constitute a felony (an offense against either a person or property), regardless of whether criminal charges were filed, and that the crime was motivated by gender and due, at least in part, to an animus based on the victim's gender (Hasenstab 2001).

4. Brzonkala claimed that the university did not treat her fairly during the proceedings because of her gender and that she had been subjected to a hostile environment.

5. Haider-Markel examined the importance of the political context through an analysis of a fifty-state data set. Using a model of policy implementation to predict state efforts to implement federal hate crime policy, Haider-Markel found that political pressures significantly influenced the adoption of hate crime policy: "Hate crime policy is largely determined by political pressures, including party competition, interest group strength, issue salience, and the strength of law enforcement bureaucracy" (1998, 85).

6. In this study, Jenness and Grattet do not provide an analysis of external factors related to the diffusion model. The authors explained: "Once the symbolic dimensions of an internal determinant model are fully investigated, especially social-movement-related variables . . . models that focus on factors external to the state must be considered" (1996, 148). Two years later, Grattet, Jenness, and Curry (1998) incorporated the diffusion model. Through an analysis of historical events, the authors found that a state's adoption of a hate crime law is "affected by both the state's internal political culture and traditions as well as by its location within the larger interstate system" (286). For instance, the authors found that states are pressured to enact hate crime laws as more and more other states do so, and that states with more innovative policy cultures are more likely to pass laws earlier than those with less innovative policy cultures (303).

7. The authors defined "perviousness" as "an organizational-environmental condition characterized by both susceptibility to environmental influence and the alignment of the

policy innovation with existing organizational culture and practices" (Jenness and Grattet 2005, 344).

8. In a comparison of the mean values for each of the variables in the models, the authors found only one significant difference between the responders and the nonresponders. On average, the nonresponding agencies were located in communities characterized by lower socioeconomic conditions As this factor was associated with not having a hate crime policy, the authors concluded that many of the nonresponding agencies did not have a hate crime policy (Jenness and Grattet 2005, 346).

3. Developing the Gender Category

1. See N.J.S. sections 2C:44-3(e), 2C:12-1(e), and 2C:33-4(d). The current statutes state that these subsections were deleted by amendment P.L. 2001, c. 443. This amendment was codified as 2C:16-1, the current statute on bias crime intimidation (see Appendix B).

2. In *R.A.V. v. City of St. Paul*, the U.S. Supreme Court unanimously held a city ordinance in St. Paul, Minnesota, to be unconstitutional because it criminalized expressive behavior protected by the First Amendment. The ordinance in question read in part: "Whoever places on public or private property a symbol, object, appellation, characterization or graffiti, including, but not limited to, a burning cross or Nazi swastika, which one knows or has reasonable grounds to know arouses anger, alarm or resentment in others on the basis of race, color, creed, religion or gender commits disorderly conduct and shall be guilty of a misdemeanor" (St. Paul, Minnesota, Legis. Code section 292.02 [1990]).

The city had utilized the ordinance to charge a juvenile who, along with several other teenagers, had placed a burning cross built out of broken chair legs inside the fenced yard of a black family. The Court based its decision on the fact that the ordinance prohibited only expressions, or "fighting words," that insulted or caused alarm due to the victim's race, color, creed, religion, or gender. The Court pointed out that expressions connected to other ideas, such as one's political affiliation or homosexuality, were not covered under the ordinance. Consequently, the ordinance violated the First Amendment as it imposed special prohibitions only on those expressed views that the city government deemed unfavorable. According to the Court's ruling, to pass constitutional muster, such statutes must be content-neutral: in other words, they cannot prohibit select viewpoints. Furthermore, such statutes cannot prohibit expressions that do not communicate ideas in a threatening or harassing manner. For example, one can say, "I hate [insert racial or religious epithet]" and not be in violation of the law. Yet if one says, "I hate [insert racial or religious epithet] and because of that, I'm going to kill you," this would be considered a threatening statement in violation of the law (Gerstenfeld 2004, 31). Put simply, the Court's decision made it clear that hate speech alone is not a criminal offense.

3. The decision in *Apprendi v. New Jersey* was the result of a 1994 case in which Charles Apprendi Jr. filed several shots into the home of Michael and Mattie Fowlkes. The State of New Jersey argued that Apprendi had committed the crime with the purpose of intimidating the Fowlkes family because they were African American. During the sentencing phase of the trial, the judge determined that the act had been motivated by racial bias and sentenced Apprendi to twelve years in prison; without the hate crime enhancement, Apprendi would have received ten years (Gerstenfeld 2004, 45). Apprendi appealed the decision, and after the New Jersey courts rejected his appeal, the case went to the U.S. Supreme Court. Apprendi argued that his due process rights had been violated because the jury had not determined the enhanced sentence under the standard of reasonable doubt; rather, the trial court judge had made the decision under the more lenient standard of preponderance of evidence. In a five-four decision, the Supreme Court ruled that the process of the penalty enhancement was indeed unconstitutional.

4. In 1993, the New Jersey state legislature enacted a civil cause of action for bias crime victims, which allows the victims to seek redress in a civil court (see N.J.S. section 2A:53A-21 in Appendix B). For example, victims can seek punitive damages, medical costs, and attorney's fees. Moreover, under this law, parents could be held liable if their conduct was found to be a significant contributing factor in a juvenile's commission of an offense. Notably, the civil statute included gender as a protected category, although gender remained absent from the criminal legal code. Governor Jim Florio signed the bill into law on June 11, 1993 (Marisco 1993b). One of the goals of this civil statute was to deter people from committing bias crimes. Governor Florio told the crowd present for the signing of the law: "Sometimes, the best deterrent is to hit people in the pocketbook. If you commit a hate crime in New Jersey, you'll pay the price."

5. This exemption is not unique to New Jersey's hate crime statute. For example, California's hate crime law reads in part: "If a perpetrator commits a sexual assault wholly or partly because of the victim's gender, a hate crime has not been committed unless the perpetrator also acts upon some animosity or other bias motivation toward the victim's gender" (California Penal Code section 422.55). Moreover, because gender was excluded from the federal Hate Crime Statistics Act, although forcible rape appeared on the list of possible crimes, the act ultimately exempted gender-motivated rapes as well.

6. Although highly publicized hate crimes can influence the development of hate crime law, this was not the case in Wyoming after the murder of Matthew Shepard, a gay college student killed because of his sexual orientation. This case received significant media attention and facilitated the creation of activist groups throughout the country. However, despite the public outcry, the state of Wyoming still does not have a hate crime law.

7. The term "University of Montreal" was used to search these two newspapers' archives and the databases used to gather the sample of articles for the content analysis of newspaper accounts written before the passage of the law.

8. As explained in the next chapter, a representative from the Coalition for Battered Women explained in an interview that the group views hate crime law as separate from the work it does with domestic violence law. Consequently, it is not surprising that this group was not involved in the discussion to include gender within the hate crime law. However, it is not clear why the New Jersey branch of the National Organization for Women did not participate in this process; unfortunately, no one from the organization responded to several inquiries about the matter.

9. Rape myths are beliefs about rape and victims of rape that are unfounded and untrue. Rape myths include the beliefs that: rape can occur only between strangers; women frequently cry rape falsely; some women ask to be raped and enjoy it; when a women says "no" to sex, she really means "maybe" or "yes;" and rape is often provoked by the victim, especially if the victim wears provocative clothing or consumes drugs or alcohol. These myths negatively affect the way sexual assaults and victims of sexual assaults are regarded by the public and handled by the criminal justice system.

4. Enforcing the Gender Category

1. The first available report is for 1999. Although gender was included in the law in 1995, the state's 1999 bias incident summary report had a column only for gender-motivated *person* offenses. The 2000 report included a column for gender-motivated *person* offenses and another column for *private property* offenses; the 2002 report added a column for *public property* offenses. As noted in the text, only four incidents were recorded under the gender category between 1999 and 2008: one in 2007 and three in 2008. It is unclear whether these cases involved gender bias or gender identity bias (which would be a crime against a transgendered person, for example); although New Jersey's bias crime statute recently added "gender identity" as a category, there is not yet a specific column for this category in the state's annual bias crime report. Since there were no cases recorded under the gender category until after the inclusion of "gender identity" in the bias crime statute, it seems likely that these four cases were gender identity–bias cases, not gender-bias cases.

The 2006 New Jersey State Police Uniform Crime Report states: "All reported offenses are compiled from a record of all criminal complaints received by police from victims or other sources, or discovered by the police during routine operations. Complaints determined to be unfounded are eliminated from this count" (New Jersey State Police 2006). The annual reports include columns for reported offenses and cases involving an arrest. The reports are available through the New Jersey State Police (http://www.nj.gov/oag/njsp/info/stats.html).

2. These numbers include both person and property offenses recorded within the bias summary reports for the years 1999 through 2008. The race-bias incidences are recorded separately from ethnic-bias incidences.

3. This is a tentative assumption because although New Jersey does not offer marriage licenses to same-sex couples, it does recognize civil unions. Therefore, it is not clear whether "spouse" is used only in cases of legally recognized marriage or for a same-sex domestic partner.

4. According to the Bureau of Justice Statistics report (Truman and Rand 2010), 79 percent of female rape or sexual assault victims identified the offender as an intimate, other relative, friend, or acquaintance.

5. The Power and Control Wheel was created in 1984 by staff at the Domestic Abuse Intervention Project (now called the Domestic Abuse Intervention Programs) in Duluth, Minnesota. Through focus groups with battered women, the staff learned about the most common ways in which batterers maintained power and control over their victims. The wheel was developed as a way to describe battering to victims, offenders, criminal justice practitioners, and the general public. For more information, see http://www.theduluthmodel.org/wheelgallery.php.

6. Research has demonstrated the apathy that the criminal justice system often shows when handling domestic violence cases (Belknap and Potter 2006; Epstein 1999; Ferraro 1993). Historically, statutes prohibiting wife abuse were rarely enforced. Such offenses were considered a private matter—in other words, not a problem to be dealt with by the criminal justice system. As a result, police were reluctant to intervene, and often no legal actions were taken against offenders. When police did respond to such calls, intimate partner abuse "was often equated with municipal ordinance violations, such as barking dogs, and labeled a 'disturbance of the peace' or as similarly minor transgressions that rarely resulted in arrest" (Belknap and Potter 2006, 172). In fact, arrest was viewed as the least desirable outcome, and officers were trained to offer crisis intervention or to simply separate the couple (Miller and Iovanni 2007, 292).

7. In the 1970s, the criminal justice system was criticized for its toleration of violence against women as the women's movement brought these issues to the forefront of public debate. Facing the threat of civil suits, the system instituted many reforms in the 1980s and 1990s for handling domestic violence cases. For instance, some jurisdictions changed the way they responded to domestic violence cases by instituting mandatory arrest policies. Instead of merely separating the couple at the scene, as they had often done in the past, police were now required to treat domestic violence as seriously as they would treat assaults by strangers (Miller and Iovanni 2007, 292), and thus were mandated to arrest the offender. However, even with the change in policies, only 15 percent to 30 percent of all dispatched calls result in an arrest (Garcia and Schweikert 2010, 8). In fact, studies show that female victims of domestic violence continue to face discriminatory practices in the legal system. For example, women are often blamed for the assaults by attorneys and judges, and police officers and judges fail to enforce protection orders (Hemmens, Strom, and Schlegel 1998). Studies also reveal that women are often dissuaded by defense

attorneys from cooperating with the system, and that some judges and police officers attempt to discourage victims from pursuing charges (Belknap, Hartman, and Lippen 2010).

8. These articles were obtained from "New Jersey News Sources" in the Lexis-Nexis database. See Appendix A for more details.

9. In the spring of 2010, an adjunct professor at Towson University was fired for using the N-word during a lecture (Mays 2010). Although the professor claimed that the word was used to illustrate a point and that he is not a racist, the university fired him after a student reported the incident to the administration. Also in the spring of 2010, an elementary school principal was fired after he quoted from a John Lennon song that contained the N-word ("Principal Fired for Using N-Word" 2010). According to the principal, the comment was taken out of context, and it had been made in his office in front of two teachers and no children.

10. There is no official record of the number or types of cases that are prosecuted as bias crimes in New Jersey. However, as Phillips (2006) discovered in her study of one county in the state, out of a total of 643 cases referred to the county's bias unit between 2001 and 2004, only 30 (less than 5 percent) were referred for prosecution as bias crimes, and of those, just 11 resulted in a conviction for a bias crime.

5. Where Do We Go from Here?

1. Although it is beyond the scope of this work to speculate how one might measure a change in prejudicial attitudes as the result of the enforcement of hate crime laws, this area of study would be worthwhile. Research has found that while hate crime laws are widely supported by the public, individuals holding conservative social and economic beliefs are less likely to support such laws, particularly if the legislation includes the category of "sexual orientation" (Johnson and Byers 2003). Lyons (2006) found similar results when exploring the influence of social status on attributions of blame in hate crimes. Thus, it would be interesting for research to document how the enforcement of hate crime law affects individuals with more conservative social beliefs.

2. According to the New Jersey State Police (2007), the majority of both offenders and victims in hate crimes were male. Specifically, there were 320 male victims and 340 male offenders, compared to 179 female victims and 71 female offenders.

3. Hopkins and Koss (2005) argue that sexual assault cases can be handled within the legal system through a restorative justice approach. The authors recognize that not all sexual assault cases would be appropriate for such programs; however, they assert that some cases, particularly acquaintance rapes, would be better addressed through programs such as victim-offender mediation. Notably, scholars have also argued that a restorative justice approach would be beneficial for hate crime victims and offenders (for example, see Shenk 2003).

4. Goldscheid and Kaufman (2001) provide a review of cases pursued under the Civil Rights Remedy (Title III) of the Violence Against Women Act. Atkins et al. (1999) also provide insights about how a specific domestic violence case was pursued as a gender-motivated bias offense under VAWA. Despite the fact that the civil remedy is no longer available under VAWA, case law can show law enforcement officials the parallels between gender-bias crimes and other forms of bias crimes.

5. The form can be found at http://www.nj.gov/oag/dcj/obccr/pdfs/biasincidentrpt.pdf.

Appendix A

1. The New Jersey news sources in the database were the *Associated Press State and Local Wire*; the *Herald News* (Passaic County); and the *Record* (Bergen County).

2. The website is www.nj.com/archive.

3. The list is available at http://www.nj.gov/oag/dcj/obccr/law_enforcement.htm. It no longer includes prosecutors or full addresses (just county names).

4. Surveys—with a pre-addressed, stamped return envelope—were first sent to the prosecutors. As this method was not effective, surveys were not mailed to the investigators.

5. After a subject agreed to be interviewed, it was unrealistic to wait to conduct the interview in order to mail or fax the informed consent form to the subject and then wait for him or her to return it, especially as it was difficult to reach the subjects by phone. After the interview, an informed consent form—with a pre-addressed, stamped return envelope—was mailed to the subject with the request that he or she sign and return the form.

6. As explained by Corbin and Strauss, saturation is reached when no new data are emerging, or when all concepts and/or categories are well defined and explained (2008, 143–45).

7. In his book on qualitative research design, Creswell states that although it is useful to use preexisting or "prefigured" codes, it is also important for qualitative researchers to be open to new codes that emerge during the analysis process (2007, 152).

Appendix C

1. The "D>" and "<A" here indicate deletions and additions that the bill's revisions will make to the text of the current statute. For example, the phrase "[A> GENDER, HANDICAP,<A]" indicates the addition of gender and handicap to the text of the statute.

Bibliography

Albonetti, C. A. 1987. "Prosecutorial Discretion: The Effects of Uncertainty." *Law and Society Review* 21 (2): 291–314.

Anderson, K. B., H. Cooper, and L. Okamura. 1997. "Individual Differences and Attitudes toward Rape: A Meta-analytic Review." *Personality and Social Psychology Bulletin* 23 (3): 295–315.

Anderson, K. L., and D. Umberson. 2001. "Gendering Violence: Masculinity and Power in Men's Accounts of Domestic Violence." *Gender & Society* 15 (3): 358–80.

Angelari, M. 1994. "Hate Crime Statutes: A Promising Tool for Fighting Violence against Women." *American University Journal of Gender and the Law* 2:63–105.

"Anti-bias Bill Forwarded." 1994. *Star-Ledger*, June 14.

Anti-Defamation League. 2001. "Hate Crimes Laws: ADL Approach to Hate Crime Legislation." New York: Anti-Defamation League (http://www.adl.org/99hatecrime/penalty.asp).

———. 2008. "Anti-Defamation League State Hate Crime Statutory Provisions." Washington: Anti-Defamation League (http://www.adl.org/99hatecrime/state_hate_crime_laws.pdf).

———. 2010. "ADL Urges FBI to Begin Collecting Hate Crimes Data on New Categories." New York: Anti-Defamation League (http://www.adl.org/combating_hate/hate_crimes_data.asp).

Associated Press. 1993. "Canada Acts to Lessen Violence on Television." *Star-Ledger*, December 1.

Atkins, D. G., J. R. Jurden, S. L. Miller, and E. A. Patten. 1999. Striving for Justice with the Violence against Women Act and Civil Tort Actions. *Wisconsin Women's Law Journal* 14:69–104.

Auerbach, C. F., and L. B. Silverstein. 2003. *Qualitative Data: An Introduction to Coding and Analysis*. New York: New York University Press.

Bachman, R., and C. Lanier. 2006. "Liberating Criminology: The Evolution of Feminist Thinking on Criminological Research Methods." In *Rethinking Gender, Crime, and Justice: Feminist Readings*, ed. C. Renzetti, L. Goodstein, and S. L. Miller, 44–56. Los Angeles: Roxbury.

Barnett, O. W., C. Y. Lee, and R. E. Thelan. 1997. "Gender Differences in Attribution of Self-defense and Control in Interpartner Aggression." *Violence against Women* 3 (5): 462–81.

Beale, S. S. 2000. "Federalizing Hate Crimes: Symbolic Politics, Expressive Law, or Tool for Criminal Enforcement?" *Boston University Law Review* 80:1227–81.

Bean, L. 1993. "Prosecuting Bias Cases: A Delicate Balancing Act." *New Jersey Law Journal* 135 (September): 4 and 30.

Becker, P. J. 1999. "The Creation of Ohio's Ethnic Intimidation Law: Triggering Events, Media Campaigns, and Interest Group Activity." *American Journal of Criminal Justice* 23 (2): 247–65.

Beckett, K. 1999. *Making Crime Pay: Law and Order in Contemporary American Politics*. New York: Oxford University Press.

Belknap, J. 2007. *The Invisible Woman: Gender, Crime, and Justice*. 3rd ed. Belmont, CA: Thomson.

Belknap, J., J. L. Hartman, and V. L. Lippen. 2010. "Misdemeanor Domestic Violence Cases in the Courts: A Detailed Description of the Cases." In *Female Victims of Crime: Reality Revisited*, ed. V. Garcia, J. E. Clifford, and R. Muraskin, 259–78). Upper Saddle River, NJ: Prentice Hall.

Belknap, J., and H. Melton. 2005. "Are Heterosexual Men also Victims of Intimate Partner Abuse?" Harrisburg, PA: VAWnet, March (http://www.biscmi.org/aquila/Male%20Victims%20NO--Belknap.pdf).

Belknap, J., and H. Potter. 2006. "Intimate Partner Abuse." In *Rethinking Gender, Crime, and Justice: Feminist Readings*, ed. C. Renzetti, L. Goodstein, and S. L. Miller, 168–84. Los Angeles: Roxbury.

Bell, J. 2002. *Policing Hatred: Law Enforcement, Civil Rights, and Hate Crime*. New York: New York University Press.

Berg, B. L. 2001. *Qualitative Research Methods for the Social Sciences*. 4th ed. Needham Heights, MA: Allyn and Bacon.

Bernard, H. R., and G. W. Ryan. 2010. *Analyzing Qualitative Data: Systematic Approaches*. Thousand Oaks, CA: Sage.

Berry, F. S., and W. D. Berry. 1990. "State Lottery Adoptions as Policy Innovations: An Event History Analysis." *American Political Science Review* 84 (2): 395–415.

Best, J. 1999. *Random Violence: How We Talk about New Crimes and New Victims*. Berkeley: University of California Press.

Black, K. A., and D. J. Gold. 2008. "Gender Differences and Socioeconomic Status Biases in Judgments about Blame in Date Rape Scenarios." *Violence and Victims* 23 (1): 115–28.

Bonner, J. R. S. 2002. "Reconceptualizing VAWA's 'Animus' for Rape in States' Emerging Post-VAWA Civil Rights Legislation." *Yale Law Journal* 111 (6): 1417–56.

Bono, M. 2001. "Judicial Limitations on Congressional Power under *United States v. Morrison*." *Loyola Journal of Public Interest Law* 2 (1): 229–54.

Boyd, E. A., K. M. Hammer, and R. A. Berk. 1996. "'Motivated by Hatred or Prejudice': Categorization of Hate-Motivated Crimes in Two Police Divisions." *Law & Society Review* 30 (4): 819–50.

Boyd, R. 2007. "When Sharpton Argued Degrading Comments Were Simply Free Speech." NewsBusters, April 12 (http://newsbusters.org/node/11986).

California Department of Justice. 2008. "Hate Crime in California 2007." Sacramento, CA: California Department of Justice (http://ag.ca.gov/cjsc/publications/hatecrimes/hc07/preface07.pdf).

Campbell, J. C., D. Webster, J. Koziol-McLain, C. R. Block, D. Campbell, M. A. Curry, F. Gary, J. McFarlane, C. Sachs, P. Sharps, Y. Ulrich, and S. A. Wilt. 2003. "Assessing Risk Factors for Intimate Partner Homicide." *NIJ Journal*, no. 250:14–19.

Carney, K. 2001. "Rape: The Paradigmatic Hate Crime." *St. John's Law Review* 75:315–55.

Casey, K. 1990. "Rutgers Vigil Addresses Sexism, Violence." *Star-Ledger*, December 7.

Catalano, S. "Intimate Partner Violence in the United States." Washington: Department of Justice (http://bjs.ojp.usdoj.gov/index.cfm?ty=pbdetail&iid=1000).

Cathcart, R. 2008. "Boy's Killing, Labeled a Hate Crime, Stuns a Town." *New York Times*, February 28.

Center for Women Policy Studies. 1991. "Violence against Women as Bias Motivated Hate Crime: Defining the Issues." Washington: Center for Women Policy Studies (http://www.centerwomenpolicy.org/publications/vawg/default.asp).

———. 2001. "Violence against Women as Bias Motivated Hate Crime: Federal and State Laws; Supplement 2001." Washington: Center for Women Policy Studies (http://www.centerwomenpolicy.org/publications/vawg/documents/VAW1.pdf).

Chappell, A. T., J. M. MacDonald, and P. W. Manz. 2006. "The Organizational Determinants of Police Arrest Decisions." *Crime & Delinquency* 52 (2): 287–306.

Ciraco, V. N. 2001. "Fighting Domestic Violence with Mandatory Arrest, Are We Winning? An Analysis in New Jersey." *Women's Rights Law Reporter* 22 (2): 169–91.

Cogan, J. C. 2003. "The Prevention of Anti-Lesbian/Gay Hate Crimes through Social Change and Empowerment." In *Hate and Bias Crime: A Reader*, ed. B. Perry, 465–77. New York: Routledge.

Conyers, J. 2007. "Hate Crimes: Federal Prosecution of Bias-motivated Incidents." *Congressional Digest* 86 (6): 160–92.

Corbin, J., and A. Strauss. 2008. *Basics of Qualitative Research*. 3rd ed. Thousand Oaks, CA: Sage.

Creswell, J. W. 2007. *Qualitative Inquiry and Research Design: Choosing among Five Approaches*. 2nd ed. Thousand Oaks, CA: Sage.

Culotta, K. A. 2002. "Does the Motive Fit the Crime? Victim, Police, and Prosecutor Decision-making in Chicago Hate Crime Cases." Ph.D. diss., University of Maryland.

Dobash, R. P., R. E. Dobash, M. Wilson, and M. Daly, 1992. "The Myth of Sexual Symmetry in Marital Violence." *Social Problems* 39 (1): 71–91.

Epstein, D. 1999. "Effective Intervention in Domestic Violence Cases: Rethinking the Roles of Prosecutors, Judges, and the Court System." *Yale Journal of Law and Feminism* 11:3–61.

Faber, J. 2007. "CBS Fires Don Imus over Racial Slur." CBS News, April 12 (http://www.cbsnews.com/stories/2007/04/12/national/main2675273.shtml).

Federal Bureau of Investigation. 1999. "Hate Crime Data Collection Guidelines." Washington: Federal Bureau of Investigation (http://www.fbi.gov/ucr/hatecrime.pdf).

———. 2007. "Hate Crime Statistics, 2006." Washington: Federal Bureau of Investigation (http://www.fbi.gov/ucr/hc2006/index.html).

———. 2008. "Hate Crime Statistics, 2007." Washington: Federal Bureau of Investigation (http://www.fbi.gov/ucr/hc2007/index.html).

———. 2009a. "2008 Crime in the United States." Washington: Federal Bureau of Investigation (http://www.fbi.gov/about-us/cjis/ucr/crime-in-the-u.s/2008).

———. 2009b. "Hate Crime Statistics, 2008." Washington: Federal Bureau of Investigation (http://www.fbi.gov/ucr/hc2008/index.html).

Ferraro, K. J. 1993. "Cops, Courts, and Women Battering." In *Violence against Women: The Bloody Footprints*, ed. P. B. Bart and E. G. Moran, 165–76. Newbury Park, CA: Sage.

"Fifth Girl Dies after Amish School Shooting." 2006. CNN, October 3 (http://www.cnn.com/2006/US/10/02/amish.shooting/).

Finn, P. 1988. "Bias Crime: A Special Target for Prosecutors." *Prosecutor* 21 (4): 9–15.

Finz, S., and K. Fagan. "Stunning Details in Stayner's Confession." SFGate.com, June 14, 001 (http://articles.sfgate.com/2001-06-14/news/17604079_1_silvina-pelosso-cary-stayner-yosemite-national-park-tourists).

Franklin, K. 2002. "Good Intentions: The Enforcement of Hate Crime Penalty-Enhancement Statutes." *American Behavioral Scientist* 46 (1): 154–72.

Freeman, A. 1994. "State Expert Calls on Jerseyans to Join in the Fight against Bias." *Star Ledger*, February 17.

Frohmann, L. 1991. "Discrediting Victims' Allegations of Sexual Assault: Prosecutorial Accounts of Case Rejections." *Social Problems* 38 (2): 213–26.

Gaffney, P. 1997. "Amending the Violence against Women Act: Creating a Rebuttable Presumption of Gender Animus in Rape Cases." *Journal of Law and Policy* 6 (1): 247–89.

Gandy, K. 2006. "School Shooters Target Girls, Point to Larger Problem of Violence against Women." Washington: National Organization for Women, October 10 (http://www.now.org/issues/violence/101006school_shootings.html).

Garcia, V., and E. J. Schweikert. 2010. "Cultural Images—Media Images: 'Doing Culture' and Victim Blaming of Female Crime Victims." In *Female Victims of Crime: Reality Revisited*, ed. V. Garcia, J. E. Clifford, and R. Muraskin, 3–19. Upper Saddle River, NJ: Prentice Hall.

"Gay Couple Say Secaucus, N.J. Firefighters Flung Rocks and Insults." 2004. *Record* (Bergen County), May 6.

Gelber, K. 2000. "Hate Crimes: Public Policy Implications of the Inclusion of Gender." *Australian Journal of Political Science* 35 (2): 275–89.

Gerstenfeld, P. B. 2004. *Hate Crimes: Causes, Controls, and Controversies*. Thousand Oaks, CA: Sage.

Goldfarb, S. F. 2000. "'No Civilized System of Justice': The Fate of the Violence against Women Act." *West Virginia Law Review* 102 (3): 499–546.

———. 2003. "Applying the Discrimination Model to Violence against Women: Some Reflections on Theory and Practice." *American University Journal of Gender, Social Policy, and the Law* 11 (2): 251–70.

Goldscheid, J. 1999. "Gender-motivated Violence: Developing a Meaningful Paradigm for Civil Rights Enforcement." *Harvard Women's Law Journal* 22:123–58.

———. 2000. "*United States v. Morrison* and the Civil Rights Remedy of the Violence against Women Act: A Civil Rights Law Struck Down in the Name of Federalism." *Cornell Law Review* 86 (1): 109–39.

———. 2003. "Advancing Equality in Domestic Violence Law Reform." *American University Journal of Gender, Social Policy, and the Law* 11 (2): 417–26.

——— and R. E. Kaufman. 2001. "Seeking Redress for Gender-based Bias Crimes: Charting New Ground in Familiar Legal Territory." *Michigan Journal of Race & Law* 6 (2): 265–84.

Gordon, M. T., and S. Riger. 1989. *The Female Fear*. New York: Free Press.

Grattet, R., and V. Jenness. 2003. "The Birth and Maturation of Hate Crime Policy in the United States." In *Hate and Bias Crime: A Reader*, ed. B. Perry, 389–407. New York: Routledge.

———. 2005. "The Reconstitution of Law in Local Settings: Agency Discretion, Ambiguity, and a Surplus of Law in the Policing of Hate Crime." *Law & Society Review* 39 (4): 893–941.

——— and T. R. Curry. 1998. "The Homogenization and Differentiation of Hate Crime Law in the United States, 1978 to 1995: Innovation and Diffusion in the Criminalization of Bigotry." *American Sociological Review* 63 (2): 286–307.

Green, D. P., L. H. McFalls, and J. K. Smith. 2001. "Hate Crime: An Emergent Research Agenda." *Annual Review of Sociology* 27:479–504.

Gusfield, J. R. 1967. "Moral Passage: The Symbolic Process of Public Designations of Deviance." *Social Problems* 15 (2): 175–88.

Hagan, J. R. 2001. "Can We Lose the Battle and Still Win the War? The Fight against Domestic Violence after the Death of Title III of the Violence against Women Act." *DePaul Law Review* 50(3): 919–92.

Haider-Markel, D. P. 1998. "The Politics of Social Regulatory Policy: State and Federal Hate Crime Policy and Implementation Effort." *Political Research Quarterly* 51 (1): 69–88.

———. 2004. "Perception and Misperception in Urban Criminal Justice Policy: The Case of Hate Crime." *Urban Affairs Review* 39 (4): 491–512.

Hamberger, L. K., J. M. Lohr, D. Bonge, and D. F. Tolin. 1997. "An Empirical Classification of Motivations for Domestic Violence." *Violence against Women* 3 (4): 401–23.

Hamel, J. 2007. "Toward a Gender-inclusive Conception of Intimate Partner Violence Research and Theory: Part 1—Traditional Perspectives." *International Journal of Men's Health* 6 (1): 36–53.

Harlow, C. W. 2005. "Hate Crime Reported by Victims and Police." Bureau of Justice Statistics Special Report. Washington: Department of Justice (http://bjs.ojp.usdoj.gov/content/pub/pdf/hcrvp.pdf).

Harutyunyan, R. 2008. "Majority of Women Fear Domestic Violence." EmaxHealth, December 19 (http://www.emaxhealth.com/2/4/27814/majority-women-fear-domestic-violence.html).

Hasenstab, D. 2001. "Is Hate a Form of Commerce? The Questionable Constitutionality of Federal 'Hate Crime' Legislation." *Saint Louis University Law Journal* 45 (3): 973–1018.

"Hate Crimes Expansion Covers Gender, Orientation, Disability." 2010. *National NOW Times* 42 (1): 3.

Haydon, T. 1992. "Bias Crime Bill Proposed to Counter Court Ruling." *Star-Ledger*, October 22.

Heise, L. 1989. "International Dimensions of Violence against Women." *Response* 12 (1): 3–11.

Hemmens, C., K. Strom, and E. Schlegel. 1998. "Gender Bias in the Courts: A Review of the Literature." *Sociological Imagination* 35 (1): 22–42.

Herbert, B. 2009. "Women at Risk." *New York Times*, August 8 (http://www.nytimes.com/2009/08/08/opinion/08herbert.html?emc=eta1).

Hester, T. 1995. "State Law on Bias Crimes Expanded to Include Handicap and Gender." *Star-Ledger*, August 16.

Hirschel, D., and I. Hutchison. 2001. "The Relative Effects of Offense, Offender, and Victim Variables on the Decision to Prosecute Domestic Violence Cases." *Violence against Women* 7 (1): 46–59.

Hopkins, C. Q., and M. P. Koss. 2005. "Incorporating Feminist Theory and Insights into a Restorative Justice Response to Sex Offenses." *Violence against Women* 11 (5): 693–723.

Hsieh, H., and S. E. Shannon. 2005. "Three Approaches to Qualitative Content Analysis." *Qualitative Health Research* 15 (9): 1277–88.

Human Rights Campaign. 2009. "About Hate Crimes." Washington: Human Rights Campaign (http://www.hrc.org/issues/hate_crimes/5895.htm).

International Association of Chiefs of Police, State and Provincial Police Division, Homeland Security Committee, and R. Fuentes. 2008. "The Demands and

Capacities of Protecting and Policing the Homeland." *Police Chief* 75 (2). (http://www.policechiefmagazine.org/magazine/index.cfm?fuseaction=display_arch&article_id=1418&issue_id=22008)

Isaacs, T. 2001. "Domestic Violence and Hate Crimes: Acknowledging Two Levels of Responsibility." *Criminal Justice Ethics*, Summer–Fall, 31–43.

Jacobs, J. B., and J. S. Henry. 1996. "The Social Construction of a Hate Crime Epidemic." *Journal of Criminal Law and Criminology* 86 (2): 366–91.

Jacobs, J. B., and K. Potter. 1998. *Hate Crimes: Criminal Law and Identity Politics*. New York: Oxford University Press.

Jenness, V. 1999. "Managing Differences and Making Legislation: Social Movements and the Racialization, Sexualization, and Gendering of Federal Hate Crime Law in the U.S., 1985–1998." *Social Problems* 46 (4): 548–71.

———. 2003. "Engendering Hate Crime Policy: Gender, the 'Dilemma of Difference,' and the Creation of Legal Subjects." *Journal of Hate Studies* 2:73–97.

——— and K. Broad. 2005. *Hate Crimes: New Social Movements and the Politics of Violence*. New Brunswick, NJ: Aldine Transaction.

Jenness, V., and R. Grattet. 1996. "The Criminalization of Hate: A Comparison of Structural and Polity Influences on the Passage of 'Bias Crime' Legislation in the United States." *Sociological Perspectives* 39 (1): 129–54.

———. 2001. *Making Hate a Crime: From Social Movement to Law Enforcement*. New York: Russell Sage Foundation.

———. 2005. "The Law-in-between: The Effects of Organizational Perviousness on the Policing of Hate Crime." *Social Problems* 52 (3): 337–59.

Johnson, M. P. 2008. *A Typology of Domestic Violence: Intimate Terrorism, Violent Resistance, and Situational Couple Violence*. Lebanon, NH: Northeastern University Press.

Johnson, S. D., and B. D. Byers. 2003. "Attitudes toward Hate Crime Laws." *Journal of Criminal Justice* 31 (3): 227–35.

Jordan, B. 1994. "'Hate Crime' Inmate Wants Time Reduced." *New Hampshire Union Leader*, May 30.

"Judge Upholds Hate-crime Law But Dismisses Charges." 2004. *New Hampshire Union Leader*, September 25.

Klarman, M. J. 2002. "Is the Supreme Court Sometimes Irrelevant?" *Journal of American History* 89 (1): 119–53.

Kohlbacher, F. 2006. "The Use of Qualitative Content Analysis in Case Study Research." *Forum: Qualitative Social Research* 7 (1): article 21 (http://www.qualitative-research.net/index.php/fqs/article/view/75/154).

Kondracki, N. L., N. S. Wellman, and D. R. Amundson. 2002. "Content Analysis: Review of Methods and Their Applications in Nutrition Education." *Journal of Nutrition Education and Behavior* 34 (4): 224–30.

Kurz, D. 1993. "Social Science Perspectives on Wife Abuse: Current Debates and Future Directions." In *Violence against Women: The Bloody Footprints*, ed. P. B. Bart and E. G. Moran, 252–69. Newbury Park, CA: Sage.

LaFree, G. D. 1989. *Rape and Criminal Justice: The Social Construction of Sexual Assault*. Belmont, CA: Wadsworth.

Lawrence, F. M. 1999. *Punishing Hate: Bias Crimes under American Law*. Cambridge, MA: Harvard University Press.

———. 2000. "Federal Bias Crime Law Symposium." *Boston University Law Review* 80 (5): 1185–90.

Levin, B. 1992–93. "Bias Crimes: A Theoretical & Practical Overview." *Stanford Law & Policy Review* 4 (Winter): 165–82.

Levin, J., and J. McDevitt. 2002. *Hate Crimes Revisited: America's War against Those Who Are Different*. Boulder, CO: Westview.

Lonsway, K. A., and L. F. Fitzgerald. 1995. "Attitudinal Antecedents of Rape Myth Acceptance: A Theoretical and Empirical Reexamination." *Journal of Personality and Social Psychology* 68 (4): 704–11.

Lyons, C. J. 2006. "Stigma or Sympathy? Attributions of Fault to Hate Crime Victims and Offenders." *Social Psychology Quarterly* 69 (1): 39–59.

MacKinnon, C. A. 1991. "Reflections on Sex Equality under Law." *Yale Law Journal* 100 (5): 1281–328.

———. 2000. "Disputing Male Sovereignty: On *United States v. Morrison*." *Harvard Law Review* 114 (1): 135–78.

Marsico, R. 1993a. "Assembly Panel Backs Bias Law Expansion." *Star-Ledger*, March 23.

———. 1993b. "Bias Crime Victims Gain Right to Sue Criminals for Damages." *Star-Ledger*, June 12.

———. 1993c. "Bias Laws Walk Tightrope between Hate, Liberty." *Star-Ledger*, April 18.

———. 1993d. "Punishing Hatred." *Star-Ledger*, May 14.

———. 1994. "Panel Endorses Crime Bill on Disability, Gender Bias." *Star-Ledger*, February 11.

Martin, S. E. 1995. "'Cross-burning Is Not Just an Arson': Police Social Construction of Hate Crimes in Baltimore County." *Criminology* 33 (3): 303–26.

———. 1996. "Investigating Hate Crimes: Case Characteristics and Law Enforcement Responses." *Justice Quarterly* 13 (3): 455–80.

——— and N. C. Jurik. 1996. *Doing Justice, Doing Gender: Women in Law and Criminal Justice Occupations*. Thousand Oaks, CA: Sage.

Mastrofski, S. D., R. R. Ritti, and D. Hoffmaster. 1987. "Organizational Determinants of Police Discretion: The Case of Drinking-driving." *Journal of Criminal Justice* 15 (5): 387–402.

Mays, J. 2010. "White Towson Professor Fired for Using N-Word." *Black Voices*, March 2 (http://www.bvblackspin.com/2010/03/02/townson-professor-fired-for-using-the-n-word/).

McCann, M. W. 1994. *Rights at Work: Pay Equity Reform and the Politics of Legal Mobilization.* Chicago: University of Chicago Press.

McPhail, B. A. 2002a. "Constructing Justice: Prosecutorial Decision Making in Hate Crime Enhancements and a Grounded Theory of Justice Construction." Ph.D. diss., University of Texas at Austin.

———. 2002b. "Gender-bias Hate Crimes: A Review." *Trauma, Violence, & Abuse* 3 (2): 125–43.

McPhail, B. A., and D. M. DiNitto. 2005. "Prosecutorial Perspectives on Gender-bias Hate Crimes." *Violence against Women* 11 (9): 1162–85.

McPhail, B. A., and V. Jenness. 2005–6. "To Charge or Not to Charge?—That Is the Question: The Pursuit of Strategic Advantage in Prosecutorial Decision-making Surrounding Hate Crime." *Journal of Hate Studies* 4 (1): 89–119.

McVeigh, R., M. R. Welch, and T. Bjarnason. 2003. "Hate Crime Reporting as a Successful Social Movement Outcome." *American Sociological Review* 68 (6): 843–67.

Melton, H. C. 2010. "Rape Myths: Impacts on Victims of Rape." In *Female Victims of Crime: Reality Reconsidered*, ed. V. Garcia, J. E. Clifford, and R. Muraskin, 113–27. Upper Saddle River, NJ: Prentice Hall.

Miller, S. L. 1994. "Gender-motivated Hate Crimes: A Question of Misogyny." *Contemporary Societies: Problems and Prospects*, ed. D. J. Curran and C. M. Renzetti, 229–35. Englewood Cliffs, NJ: Prentice Hall.

———. 2005. *Victims as Offenders: The Paradox of Women's Violence in Relationships.* New Brunswick, NJ: Rutgers University Press.

——— and L. Iovanni. 2007. "Domestic Violence Policy in the United States: Contemporary Issues." In *Gender Violence: Interdisciplinary Perspectives*, ed. L. L. O'Toole, J. R. Schiffman, and M. L. K. Edwards, 287–96. 2nd ed. New York: New York University Press.

Minnesota Department of Public Safety. 2009. "2007 Minnesota Crime Information." Saint Paul, MN: Minnesota Department of Public Safety (http://www.dps.state.mn.us/bca/CJIS/documents/Crime2007/2007%20MN%20Crime%20Book%20Revised%202010-2009.pdf).

Moore, T. 2007. "Filthy, Degrading Lyrics Paying Huge Dividends." *New York Daily News*, April 15 (http://www.nydailynews.com/entertainment/music/2007/04/15/2007-04-15_filthy_degrading_lyrics_paying_huge_divi.html).

New Jersey, Office of the Governor. 1993. "New Law Strengthens Protection from Bias Crimes." Trenton: Office of the Governor, June 11.

New Jersey State Police. 2000. "Bias Incident Summary." In "Crime in New Jersey: 1999 Uniform Crime Report, for the Year Ending December 31, 1999," 211–23. Trenton,

NJ: State of New Jersey, Office of the Attorney General (http://www.state.nj.us/njsp/info/ucr99/sec12_99.pdf).

———. 2006. "Bias Incident Summary." In "Crime in New Jersey: 2005 Uniform Crime Report, for the Year Ending December 31, 2005," 211–23. Trenton, NJ: State of New Jersey, Office of the Attorney General (http://www.state.nj.us/lps/njsp/info/ucr2005/pdf/2005-ucr.pdf)

———. 2007. "Bias Incident Summary." In "Crime in New Jersey: 2006 Uniform Crime Report, for the Year Ending December 31, 2006," 211–23. Trenton: NJ: State of New Jersey, Office of the Attorney General (http://www.state.nj.us/lps/njsp/info/ucr2006/pdf/2006-sect-12.pdf).

———. 2008. "State of New Jersey Bias Incident Offense Report for the Year Ending December 31, 2007." Trenton, NJ: State of New Jersey, Office of the Attorney General (http://www.state.nj.us/lps/njsp/info/pdf/2007_bias_incident.pdf).

Nolan, J. J., and Y. Akiyama. 2004. "An Analysis of Factors That Affect Law Enforcement Participation in Hate Crime Reporting." In *Crimes of Hate: Selected Readings*, ed. P. B. Gerstenfeld and D. R. Grant, 93–104. Thousand Oaks, CA: Sage.

Novak, K. J., J. Frank, B. Smith, and R. S. Engle. 2002. "Revisiting the Decision to Arrest: Comparing Beat and Community Officers. *Crime & Delinquency* 48 (1): 70–98.

O'Neill, J. 1992. "Judge Rules Jersey's Hate Crimes Law Violates Teen's Right to Free Speech." *Star-Ledger*, September 26.

O'Toole, L. L., J. R. Schiffman, and M. L. K. Edwards, eds. 2007. *Gender Violence: Interdisciplinary Perspectives*. 2nd ed. New York: New York University Press.

"Panel Votes to Include Gender, Handicap in Bias Crimes Law." 1993. *Star-Ledger*, May 25.

Peet, J. 1990. "Students Become More Cautious as Bias, Intolerance Rise on Campus." *Star-Ledger*, November 19.

Pendo, E. A. 1994. "Recognizing Violence against Women: Gender and the Hate Crimes Statistics Act." *Harvard Women's Law Journal* 17:157–83.

Pepitone, J. 2010. "Waldo Rapes Leave UMKC Students, Faculty Feeling Uneasy about Safety." Fox 4, March 2 (http://www.fox4kc.com/news/wdaf-story-waldo-rapes-umkc-030210,0,2017861.story).

Perilla, J., K. Frndak, D. Lillard, and C. East. 2003. "A Working Analysis of Women's Use of Violence in the Context of Learning, Opportunity, and Choice." *Violence against Women* 9 (1): 10–46.

Perry, B. 2001. *In the Name of Hate: Understanding Hate Crimes*. New York: Routledge.

———. 2003. "Part 5: Introduction." In *Hate and Bias Crime: A Reader*, ed. B. Perry, 385–88. New York: Routledge.

Perry, T. 2000. "Jury Convicts Man in Hate Crime Case." *Los Angeles Times*, March 3.

Phillips, N. D. 2006. "Prosecution of Bias Motivated Crimes in a New Jersey County, 2001–2004." Ph.D. diss., City University of New York.

Pollard, P. 1992. "Judgments about Victims and Attackers in Depicted Rapes: A Review." *British Journal of Social Psychology* 31 (4): 307–26.

Polletta, F. 2000. "The Structural Context of Novel Rights Claims: Southern Civil Rights Organizing, 1961–1966." *Law & Society Review* 34 (2): 367–406.

"The Price of Hatred." 1993. *Star-Ledger*, June 12.

"Principal Fired for Using N-Word." 2010. Boston Channel, March 26 (http://www.thebostonchannel.com/news/22966514/detail.html).

Reed, E., A. Raj, E. Miller, and J. G. Silverman. 2010. "Losing the 'Gender' in Gender-based Violence: The Missteps of Research on Dating and Intimate Partner Violence." *Violence against Women* 16 (3): 348–54.

Regan, C. J. (1999). "A Whole Lot of Nothing Going On: The Civil Rights 'Remedy' of the Violence against Women Act." *Notre Dame Law Review* 75 (2): 797–816.

Reilly, M. 1993. "Study Calls for Creation of Council to Fight Racism, Hate Crimes in State." *Star-Ledger*, December 23.

Renzetti, C. 1992. *Violent Betrayal: Partner Abuse in Lesbian Relationships*. Thousand Oaks, CA: Sage.

———. 1998. "Connecting the Dots: Women, Public Policy, and Social Control." In *Crime Control and Women: Feminist Implications of Criminal Justice Policy*, ed. S. L. Miller, 181–89. Thousand Oaks, CA: Sage.

"Reward Offered for Leads in Paintball Gun Assault." 2003. *Associated Press State and Local Wire*, July 17.

Scully, D., and J. Marolla. 1985. "'Riding the Bull at Gilley's': Convicted Rapists Describe the Rewards of Rape." *Social Problems* 32 (3): 251–63.

Seale, C. F. 2003. "Computer-assisted Analysis of Qualitative Interview Data." In *Inside Interviewing: New Lenses, New Concerns*, ed. J. A. Holstein and J. F. Gubrium, 289–308. Thousand Oaks, CA: Sage.

Senn, C. Y., and K. Dzinas. 1996. "Measuring Fear of Rape: A New Scale." *Canadian Journal of Behavioural Science*. April (http://findarticles.com/p/articles/mi_qa3717/is_199604/ai_n8750165/?tag=content;col1).

Sheffield, C. 1992. "Hate Violence." In *Race, Class, Gender in the United States: An Integrated Study*, ed. P. S. Rothenberg, 388–97. New York: St. Martin's.

Shenk, A. H. 2003. "Victim-Offender Mediation: The Road to Repairing Hate Crime Injustice." In *Hate and Bias Crime: A Reader*, ed. B. Perry, 439–54. New York: Routledge.

Sherman, L. W. 1980. "Causes of Police Behavior: The Current State of Quantitative Research." *Journal of Research in Crime and Delinquency* 17 (1): 69–100.

Softas-Nall, B., A. Bardos, and M. Fakinos. 1995. "Fear of Rape." *Violence against Women* 1 (2): 174–86.

Soule, S. A., and J. Earl. 2001. "The Enactment of State-level Hate Crime Law in the United States: Intrastate and Interstate Factors." *Sociological Perspectives* 44 (3): 281–305.

Spears, J., and C. Spohn. 1997. "The Effect of Evidence Factors and Victim Characteristics on Prosecutors' Charging Decisions in Sexual Assault Cases." *Justice Quarterly* 14 (3): 500–24.

Spohn, C., D. Beichner, and E. Davis-Frenzel. 2001. "Prosecutorial Justifications for Sexual Assault Case Rejection: Guarding the 'Gateway to Justice.'" *Social Problems* 48 (2): 206–35.

Stanko, E. A. 1993. "Ordinary Fear: Women, Violence, and Personal Safety." In *Violence against Women: The Bloody Footprints*, ed. P. B. Bart and E. G. Moran, 155–64. Newbury Park, CA: Sage.

Steen, S., and M. A. Cohen. 2004. "Assessing the Public's Demand for Hate Crime Penalties." *Justice Quarterly* 21 (1): 91–124.

Stolz, B. A. 1999. "Congress, Symbolic Politics and the Evolution of 1994 'Violence Against Women Act.'" *Criminal Justice Policy Review* 10 (3): 401–28.

Strauss, A., and J. Corbin. 1998. *Basics of Qualitative Research: Techniques and Procedures for Developing Grounded Theory*. 2nd ed. Thousand Oaks, CA: Sage.

Swatt, M. 2006. "Exploring the Difference between Male and Female Intimate Partner Homicides." *Homicide Studies* 10 (4): 279–92.

Taslitz, A. E. 1999. *Rape and the Culture of the Courtroom*. New York: New York University Press.

Taylor, K. L. 1996. "Treating Male Violence against Women as a Bias Crime." *Boston University Law Review* 76 (3): 575–604.

"Three Pennsylvania Women Killed in Hate Crime." 2009. *Feminist News*, August 6 (http://www.feminist.org/news/newsbyte/uswirestory.asp?id=11865).

Tjaden, P., and N. Thoennes. 2006. *Extent, Nature, and Consequences of Rape Victimization: Findings from the National Violence against Women Survey*. Washington: U.S. Government Printing Office.

Truman, J. L., and M. R. Rand. (2010). "Criminal Victimization, 2009." *Bureau of Justice Statistics Bulletin*, October. Washington: Department of Justice (http://bjs.ojp.usdoj.gov/content/pub/pdf/cv09.pdf).

Uris, R. 1997a. "DMV Clerk Faces Bias Accusation; Use of Racial Epithet Alleged." *Record* (Bergen County), August 20.

———. 1997b. "DMV Clerk in Bias Case Apologizes, But Loses Job." *Record* (Bergen County), August 21.

———. 1997c. "Ex-DMV Worker Cited for Racial Slurs Files Own Complaint." *Record* (Bergen County), August 28.

Vago, S. 2003. *Law and Society*. 7th ed. Upper Saddle River, NJ: Prentice Hall.

Valente, R. L., B. J. Hart, S. Zeya, and M. Malefyt. 2001. "The Violence against Women Act of 1994: The Federal Commitment to Ending Domestic Violence, Sexual Assault, Stalking, and Gender-based Crimes of Violence." In *Sourcebook on Violence against Women*, ed. C. M. Renzetti, J. L. Edleson, and R. K. Bergen, 279–301. Thousand Oaks, CA: Sage.

Vitale, J. 2002. "Reflections on Legislation: The Evolution of New Jersey's Bias Crime Law. *Seton Hall Legislative Journal* 26 (2): 363–90.

Walker, J. L. 1969. "The Diffusion of Innovations among the American States." *American Political Science Review* 63 (3): 880–99.

Wang, L. 1999. "The Complexities of 'Hate.'" *Ohio State Law Journal*, 60 (3): 799–900.

Warr, M. 1985. "Fear of Rape among Urban Women." *Social Problems* 32 (3): 238–50.

Weisburd, S. B., and B. Levin. 1993–94. "'On the Basis of Sex': Recognizing Gender-based Bias Crimes." *Stanford Law & Policy Review* 5 (2): 21-47.

Wethington, J. L. 2001. Constitutional Law—Commerce Clause: Violence against Women Act's Civil Rights Remedy Exceeds Congress's Powers to Regulate Interstate Commerce." *University of Arkansas at Little Rock Law Review* 23 (2): 485–510.

Whatley, M. A. 2005. "The Effect of Participant Sex, Victim Dress, and Traditional Attitudes on Casual Judgments for Marital Rape Victims." *Journal of Family Violence* 20 (3): 191–200.

Yearwood, D. L., and S. Freeman. 2004. "Analyzing Concerns among Police Administrators: Recruitment and Retention of Police Officers in North Carolina." *Police Chief* 71 (3) (http://www.policechiefmagazine.org/magazine/index.cfm?fuseaction=display&article_id=253&issue_id=32004).

Index

acquaintance rape, 73–74, 158n4. *See also* intimate partner violence
Akiyama, Yoshio, 36
Alaska, 4, 16
American Civil Liberties Union, 55
American Jewish Committee, 55
American Jewish Congress, 55
Angelari, Marguerite, 22, 78–79
Anti-Defamation League, 4–5, 33, 55–56
anti-hate-crime movement, 27–28
Apprendi v. New Jersey, 530 U.S. 466, 44, 80–81, 156n3

Bachman, Ronet, 113
Becker, Paul J., 32–33, 114
Belknap, Joanne, 158n6
Bell, Jeannine, 16–17, 36–37, 39–40
Bennett, John O., 44
Berk, Richard, 35–36
Best, Joel, 3
bias crime. *See* hate crime
Boyd, Elizabeth, 35–36
Brzonkala, Christy, 25–26, 154n4
Bush, George W., 100
Byrd, James, Jr., 40, 69

California: bias-crime enforcement in, 37–38, 110; Billy Dean McCall conviction, 94; California gay student murder of 2008, 102; gender-bias crime statistics, 15, 153n11; gender exemption in, 156n5; hate crime law of 1978, 3–4, 16; random bias-assault conviction in, 81
Canada, 1, 12, 54–55, 70
Carney, Kathryn M., 11, 105
Center for Women Policy Studies, 95–96
Chadwick, Roger, 106
civil rights movement, 27–28, 47, 114
Coalition Against Sexual Assault, 48–49, 57
Coalition for Battered Women, 48–49, 57, 157n8
Coalition on Hate Crimes Prevention, 21
Cole, Lorraine, 7
Commission on Sex Discrimination in the Statutes, 56
Connecticut, 78–79
Corbin, Juliet M., 118, 121, 160n6
Crawford, James, 1, 25–26
crimes/incidents (chronology of hate crimes): University of Montreal shootings (1989), 1, 12, 54–55, 70; University of Florida murders (1990), 7; Apprendi assault on Fowlkes family (1994), 156n3; Virginia Tech dormitory assault (1994), 25–26, 154n4; New Jersey DMV harassment case (1997), 86–88; James Byrd murder (1998), 40, 69; Matthew Shepard murder (1998), 28, 69–70; Billy Dean McCall conviction (2001), 94; attack of white New Jersey homeless man (2003), 85–86; New Jersey firefighter harassment of gay couple

175

crimes/incidents (*continued*)
(2004), 86; Amish school shooting (2006), 12, 15; Don Imus basketball slurs (2007), 87–88; California gay student murder (2008), 102; Pittsburgh health club shooting (2009), 12–13, 15, 69; University of Missouri at Kansas City rapes (2009–2010), 7

cross burning: collective victimization and, 5–6; fear of victimization and, 103; motivation in, 39; St. Paul ordinance conviction and, 155n2; as triggering event, 33; as "typical" bias crime, 9, 36, 58

Curry, Theodore R., 31–32, 154n6

Del Tufo, Robert, 46–47
Derman, Harriet E., 44, 48
DiFrancesco, Donald, 99
DiNitto, Diana M., 40–42
disability, 4–5, 21, 64
domain expansion, 97
Domestic Abuse Intervention Programs, 158n5
domestic violence. *See* intimate partner violence

Earl, Jennifer S., 31–32
education/advocacy: bias crime education, 17, 80, 109–11; policy recommendations for, 106–10; symbolic purpose of bias-crime legislation, 29–31, 47–49, 91–92, 96, 101–2; training of criminal justice personnel, 108–9
enforcement (of bias crime statutes): overview, 33–34, 64; awareness of gender category and, 64–65; bias crime enforcement units, 34–35; "civil arena" argument against, 82–83, 100–101; consequences of non-enforcement, 94–95; difficulty of proof, 71–72; domestic violence enforcement, 10, 158–59n6–7; factors influencing enforcement, 36–37; ideological resistance to, 95–96; juvenile bias rehabilitation, 17; overcharging and, 74; pattern-of-violence as prosecution strategy, 108; police opposition to bias crime laws, 35–36; pragmatic consequences of, 61; prosecutor bias and, 41; prosecutorial rationale, 16, 38–41, 68–72; "redundancy argument" against, 12, 72, 75, 78–79, 90, 101; resistance to enforcement from citizenry, 37; restorative justice approach, 159n3; VAWA civil rights remedy and, 24–26, 154n3. *See also* legislation; motivation/intent; Office of Bias Crime and Community Relations; reporting; sentencing

family violence approach, 152n8
feminism, 14, 27–28, 152n8. *See also* women
Finn, Peter, 38–39
Florida, 7
Florio, Jim, 46, 99, 156n4
Freeman, Stephanie, 100
Freeman, Steven M., 5

Gelber, Katharine, 10–11
gender: gender essentialism, 84, 111; gender stereotypes, 9; male privilege in relationships, 79–80; non-gender-based violence against women, 5; as protected group, 4–5, 7–9, 21; rape victim blaming and, 151n5; as "risk factor," 2; symbolic consequences of gender exemption, 62–63; views of domestic violence as a bias crime, 78–79
gender-bias crime: gender as bias crime category, 44–45; HCPA coverage of, 21–22; normalization of violence against women, 69; preemption by other categories, 84, 87–88; reporting of, 15–16; statistics for, 15; Texas hate-crime law and, 13, 16
gender exemption (in bias-crime laws): overview, 45, 57–58, 104–5; California

176 | Index

exemption text, 156n5; domestic violence exclusion from, 75; New Jersey exemption text, 45, 124; policy recommendations for, 106–7; pragmatic concerns, 61–62; symbolic consequences of, 62–63; "typical" hate crime model and, 58–61; views of, 71–72, 75
gender symmetry approach, 152n8
Gerstenfeld, Phyllis B., 8, 29, 102
Goldscheid, Julie, 8
Goodman, Kenneth, 49–50
Grattet, Ryken, 27–32, 37–38, 97, 101–2, 114, 154n6
Gusfield, Joseph R., 101

Haider-Markel, Donald P., 151n4, 154n5
Hammer, Karl, 35–36
Harvey, Peter, 85–86
Hatch, Orin, 9
hate crime: defined, 3–4, 151n2; analytical models for, 67–68; bias category conflicts, 84, 86–88, 111; bias factors in, 8; collective victimization and, 6–7, 58, 60–61, 79; fear of victimization as consequence, 2–3, 103; hate/animus as component of, 8–9, 67–70; historical development of concept of, 27–28; history of legislative actions, 3–4; non-gender-based violence against women, 5; protected groups, 4–5; randomness vs. intimacy and, 10–11, 81; social hierarchy and, 9, 12, 59, 66–68; types of crimes, 21. *See also* motivation/intent; "typical" hate crimes
Hate Crimes Prevention Act (HCPA, 2009), 5, 20–22, 26–27, 100
Hate Crimes Sentencing Enhancement Act (1994), 22, 99–100
Hate Crimes Statistics Act (HCSA, 1990): gender exclusion from, 46; gender exemption in, 156n5; opposition to, 96–97; passage of, 7, 20–21, 49, 99–100
Henry, Jessica S., 29–30
Herbert, Bob, 13, 15

homosexuality. *See* sexual orientation
Hopkins, C. Quince, 159n3

Imus, Don, 87–88
interpersonal violence, 3
intimate partner violence: acquaintance rape convictions, 73–74; control/domination of partners with, 10; emotional violence, 10; feminist approach to, 152n8; as gender-bias offense, 75, 157n8; history of enforcement neglect, 158–59n6–7; intimacy as preclusion of group hate, 10–11; power as fundamental to, 3, 76–77, 158n5; prevalence of male perpetrators, 13–14, 70–71, 158n3–4; *State of Massachusetts v. Aboulez* bias conviction, 107–8; statistics for, 1–2, 70–71; women as perpetrators, 152nn8–9. *See also* rape; sexual assault
intimidation: bias intimidation as crime, 43, 77; ethnic intimidation laws, 32, 43, 46, 121; motivation as factor in, 59
Isaacs, Tracy, 10

Jacobs, James B., 29–30
Jenness, Valerie: on factors affecting legislation, 27–32, 154–55nn6–7; on "law-in-between," 37–38; on prosecutor rationale, 16; on rights movements, 114; on the symbolic value of bias laws, 101–3; on Texas bias law implementation, 40; on VAWA, 96–97
justice system. *See* enforcement
juvenile crime, 17

Kady, Louis, 49
Koss, Mary, 159n3
Kyrillos, Joseph, 44

LaFree, Gary, 73
Lanier, Christy, 113
law enforcement. *See* enforcement
Lawrence, Frederick M., 6–7, 67

legislation (hate crime legislation): civil remedy laws, 46–47, 99; constitutional issues in, 49–50, 53, 96, 154n2, 155n2; deterrent value of, 92–93; diffusion model of, 154n6; domain expansion, 97; economy effect on, 30–31; educational value of, 17, 80, 92–93; examples of exempted hate crimes, 12–13; history of legislative actions, 4; intent-to-intimidate as concept in, 43, 53; "organizational perviousness" toward bias policies, 38, 154–55n7; patriarchal values effect on, 103; penalty-enhancement statutes, 79, 97–98; political context of, 31, 46–48, 98–100, 104, 154n5, 159n1; regional infectiousness patterns, 31–32; state hate crime legislation, 97–98, 151n3, 151n6; symbolic purpose of, 29–31, 47–49, 91–92, 96, 101–2; theories of crime legislation, 28–31; triggering events, 32–33, 53–56, 70, 156n6. *See also* enforcement; gender exemption; reporting; *particular laws; particular states*

Lepine, Marc, 1, 12

Levin, Brian, 67, 105

"lifestyle" groups, 4

Local Law Enforcement Hate Crimes Prevention Act. *See* Matthew Shepard and James Byrd, Jr. Hate Crimes Prevention Act

lynching, 9

Marolla, Joseph, 9

Martin, Susan E., 34–35, 84

Maryland, 34–35

Massachusetts, 10, 107–8

Matthew Shepard and James Byrd, Jr. Hate Crimes Prevention Act. *See* Hate Crimes Prevention Act

McDevitt, Jack, 11

McGreevey, James, 99

McPhail, Beverly A.: on the gender category, 8–9; on hate crime prosecutorial rationale, 16; on HCPA bias coverage, 21; on power/control as fundamental motive, 76; on prosecutor rationale, 10, 40–42; on random vs. intimate victims, 11; on status categories, 84; on study methodology, 121

media: bias crime reporting by, 52–53; content analysis of, 118–19; effect on hate-crime legislation, 31, 50–51; investigative role of, 88–89; neglect in gender-bias coverage, 85–87; public education campaigns and, 109–10

men: as crime victims, 2; as domestic violence victims, 13; as gender-bias crime victims, 152n7; male privilege in relationships, 79–80; male support for gender exemption, 62, 75; purposes of interpersonal violence by, 14

methodology, 17–18, 113–22, 146–50, 152n8

Miller, Jeffrey, 12

Miller, Susan L., 11–12, 152nn8–9

Minnesota, 4, 15, 110. *See also R.A.V. v. City of St. Paul*

misogyny, 2–3, 50, 86–88, 101, 107–8

Missouri, 4, 7

Morrison, Antonio, 1, 25–26

motivation/intent (in hate crimes): difficulty of determination of, 9; in domestic violence, 75–77, 100; FBI guidelines for, 153–54n1; gender symmetry approach and, 152n8; hate/animus as motive, 8–9, 67–70, 106; misogynist slurs as evidence of, 86–88, 101, 107–8; power/control as motive, 3, 40–41, 59–61, 76–77, 158n5; in rape, 100; social hierarchy and, 9, 12, 59, 66–68; in "typical" hate crimes, 100

National Coalition against Domestic Violence, 21, 106–7

National Crime Victimization Survey, 152n8

National Organization for Women, 21–22, 48–49, 107, 157n8

National Violence Against Women Survey, 2, 152n8

New Hampshire, 10, 106, 108, 110
New Jersey: attitudes toward discrimination in, 46; bias crime statute enforcement, 64, 157n1, 159n10; as case-study state, 16–17; hate crime legislation, 43–50, 70, 97–98; media coverage of hate crime, 50–51, 85–87; political support for bias legislation, 47–48, 98, 104; reporting procedures in, 16; sexual assault convictions, 73
New Jersey Bias Crime Officers Association, 116
New Jersey bias statutes: original hate crime law (1981), 16, 43–44, 45; Ethnic Intimidation Act (1990), 43, 46; civil remedy law (1993), 46–47, 97, 99, 124–29, 156n4; hate crime law (1995), 16, 43–44, 64, 129–35, 157n1; bias intimidation law (2002), 43–44, 90, 123–24; bias crime law (2008), 136–45; "gender identity or expression" protection statute (2008), 110, 153n12, 157n1
New Jersey County Prosecutors Association, 116
New Jersey State Commission on Racism, Racial Violence and Religious Violence, 50–51
New York, 4, 16, 34–35
Nolan, James J., 36

Obama, Barack, 27
Office of Bias Crime and Community Relations (OBCCR), 17, 46–47, 52, 97, 99, 108, 115, 153n15
Ohio, 32–33, 114, 121
Okechukwu, Christopher, 86–88
Oklahoma, 151n4

penalty-enhancement statutes, 79, 97–98
Pennsylvania, 12–13, 15, 69
Perilla, Julia, 14
Phillips, Nickie D., 159n10
plea bargaining, 74, 81–82, 106
police. *See* enforcement

policy recommendations, 103–9
political parties: conservative support for legislation, 47–48, 159n1; effect on hate-crime legislation, 31; hate crime legislation as liberal issue, 27–28, 47; New Jersey law as bipartisan, 98
Potter, Hillary, 158n6
power: as bias crime motive, 3, 40–41, 59–61, 76–77, 158n5; in interpersonal violence, 3, 76, 158n5; relationship with hate, 59–60; in same-sex relationships, 14
protected groups: civil rights movement and, 27–28; constitutional issues and, 49–50, 53, 96, 155nn2–3; crime incidence related to, 21; gender as a protected group, 7–9; history of recognition of, 4–5; random vs. intimate violence and, 10–11, 81; social hierarchy and, 9, 12, 59, 63, 66–68

race: as protected group, 4; race-bias crimes, 9; race-bias crime statistics, 15, 64, 65; racial harassment, 83; racial slurs, 87–88, 159n9; resistance to race-bias crime enforcement, 37; "typical" hate crimes and, 58, 83, 84
rape: collective victimization and, 9–10, 105–6; difficulty of victimization in, 90, 151n5; gender hate and, 60–61; prosecution as hate crime, 72–73; sentencing for, 105; statistics for, 2; stranger rape as bias crime, 11. *See also* intimate partner violence; rape myth; sexual assault
rape myths: defined, 157n9; bias legislation as counter to, 63, 105; effect on policy makers, 9, 74–75; public education campaigns and, 109; understanding of power motive and, 60–61; victim blaming and, 60, 74, 90
R.A.V. v. City of St. Paul, 505 U.S. 377: overview, 53–54, 98; effect on legislation, 43–44, 52, 57; motivation as factor in, 6; text of original ordinance, 155n2

Index | 179

Reed, Elizabeth, 14
rehabilitation, 17
Rehnquist, William, 26
religion: as protected group, 4; religious bias crime, 5–6; religious-bias crime statistics, 15, 64, 65; religious harassment, 83; swastikas-on-synagogues as "typical" bias crime, 58, 80, 83
reporting (of bias crimes): barriers to victim reporting, 34, 39; barriers to witness reporting, 39; city/state public image and, 16–17; factors influencing reporting, 36; of gender-bias crime, 15–16; HCPA provisions for, 27; media reporting of bias crime, 52–53; New Jersey reporting procedure, 16; as 'shield' from criminalization, 31–32; state HCSA compliance, 22; training/policies effect on, 35–37; "typical" hate crimes and, 65–67. *See also* enforcement; legislation; statistics
restorative justice, 159n3
Roberts, Charles Carl, 12, 15

Sadofski, Joseph E., 54
Scott, John, 51
Scully, Diana, 9
sentencing: *Apprendi* decision on jury sentencing, 43, 80–81; bias crime enhanced penalties, 79, 97–98; Hate Crimes Sentencing Enhancement Act, 22; leniency in partner violence sentencing, 24; plea bargaining and, 74, 81–82, 106; rape and sexual assault sentencing, 105; state domestic violence sentencing, 10; state hate crime sentences, 4; VAWA civil rights remedy, 24–26, 154n3. *See also* enforcement
sexual assault: collective victimization and, 9–10, 58, 60–61; conviction rate for, 73; gender hate and, 59–61; non-gender-based sexual assault, 5; recognition of bias in, 61; sentencing for, 105; statistics for, 2. *See also* intimate partner violence; rape
sexual harassment, 83
sexual orientation: avoidance of victimization and, 12; bias crime legislation and, 22, 110, 151n4, 159n1; gay/lesbian rights movement, 27–28; lesbian same-sex interpersonal violence, 14; as protected group, 4–5; sexual orientation bias crimes, 28, 69–70, 86, 102; sexual-orientation-bias crime statistics, 15, 64, 65; transgender bias crime victims, 152n7, 153n12
Sheffield, Carole, 22
Shepard, Matthew, 28, 69–70, 156n6
Sinagra, Jack, 18, 44, 54, 116, 117
Sodini, George, 12–13, 15, 69
sodomy, 32
Soule, Sarah A., 31–32
State of Massachusetts v. Aboulez (No. 94-0985H), 107–8
statistics: FBI Uniform Crime Report Program, 153n14; gender symmetry approach and, 152n8; Hate Crimes Statistics Act, 7, 20–21; media coverage of hate crime, 85; New Jersey bias crime statute enforcement, 64, 157n1, 159n10; prevalence of male perpetrators, 13–14, 70–71, 158n3–4; random vs. intimate violence, 11; rape and sexual assault sentencing, 105; sexual assault incidences, 1–2; state gender-bias crime statistics, 15. *See also* reporting
Stayner, Cary, 1, 12
stereotypes, 9, 84
Stolz, Barbara A., 30, 114
Strauss, Anselm L., 118, 121, 160n6
Swatt, Marc L., 152n9

Taslitz, Andrew E., 90
Texas, 13, 16, 40–42, 69
"three strikes" laws, 61
Towne, Richard, 10

triggering events (influencing legislation), 28, 32–33, 53–56, 70, 156n6
"typical" hate crimes: bias crime reporting and, 65–67; domestic violence compared with, 80; effect on hate-crime legislation, 100; gender crimes and, 8, 16, 40; juvenile crime association with, 66; New Jersey gender exemption and, 45, 58–61; prevalence of male-on-male crimes as, 103, 159n2; sexual assault compared with, 65; workplace as gender-bias context, 83

United States v. Morrison (VAWA civil rights remedy), 25–26, 75, 154n2

Vago, Steven, 95
Valente, Roberta, 25
VAWA. *See* Violence Against Women Act
Veggian, Pia, 86–88
victimization: barriers to reporting crimes, 34; collective victimization, 5–7, 9–10, 58, 60–61, 79; fear of victimization, 2–3, 103; VAWA testimony on, 23–24; victim blaming, 74–75, 90, 151n5

victims rights movement, 27–28
Violence Against Women Act (VAWA): overview, 23–24; civil rights remedy, 24–26, 154n3; opposition to, 9, 96–97; passage of, 3, 79; political context of, 46; remedies for state statute deficiencies, 151n1; symbolic purpose of, 30; *U.S. v. Morrison* challenge to, 75
Virginia, 25–26, 154n4
Vitale, Joseph, 45

Warsh, Jeffrey A., 44, 48
Weisburd, Steven Bennett, 67, 105
Whitman, Christine Todd, 16, 44–45, 99
Wisconsin v. Mitchell (1993), 98
women: feminism, 14, 27–28, 152n8; gender essentialism and, 84, 111; interpersonal violence by, 14; as intimate partner violence perpetrators, 152nn8–9
Wyoming, 8, 28, 69, 156n6

Yard, Molly, 22
Yearwood, Douglas L., 100

LIBRARY OF CONGRESS CATALOGING-IN-PUBLICATION DATA

Hodge, Jessica P.
 Gendered hate : exploring gender in hate crime law / Jessica P. Hodge.
  p. cm. — (The Northeastern series on gender, crime, and law)
 Includes bibliographical references and index.
 ISBN 978-1-55553-751-7 (cloth : alk. paper) — ISBN 978-1-55553-747-0 (pbk. : alk. paper) — ISBN 978-1-55553-757-9 (e-book)
  1. Women—Crimes against—United States. 2. Hate crimes—United States. I. Title.
 KF9304.H63   2011
 345.73'025—dc22   2011004037